Development of China's Financial Supervision and Regulation

Bin Hu • Zhentao Yin • Liansheng Zheng
Editors

Development of China's Financial Supervision and Regulation

palgrave
macmillan

Editors
Bin Hu
Chinese Academy of Social Sciences
Beijing, China

Liansheng Zheng
Chinese Academy of Social Sciences
Beijing, China

Zhentao Yin
Chinese Academy of Social Sciences
Beijing, China

ISBN 978-1-137-52224-5   ISBN 978-1-137-52225-2 (eBook)
DOI 10.1057/978-1-137-52225-2

Library of Congress Control Number: 2016936091

© The Editor(s) (if applicable) and The Author(s) 2016
This work is subject to copyright. All rights are solely and exclusively licensed by the Publisher, whether the whole or part of the material is concerned, specifically the rights of translation, reprinting, reuse of illustrations, recitation, broadcasting, reproduction on microfilms or in any other physical way, and transmission or information storage and retrieval, electronic adaptation, computer software, or by similar or dissimilar methodology now known or hereafter developed.
The use of general descriptive names, registered names, trademarks, service marks, etc. in this publication does not imply, even in the absence of a specific statement, that such names are exempt from the relevant protective laws and regulations and therefore free for general use.
The publisher, the authors and the editors are safe to assume that the advice and information in this book are believed to be true and accurate at the date of publication. Neither the publisher nor the authors or the editors give a warranty, express or implied, with respect to the material contained herein or for any errors or omissions that may have been made.

Cover illustration: © Peter Scholey / Alamy Stock Photo

Printed on acid-free paper

This Palgrave Macmillan imprint is published by Springer Nature
The registered company is Nature America Inc. New York

Acknowledgements

Financial Regulation in China: Shadow Banking, Securities and the Foreign Exchange Regime has become available to our readers, thanks to the hard work of dozens of dedicated scholars. We are indebted to Dr. Gang Wang from the Development Research Center of the State Council; Dr. Zuqing Mao from the China Banking Regulatory Commission; Dr. Xiaochuan Zhang, Dr. Yongdong Pan and Dr. Limei Wan from the China Securities Regulatory Commission; Dr. Liu Tang from the Institute of Finance and Banking Chinese Academy of Social Sciences; Dr. Qian Xie from the Institute of Economics, Chinese Academy of Social Sciences; and Dr. Jianjun Li from Bank of Kunlun.

Mr. Junfeng Zheng and Ms. Lee Bi Ling Stella made major contributions to the tasks of translation and final polishing.

Finally, we would like to thank all the organizations and individuals, particularly Ms Li Zhou, Ms Yanling Li and Dr. Xue Bai, who have supported this book so warmly.

Contents

1 China's Shadow Banking System—Scale, Risks and Regulation: Research from the Perspective of Non-Traditional Credit Financing   1
Bin Hu and Liansheng Zheng

2 Internet Finance: Definition, Models, Risk, and Regulation   31
Bin Hu and Liansheng Zheng

3 Annual Developments in Banking Regulation   59
Gang Wang and Zhuqing Mao

4 Annual Developments in Securities Regulation   101
Xiaochuan Zhang and Yongdong Pan

5 Annual Report on Foreign Exchange Administration   153
Liu Tang

6 Research on the Financial Reform and Innovation and Corresponding Regulation in China (Shanghai) Pilot Free Trade Zone   189
Qian Xie

7 Shanghai–Hong Kong Stock Connect: Main
   Characteristics, Strategic Significance,
   and Regulatory Response   209
   Jianjun Li

8 Stock-Issue Registration System Reform:
   International Experience and China's Choice   229
   Limei Wan

Index   247

Editors and Authors

Bin Hu PhD in law, is a professor in and deputy director general of the Institute of Finance and Banking (IFB), Chinese Academy of Social Sciences (CASS), and director general of the Research Center for Financial Law and Regulation, CASS. He has hosted more than 40 research projects from government departments, financial regulators and financial institutions, published over 80 papers on leading law and economics journals in China and been the editor-in-chief for the Annual Report on China's Financial Supervision and Regulation for nine years. Hu has extensive experience and professional knowledge of financial laws and regulations. He was awarded the Youth Innovation Award by Central State Organs Work Committee. He has been selected in the National Hundred, Thousand and Ten Thousand Talent Project, appointed the state's young and middle-aged expert with outstanding contribution and held Special Government Allowance of the State Council from 2014. His main research areas are financial regulation, financial law and securitization.

Zhentao Yin Zhentao Yin has a PhD in economics, and is Senior Research Fellow and Associate Professor at the Chinese Academy of Social Sciences. He is the Deputy Director of the Law and Finance Department of the Institute of Finance and Banking, CASS, and a deputy director of the Research Center for Financial Law and Financial Regulation at CASS.

Liansheng Zheng Liansheng Zheng has a Ph.D. in economics, and is Senior Research Fellow and Associate Professor at the Chinese Academy of Social Sciences. He is a deputy director of the Research Center for Financial Law and Financial Regulation, CASS.

List of Figures

Fig. 1.1	The definition of China's shadow banking system	9
Fig. 5.1	RMB exchange-rate trend in 2014	156
Fig. 5.2	Scale and proportions of short-term debt in China	176
Fig. 5.3	2009–2014 balances of capital and financial accounts	179
Fig. 6.1	Operation of the separate accounting systems in Shanghai Free Trade Zone	199
Fig. 6.2	Interest rate determination mechanism under dual pricing system	201
Fig. 7.1	Transaction structure of Shanghai-Hong Kong Stock Connect	210
Fig. 7.2	The quota limits of Shanghai-Hong Kong Stock Connect are close to QFII volumes, etc	215
Fig. 7.3	RMB deposit scale in Hong Kong	222

List of Tables

Table 1.1	Categories of non-traditional financial products/tools	7
Table 1.2	The three levels of China's shadow banking system	11
Table 5.1	China capital account convertibility restriction list	161
Table 5.2	Offshore foreign exchange transactions of the BRIC countries in 2013	165
Table 5.3	Current foreign debt management model in China	175
Table 6.1	Degree of openness in various sectors of China's service industry, percentage	194
Table 6.2	Documents issued after the establishment of Shanghai Free Trade Zone and their core contents	195
Table 6.3	Comparison of cross-border financing systems in four places around China and evaluation of the cross-border financing system in the pilot free trade zone	203
Table 6.4	Overall evaluation and comparison: The foreign exchange management system within and outside the free trade zone	204
Table 7.1	Relevant provisions and main arrangements of Shanghai-Hong Kong Stock Connect	212
Table 7.2	Comparison of Shanghai-Hong Kong Stock Connect and QFII/QDII/RQFII	213
Table 7.3	Cooperative regulation in Shanghai-Hong Kong Stock Connect	226
Table 8.1	Examples of three kinds of issue systems	233
Table 8.2	The three-level legal system in the USA	234

CHAPTER 1

China's Shadow Banking System—Scale, Risks and Regulation: Research from the Perspective of Non-Traditional Credit Financing

Bin Hu and Liansheng Zheng

The explosive growth of shadow banking has raised both intrigue and concern among experts, as it has significantly changed the structure of the global financial system. Since the 2008 financial crash, international regulatory agencies and organizations have been conducting extensive research on the topic. Shadow banking in China has sparked huge debate over its definition, scale and potential off-balance-sheet risks. The China Banking Regulatory Commission (CBRC) has issued Regulatory Document no. 8, concerning off-balance-sheet wealth management products, and

---

Bin Hu, PhD in law, is a Professor at CASS, Deputy Director General of the Institute of Finance and Banking (IFB), CASS, and Director of Research Center for Financial L-aw and Regulation (RCFLR), whose main research interests include financial regulation, financial law, and asset securitization; Liansheng Zheng, PhD in economics, is an Associate Professor in the IFB Law and Finance Department, CASS, and a deputy director of RCFLR, whose main research interests include financial regulation, financial innovation and macroeconomics.

B. Hu (✉) • L. Zheng
Institute of Finance and Banking, Chinese Academy of Social Science, Beijing, China

© The Editor(s) (if applicable) and The Author(s) 2016
B. Hu et al. (eds.), *Development of China's Financial Supervision and Regulation*, DOI 10.1057/978-1-137-52225-2_1

Document no. 107 ("Notice of the General Office of the State Council on Enhancing Regulation of Shadow Banking"). Since publication of these documents the focus has shifted from systemic financial risks arising out of the shadow banking system to the division of regulatory responsibilities and the coordination of regulation.

This chapter clarifies the basic concepts, scale and risks of shadow banking in China. It also offers several policy suggestions to tackle regulatory issues.

1.1 Shadow Banking System: Controversy and Evolution

American economist Paul McCulley coined the term shadow banking in 2007. A year later, Timothy Geithner, then president of the Federal Reserve Bank of New York, called it "the parallel banking system." Shadow banking refers to non-banking financial institutions. Examples include investment banks, private equity funds, money-market mutual funds, mortgage intermediaries, hedge funds, bond insurance companies, and structured investment vehicles.

In 2012, the European Central Bank described shadow banking as a credit intermediary outside the regulated banking system. The popular "originate-to-distribute" model allows the bank to transfer a regulated asset on the balance sheet to an unregulated off-balance sheet. With the widespread application of securitization vehicles, the evasion of relevant regulation is of particular significance.

Scholars are divided when it comes to the definition of shadow banking. The most authoritative description so far comes from the Financial Stability Board (FSB). It provides a broader definition of shadow banks to include all entities outside the regulated banking system that perform credit intermediation. The FSB established four fundamental features of shadow banking: maturity transformation, liquidity transformation, leverage, and credit-risk transfer. The FSB's definition of shadow banking has gained worldwide recognition. However, since the FSB only follows the Eurozone and 25 other economies, its definition may not apply to all economies and policy frameworks.[1]

Chinese researchers also have mixed views on the subject. There are three main debates. The first is whether shadow banking is subject to regulation. The second is whether it can cause systemic financial risk. The third looks at whether non-traditional credit financing is different from traditional banking.

Those who agree with the FSB's definition, according to which China's shadow banking system only includes private lending and third-party wealth management on an estimated scale of 400 billion USD in 2010, believe it is a common "misunderstanding" to classify financial products and trust products as shadow banking.[2] In January 2014, China's State Council issued a directive called the "Notice of the General Office of the State Council on Enhancing Regulation of Shadow Banking" (Document no. 107). This was regarded in various circles as the first comprehensive definition. The notice clarified three categories of shadow banking. The first are intermediaries who do not have a financial operating license and are not part of the regulation system. Independent financial advisors and Internet finance firms are examples of this. The second are those without licenses who are only partly regulated, such as credit-guarantee companies and small loan firms. The third type are those that have licenses but face inadequate regulation in such areas as money-market funds, securitization, and some wealth management services.

The second debate is around the potential risks of shadow banking. The chief advisor of the China Banking Regulatory Commission, Shen Liantao, believes that macroscopic, structural, and microscopic issues may lead to major financial risks. Research areas include wealth management, trust, and the interbank sector as part of shadow banking.[3] Corporate bonds have also been recognized as part of the shadow banking category because of the risk of local debt. This view considers internal financial risks and the potential ripple effect. Some scholars have even classified corporate bonds as shadow banking in view of the risk of local debt (Wang Tao et al. 2012). Therefore, different definitions result in different measurements of the scale of shadow banking, ranging from 3,000–4,000 billion yuan to 36 trillion yuan.[4] This topic is particularly concerned with the contagiousness of financial risks and internal relations within the financial system.

The third debate looks at non-traditional credit financing as the core of shadow banking and compares it with credit intermediaries in the traditional banking system. Li, Hu et al. discuss the inevitability and risk of the development of non-traditional credit financing from the financial innovation perspective.[5] Though subjection to regulation is not the core criterion for shadow banking under this definition, expounding the shadow banking business and risk follows a similar logic to the FSB's tracking, estimation, and data gathering in relation to shadow banking[6] through other financial intermediaries or non-bank financial intermediation,[7] although the scope of non-traditional credit financing is larger than that of non-bank financial intermediation..

The FSB's definition is the most original and least controversial assessment of the shadow banking system. A single perspective cannot reflect the system as a whole, due to the differences in financial structures across the globe. The FSB's statistical approach neglects some imperative factors relating to China's financial products and more importantly, fails to cover major structural issues such as the change of credit intermediaries within China's banking system.

Document no. 107 is an extension of regulation theory and incorporates financial products within the regulation system. To define shadow banking in regulatory terms does not fully allow for changes of structure and distribution of risks in China's financial system. The definition pertaining to risks neglects crucial factors and often leads to a generalization of the system.

1.2 China's Shadow Banking System from the Perspective of Non-Traditional Credit Intermediaries

The features of China's financial system are different to those of other countries and an analysis of them is important to paint a clear picture of China's shadow banking system.

1.2.1 Features of China's Financial System

The overall level of development of finance in China has been relatively slow, lagging behind the real sector. Its particular structure reflects the transition from financial repression in a planned economy to a fully functional financial system in a market economy.

(a) Non-traditional credit intermediaries have changed China's banking system. Indirect financing remains the core of banking. Almost all types of non-traditional credit financing are closely related to the banking system, which is usually the main purchaser or main channel of distribution of financial products. This close relationship means that if one financial product is at risk, then it is bound to have a potential impact on the banking system.

(b) Non-traditional credit services provided by financial institutions are growing rapidly. They are providing large amounts of liquidity buffers for the real economy but also create systemic risk in the financial system.

Policy changes by central banks have led to a decline in the capital support provided by traditional finance for the economic development of society. Non-traditional credit intermediaries have been able to provide financing for investments and economic development by gradually breaching restrictions on financial regulation and credit control. Liquidity risks caused by maturity mismatch (long-term asset vs. short-term debt) of non-traditional credit financing are increasing as the market expands, threatening the stability of the financial system.

(a) Incompatibility between mixed operations and separate regulation structures

In so far as the current stage of China's financial industry is concerned, the divided regulation system is effective. Limited resources and experience allow regulators to focus on each specific field of finance, as well as making regulation more efficient, by separating the professions. The growing trend towards mixed operations in the financial industry has caused the boundaries between various financial products to become indistinct, making it difficult for a single regulatory entity to supervise these products. Regulatory agencies have different stances and there is a lack of coordination and cooperation between them. Such differences can easily result in regulatory arbitrages and regulatory vacuums.

(b) Financial innovation suppressed under strict administrative regulation in the financial market, non-complex and underdeveloped asset securitization, and relatively low leverage

Without highly leveraged operations or complex asset securitization, China's non-credit financing business depends more on ways of distinguishing off-balance-sheet business from on-balance-sheet business. As a result, domestic non-traditional credit financing basically corresponds to assets and liabilities on the balance sheet. Investments in non-standard assets and highly leveraged operation have been largely restricted since the CBRC issued a large number of regulations. In terms of interbank business, some institutions have a higher leverage ratio than others. However, the single-digit leverage ratio of China's financial institutions cannot be compared with that in the USA, which can easily reach 20–30 times. China's asset securitization is not as developed and has not yet acquired the complex structural investment vehicles that decrease the fragility of the system.

Overall, the rapid development of non-traditional credit financing causes systemic risks for the financial system. The dominant position of banking within the financial system also means that the risk will first emerge within the banking system. The existing separate regulation system is not compatible with the objective requirements of the development of mixed operations in the financial industry. Even though securitization products lack regulation, and are highly leveraged and complex in structure, they do not pose obvious problems in China. All these aspects demonstrate the internal coherence of the definition of China's shadow banking system from the perspective of non-traditional credit financing.

1.2.2 Non-Traditional Credit Financial Products and the Shadow Banking System

Shadow banking is an extremely complex system involving a "trinity" of product/tool, institution, and market. Maturity transformation, liquidity transformation, and credit transfer are the key features of credit intermediaries that offer financial services and constitute three of the four features of the shadow banking system as defined by the FSB. Under this definition, non-financing businesses such as interbank businesses, asset management plans, and financial companies should not be included in the shadow banking system.

1.2.2.1 Non-Traditional Credit Financial Products with Typical Characteristics of Shadow Banking

China's shadow banking system and traditional commercial banking system have been organically integrated, therefore, we can classify non-traditional credit financial products that have shadow banking's characteristics of maturity transformation, liquidity transformation and credit transfer on two levels. The first are credit intermediaries outside the banking system, and the second are non-traditional credit intermediaries within the banking system. The two combined make up non-traditional credit financing. In other words, non-traditional credit financing can be divided into two groups: credit intermediaries outside the banking system (as defined by the FSB); and non-traditional credit financing within the banking system (considering China's special characteristics).

Wealth management services are of particular note, as they are the fastest-growing business in the banking sector. Capital-protected products are subject to the strictest risk controls as they appear on banks' balance sheets. Although most non-protected wealth management services are recorded as a bank's agent service, they actually provide channels or agent services for financing activities outside the banking system. In order to differentiate financing activities within the banking system from those outside it, we have classified wealth management services as a credit supply mechanism outside the banking system (Table 1.1).

Table 1.1 Categories of non-traditional financial products/tools

Credit mechanism	Category	Product/tool	Characteristics of regulation	Within the shadow banking system or not
Credit supply within the banking system	Traditional credit financing	Various loans and discount notes	Strictly regulated	No
	Off-balance-sheet non-traditional credit financing	Bank acceptance L/C Payables and payment services Bank guarantees Loan commitment	Insufficiently regulated	Mostly no. Only a few businesses—such as some acceptance bills, letters of credit, payment service, etc.—as an overlapping link of shadow banking business fall within the scope of shadow banking.
	On-balance-sheet non-traditional credit financing	Investment (standard and non-standard)	Insufficiently regulated	Non-standard investment is classified as shadow banking. Interbank business is the core of shadow banking in the broad sense; the others are not.
		Central bank reserves	Strictly regulated	
		Non-interest-earning assets	Regulated	
		Interbank business	Insufficiently regulated	

(*continued*)

Table 1.1 (continued)

Credit mechanism	Category	Product/tool	Characteristics of regulation	Within the shadow banking system or not
Credit supply outside the banking system	Licensed financial services	Trust	Relatively insufficiently regulated	Classified as shadow banking in the narrow sense
		Wealth management	Insufficiently regulated	
		Money-market funds	Insufficiently regulated	
		Asset management		
		Asset securitization		
		Financing through fund and insurance subsidiaries	Insufficiently regulated	
		Finance companies	Insufficiently regulated	
		Bond (national debt excluded)	Slightly insufficiently regulated	
		Insurance asset management	Strictly regulated	No
		Equity financing	Strictly regulated	
		Fund asset management	Strictly regulated	
	Unlicensed financial services	Small loans	Relatively insufficiently regulated	Classified as shadow banking in the narrowest sense
		Financing guarantee		
		Online credit financing	Unregulated	
		Unregistered private equity fund		
		Third-party wealth management		
		Private lending		

Source: Summary by the authors

1.2.2.2 The Three Levels of China's Shadow Banking System, and an Evaluation of Its Scale

Shadow banking in China can be defined on three levels from the perspective of non-traditional credit financial products. The first level corresponds in a narrow sense to the domestic definition of shadow banking:whether or not it is subject to regulation. The second, also narrower level con-

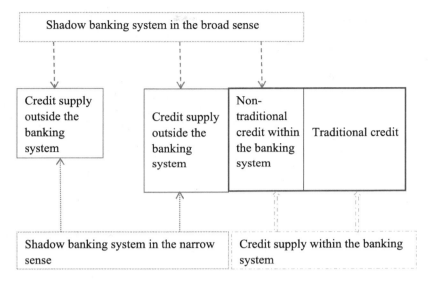

Fig. 1.1 The definition of China's shadow banking system

cerns credit intermediaries outside the banking system. The third level broadly combines the narrow sense with non-traditional credit financing within the banking system. Fig. 1.1 demonstrates the definition of China's shadow banking system.

Non-traditional credit financial products in the narrowest sense of the shadow banking system include private lending,[8] third-party wealth management, Internet credit financing, unregistered private equity funds, small loans, and financing guarantee. One relevant report showed that the scale of unregulated or unlicensed funding reached approximately 3 trillion yuan at the end of the third quarter of 2011. Unlicensed and insufficiently regulated small loans and financing guarantees hit around 2.17 trillion yuan by the end of 2012.[9] The scale of non-traditional financing involved in the shadow banking system in its narrowest sense is estimated at 6 trillion yuan.

Following the increasing amount of regulation introduced over the last two years, the scale of non-traditional financing in the shadow banking system in its narrowest sense is estimated at 6 trillion yuan.

Non-traditional credit financial products involved in the shadow banking system in its narrow sense include wealth management, trust, finance companies, money-market funds, asset management for clients, fund financing, insurance subsidiaries, asset securitization, etc. By the end of September 2013, the scale of trust assets had reached 10.13 trillion yuan,[10] the balance of wealth management funds was 9.92 trillion yuan,[11] the scale of financial companies' assets was 4.14 trillion yuan,[12] and asset management plans of securities brokers exceeded 3.89 trillion.[13] Fund subsidiaries' assets probably exceeded 1 trillion yuan by the end of 2013.[14] Money-market funds hit 0.74 trillion yuan at this time, with the four quarters experiencing a surge of 50%.[15] These figures come to a total of 29.82 trillion yuan. In its narrowest sense, the size of non-traditional financing involved in China's shadow banking system is about 36 trillion yuan, which is towards the top end of different estimates of the scale of shadow banking domestically.[16] The scale of asset securitization has been quite limited so far and is therefore omitted here.

However, this figure is a gross overestimate: first because assets of wealth management all come from other financing tools, leading to duplicate calculations; second, financial companies deal with a relatively smaller proportion of financing business; and third, there are also duplications between the financing business of securities brokers, fund subsidiaries, and trusts. The proportion of financing business of financial companies is approximately 30%, assuming that wealth management assets are collected entirely from other non-traditional credit financing tools. The non-duplicate part of the financing business of securities brokers and fund subsidiaries is 50%. It can be estimated that the scale of the shadow banking system on this level is 14.6 trillion yuan, adding up to about 21 trillion yuan plus the part of the shadow banking in the narrowest sense.[17] This process of elimination and differentiation is based on the three basic functions of the shadow banking system: maturity transformation, liquidity transformation, and credit-risk transfer.

Non-traditional credit financial products involved in shadow banking in the broad sense include non-traditional credit financing and related innovations within the banking system such as interbank business and a small portion of L/C, drafts, and payment services. Statistics, however, can only take interbank business into account. Interbank business in 2012 was 10 trillion yuan. The interbank assets of sixteen listed banks reached 11.6 trillion yuan[18] by the end of September 2013. The scale of interbank business in 2013 exceeded approximately 12 trillion. Based on these figures, the scale of the system in the broad sense is estimated at 33 trillion yuan, or 23% of the total assets of 143 trillion yuan in the banking system. However, this is an overestimate because a large proportion of interbank

Table 1.2 The three levels of China's shadow banking system

	Characteristics	Non-traditional credit financing activities involved	Estimated scale (trillion yuan)
The narrowest sense	Unregulated or unlicensed	Private lending, third-party wealth management, online credit financing, unregistered private equity funds, small loans, financing guarantee	6
The narrow sense	Credit supply under insufficient regulation outside the banking system	Products involved in the narrowest sense of shadow banking, plus wealth management, trust, finance companies, money-market funds, asset management for clients, financing of funds and insurance subsidiaries, asset securitization, etc.	21
The broad sense	Non-traditional credit financing within the banking system that is subject to relatively insufficient regulation or circumvents regulation	Interbank business, and a small portion of L/C, drafts, and payment services	27

Source: Summary by the authors

businesses act as normal interbank fund transfers and do not conduct financing activities. Since banks have not collected statistics, if 50% is set as the proportion of quasi-credit, then the scale of non-traditional credit financing involved in the shadow banking system in the broad sense would reach about 27 trillion yuan. Its proportion to the assets of the banking system would decrease to 19%. The overall scale of China's non-traditional credit financing is small in comparison to that of the USA before the financial crash, where the shadow banking system was equal to the commercial banking system in terms of assets (Table 1.2).

1.2.3 Perception of the Scale and Risks of China's Shadow Banking System

In terms of scale, the assets of China's shadow banking system, even if defined in the broad sense, account for only about 20% of the total banking industry. Nonetheless, the development of the shadow banking system has substantially changed China's financial industry. However, the core risks, regulatory policies, development, position, and complementary reforms of China's shadow banking system are more important than its scale. Currently, on-balance-sheet risks are a crucial link as they greatly improve the inner relations of risks.

1.2.3.1 The Scale of Shadow Banking Is Not the Most Important

First, the limited scope and the design of balance sheets of financial institutions in China make it difficult to accurately determine the scale of shadow banking. Present calculations are only estimates and there is inevitably some duplication.

Second, changes in the scale of shadow banking reflect the structural transition from bank-dominated indirect financing to diversified means of financing. However, such changes fail to expose the accumulation of systemic risks across the whole financial system. Although it is the quantity of financial risks that are usually cited, the true risks of shadow banking, especially the on-balance-sheet and off-balance-sheet risks of banks and other institutions, reside in the "quality."

1.2.3.2 Credit Expansion Mechanisms Based on Interbank Business Is the Key to the Risks of China's Shadow Banking System

"An important feature of shadow banking is the historical and continuing involvement of commercial and clearing banks—that is, more 'traditional' banking institutions."[19] Practical research and theoretical study have revealed that the financial risks of China's interbank business mainly manifest themselves in the following ways. The first is non-traditional credit financing with interbank business as the core. This involves, to a certain extent, idle funds that do not serve the real economy. The second is the large, 1.8 billion yuan gap between the assets and liabilities of interbank business, which indicates highly leveraged operations in some institutions. The third is interbank business that mostly evades regulation and resorts to regulatory arbitrage. It eliminates regulation of scale of financing, capital and risk provision through managed liabilities and balance-sheet transfer. Fourth, control of the financing scale during interbank operations is broken. Credit funding runs counter to policy direction, flowing to high-risk fields including industries with overcapacity, real estate, financing platforms, etc. Interbank businesses grant long-term loans with short-term deposits, leading to severe maturity mismatch. The final aspect is that some interbank businesses intentionally conceal credit risks and risk weightings in quasi-credit financial services. This leads to non-transparency of information.

Fundamental changes have occurred in the banking system's risk structure due to the rapid expansion of interbank business which has expanded the scope of credit funding and changed its direction. It also hides the credit risks of some banking businesses, increases the leverage and intensifies the inner relations of the banking system. Therefore, financial risks can be contagious and pose larger potential systemic risks than the bank-dominated single system. Future regulation should focus on interbank business as it is the key to risks in the shadow banking system.

1.2.3.3 *Against the Background of Rapid Expansion of Interbank Business, Shadow Banking Risk First Manifests Itself as Liquidity Risk of the Capital Market*

Under the expansion mechanism of non-traditional credit financing, shadow banking risk will first manifest itself as a liquidity risk of the capital market. As non-traditional credit financing within the banking system relies increasingly on the wholesale capital market, the severe mismatch maturity of interbank business in particular is maintained through the wholesale interbank lending market. Liquidity is weak as it fluctuates in the wholesale market. Once risks erupt in the lending market, banks or other financial institutions that depend heavily on the wholesale capital market will face a liquidity crisis. This triggers contract violation and severe credit problems and could lead to a balance-sheet crisis in the banking system, in other words, the bankruptcy of a bank. The "money drought" on June 20, 2013 demonstrated the risks involved in shadow banking, and the continuous rise of interest rates in the interbank lending market.

1.2.3.4 *Risks of Shadow Banking Can Easily Trigger Systemic Financial Risks*

A series of new problems and risks have appeared due to the rapid development and excessive financial innovation of the shadow banking system.

There is an inherent problem with shadow banking and the non-traditional credit financing business. Maturity mismatch, rate of return mismatch, and information asymmetry would produce liquidity risks, credit default, and moral hazard, which mainly consist in incomplete infrastructure, information asymmetry, overdraft of institutional credit, etc. Domestic financial institutions are unable to clearly understand the risk of such businesses. The "rationality of individual vs. fallacy of composition" mismatch may also result.

The other problem is the greatly enhanced inner relationship of the financial system with the fast development of interbank business. China's shadow banking system involves several industries including banks, trusts, securities, and insurance. It also spans several financial markets—money, credit, capital, insurance, and wealth management. Closer relations develop and risk contagion among financial institutions and in the financial system increases exponentially. Once a larger risk has arisen from shadow banking, it can quickly spread to the banking sector and the real economy through the money market and credit market, causing systemic financial risk. In a certain sense, close relationships and contagion are the largest hidden dangers of systematic risk in China's financial system.

1.3 The Regulation of China's Shadow Banking System: Development and Review

1.3.1 2008–2009: Emphasis on the Regulation of Wealth Management Products

The CBRC carried out regulation in 2009, during a time of rapid growth for wealth management products. It was aimed at financial risks caused by wealth management products with a focus on report management and investment management of wealth management services.

During the development of wealth management services, some financial institutions in the banking industry transferred existing loans and new loans off their balance sheet through financial innovation. The design and distribution of credit-type wealth management products in particular was used to evade regulatory requirements for capital supervision, provisions, etc. It can be seen that bank loans have been transferred off the balance sheet. Banks continue to take responsibility for post-loan management, loan recovery and other substantial legal responsibilities and risks. However, capital requirements are reduced and corresponding provisioning is circumvented as a result. The potential risks of this type of balance-sheet transfer are not to be ignored. Meanwhile, regulation of wealth- management services, information disclosure management, investment management, etc. have not been established.

In 2008, as wealth management services flourished and the above-mentioned problems were revealed, the CBRC issued the "Notice on Further Regulating Relevant Issues concerning Personal Wealth Management Services of Commercial Banks." The document provided risk warnings and regulations on various aspects including product design, client evaluation, information disclosure, risk assessment, and sales conformity. In 2009, wealth management experienced explosive growth, making those problems increasingly apparent. The CBRC issued the "Notice on Further Regulating Relevant Issues concerning Reporting Management of Personal Wealth Management Services of Commercial Banks" on April 28, 2009 to regulate the reporting system for wealth management services. It then issued the "Notice on Further Regulating Relevant Issues concerning Investment Management of Personal Wealth Management Services of Commercial Banks" on July 6, 2009. This publication in particular involves broader adjustments and stricter regulations on principles, methods and directions of investment management compared with the previous policies and practices.

During the release and implementation of the regulatory documents, related departments made full use of the flexibility of the regulatory framework. They produced policies that were effective, timely and pertinent to regulation over the development, changes and risk distribution of the wealth management market. The publication discussed the relationship between development and stability on the basis of encouraging development and preventing risks. However, these are mostly regulatory documents that focus at the level of the CBRC or its general office, and involve quite limited measures for inner relations of risks in wealth management services. At the same time, the frequent release of regulatory documents led to "response overload" for relevant agencies.

1.3.2 2010: Strengthened Regulation of Bank–Trust Cooperation

The expansion of wealth management by commercial banking companies slowed down, following the introduction of relatively effective risk controls. Commercial banks began to focus on innovative business outside the scope of regulation. Meanwhile, the basic tone of China's macroeconomic policy became more tightly controlled. As an approach to escape regulation, some wealth management cooperation between banks and trust companies developed quickly. Bank–trust wealth management cooperation avoided relevant regulation through the introduction of trust plans. Although risks were not substantially reduced or eliminated, internal relationships within the financial system improved.

In 2010, regulation focused on the financial risks of bank–trust wealth management cooperation. As money was tight, there was some control over credit financing, while bank–trust quasi-credit financing experienced massive growth. This produced relatively high macro-economic and financial risks. In August 2010, the CBRC issued the "Notice on Regulating Relevant Matters concerning the Wealth Management Cooperation between Banks and Trust Companies," which strengthened regulation of bank–trust wealth management cooperation. It stressed the principle of self-management of trust companies and introduced balance-ratio management (no larger than 30% of total assets) for financing business, calling a halt to open and non-listed companies' equity investment products. Commercial banks were also required to transfer off-balance-sheet assets to their balance sheets within two years. In the notice, the CBRC also stated that a daily monitoring system for bank–trust wealth management cooperation would be established. On January 13, 2011, the CBRC published new regulations on bank–trust wealth management cooperation, the "Notice on Further Regulating Wealth Management Cooperation between Banks and Trust Companies." This clarified the risk attribution of bank–trust wealth management cooperation and required bank-trust wealth management cooperation businesses to transfer off-balance-sheet assets to the balance sheet by the end of 2011, eight months earlier than the previous notice. For loans between commercial banks and trust companies that were not transferred to the balance sheet, trust companies would need to provide for risk capital at the rate of 10.5%.

The regulation of bank–trust cooperation was timely and effective. In particular, the stipulations concerning balance-ratio management, the transfer of off-balance-sheet assets, the clarification of risk attribution and risk capital provision, played a relatively positive role in reducing banks' hidden off-balance-sheet risks. It also increased the separation between banks and trust companies.

1.3.3   2011: New Emphasis on Overall Regulation and Control of Off-Balance-Sheet Business Risk

With the tone of macro-economic adjustment continued moderate to tight, the real economy's thirst for capital was becoming increasingly acute. The rapid increase in risk caused by innovation and accelerated development in non-traditional credit financing, combined with the rapid expansion of banks' off-balance-sheet business, forced banks to emphasize the role of regulation in the latter.

In 2011, regulatory authorities faced a multi-dimensional task in the regulation of non-traditional credit financing. At the Work Conference on the Regulation of Non-banking Financial Institutions took place in April 2011, the CBRC's cautious and evidence-based proposals stressed the basic logical principles of preventing risks while encouraging development. To promote the development of non-banking financial institutions and services, the CBRC required comprehensive control of off-balance-sheet risks, continued regulation of bank–trust cooperation, and strengthened regulation of off-balance-sheet business including wealth management, credit asset transfer, interbank payment services, etc. It also sought to rectify irregular commercial paper business, and strictly prevented regulatory arbitrage and risk transfer. Three regulatory tasks were specified by the CBRC. The first was to continue the regulation of bank–trust cooperation by urging the banking industry to strictly implement the regulations on inclusion of risk-weighted assets, observe the principles of "true sale" and "cost symmetry," and realize the total transfer of risks and returns. On April 15 and October 28, the special topic of consolidated supervision was discussed. The second task was to strengthen the regulation of wealth management services, and further the construction of systems of wealth management product sales and risk management. On August 24, the departmental regulation "Measures on the Administration of the Sales of Wealth Management Products of Commercial Banks" was issued. Another document was issued on September 30, called the "Notice on Relevant Issues concerning Further Strengthening Risk Management of Wealth Management Services of Commercial Banks." The third task rectified irregular commercial paper business by focusing on bank acceptance with comprehensive supervision and regulation of its trade background, regularity of money flow, and accounting compliance. This was to ensure regulation, to a great extent, of reverse-repo commercial paper services. At the end of June, the CBRC ended irregular discount note operations with relevant accounting errors.

In 2011 regulation became very difficult due to a change in macro-economic policies, strong capital demands by meso-economic areas, and the powerful dynamics of micro-economic innovation. At this time, regulators began to worry about the rise of shadow banking in China.

1.3.4 2012–2013: Overall Regulation of Non-Traditional Credit Financing in the Form of Non-Standard Assets, Credit Assets Transfer, and Interbank Business

The next focus of regulators was interbank payment services, credit asset transfers, and cross-industry non-traditional credit financing. In April 2012, the CBRC required commercial banks to carry out self-examination and to rectify irregular interbank payment services.August saw the publication ofthe "Notice on Regulating the Administration of Interbank Payment Services" which emphasized the regulation of accuracy, accounting systems, and risk management. Settlements due before the end of 2012 would automatically be cleared while those due after the end of 2012 should be rectified before December 31, 2012. At the same time, the CBRC urged commercial banks to carry out strict inspection of cross-industry cooperation with trusts, securities, funds, and insurance in respect of credit strength, direction of capital flow, and risk controls, and to establish appropriate risk separation and risk compensation mechanisms to prevent risks from transferring to the balance sheets of banks and prevent regulatory arbitrage. The CBRC also set out rules for the design, sale, and investment direction of wealth management products and credit asset transfers, put an end to interbank deposit and note trust services of trust companies, and further regulated commercial paper deals. Although the CBRC still used off-balance-sheet risks to summarize non-traditional credit financing risks, it is questionable whether interbank business such as interbank payment and deposits actually are off balance sheet, and we are inclined to include interbank business in the on-balance-sheet category.

In 2013, interbank business was focused on non-standard credit assets and reverse repo became the main topic of regulation of non-traditional credit services. It included wealth management, bank–trust cooperation, commercial paper deals, interbank payments, etc. The "Notice on Relevant Issues concerning the Regulation of the Investment Operation of Wealth Management Services of Commercial Banks" (Document no. 8)[20] issued in March 2013 placed restrictions on the investment operations of commercial banks' wealth management services, requiring in particular the regular administration of non-standard credit assets. The financial risks of bank wealth management products and related non-standard credit assets decreased as a result of the document. It clarified the identification of non-standard credit assets. The upper limit of a bank's investment in non-standard credit assets was controlled. Operation, administration and risk management mechanisms of non-standard assets were established. Information transparency was improved through a transaction counterpart list. Inter-institutional guarantee mechanisms were regulated.

We believe there are six crucial regulatory questions concerning the administration of interbank financing. The first is whether to implement standard and transparent supervision, and to restore true credit risks and risk weighting of quasi-credit assets according to information transparency principles. The second is whether to include interbank business in the unified credit granting system of the banking industry to prevent excessive risk in branch institutions and to strengthen the breakdown management of banking institutions' balance sheets. The third is whether to propose corresponding capital requirements and provision for true credit risks and risk weightings in accordance with the "penetration principle." The fourth is whether to prohibit banks from providing explicit or implicit third-party guarantees. The fifth is whether to establish the transaction counterpart list as provided for by Document no. 8. The final question is whether to implement concentration-ratio control and carry out categorized concentration-ratio management in sole financial institutions, non-banking financial institutions, and all corporations.

There are two kinds of perspective on interbank regulation. Some believe Document no. 9 should be issued in order to execute strict supervision. The other view is to strengthen regulation of principles through window guidance or negative list management. Either way, we believe those six aspects should be included in relevant regulations to prevent possible regional or systemic risks in non-traditional credit within the banking system. The technical details of interbank business should be considered as interbank business is equally important to liquidity, term, and return for banks and other financial institutions. An example of this is the relatively low credit risks among transaction counterparts.

1.3.5 2014: Shadow Banking as a Whole as a Significant Area of Regulation

The concept of shadow banking first appeared in the 2011 annual report of the CBRC, which clarified its definition in the form of columns. It also pointed out six categories of non-banking institutions that did not fall into the category of shadow banking: trust, finance company, car finance, finance lease, money brokers, and consumer finance. However, the CBRC has always summarized China's shadow banking risks as off-balance-sheet risks. In 2013, shadow banking appeared again in the monetary policy implementation report of the People's Bank of China. As experts developed a deeper understanding of the definition, business, products, market, and risks of China's shadow banking system, the whole non-traditional credit financing system gradually became recognized by the regulatory authorities.

Document no. 107 is the most comprehensive regulatory policy aimed at China's shadow banking system. Implementing its policies would greatly influence the macro-economy and financial market. The document defined the scope of China's shadow banking system for the first time, naming three categories: credit intermediaries without financial services licenses and totally free from regulation; credit intermediaries without financial service licenses under defective regulation; and relevant financial services license holders whose financial businesses are defectively regulated or are attempting to evade regulation. The document continues the basic principle "everyone is responsible for their own children," and specifies arrangements and responsibilities of shadow banking regulation authorities. It also divides regulatory duties into "one bank and three commissions" (i.e., People's Bank of China, China Banking Regulatory Commission, China Securities Regulatory Commission, and China Insurance Regulatory Commission), according to the principle that "each is responsible for the institutions approved by them." The unification rule applies to those that have been put under the regulation of local governments. For cross-industry and cross-market business, the inter-ministerial joint conference system should be brought into play.

Document no. 107 has not been recognized in academic and business circles, even though it discusses overall regulation of shadow banking. Its definition still follows the principles of not being subject to regulation, based on the original definition of the FSB, but the FSB's statistics have shifted to the center of non-banking credit. The definition of shadow banking also fails to reflect changes in the structure and risk distribution of China's financial system. For example, wealth management, trust, and interbank business are not included under shadow banking. However, these businesses have profoundly changed China's financial institutions, products, markets, and risk features. Finally, the document continues the previous regulatory system's principle of separate regulation for different institutions. Along with the rise of non-traditional credit financing, the ongoing development of mixed operations among these businesses has caused a severe mismatch between the mixed operation mode and the divided regulatory systems. The regulatory system must strengthen comprehensive regulation, as regulation of separate institutions may fail to address the overall risks of non-traditional credit financing, especially the rapid increase of new relationships arising from mixed operations.

1.3.6 Review of Regulatory Policies

The development of China's shadow banking system has led to numerous problems. For example, wealth management service investment and reporting systems, sales of wealth management products, idle funds, false note discounts, nonconformity of capital investment with policies of macro adjustment and control, fraudulent interbank payments, the excessive expansion of reverse repo, etc. may all lead to moral hazard, market risks, liquidity risks, and maturity risks. Regulatory authorities are not only trying to adapt to the development of the prosperous and innovative shadow banking system, but also striving to improve regulatory measures and perfect the regulatory system.

1.3.6.1 Current Regulation of the Shadow Banking System Is Generally Timely and Effective

Since 2009, innovative businesses have gradually broken through and even crossed the boundaries of the regulatory system. To avoid significant regulatory loopholes or oversight, the financial authorities have issued a series of dynamic, timely, and effective regulatory measures against prominent issues concerning wealth management products, non-standard assets, interbank payments, and reverse repo. These measures cater to the trend of the development of non-traditional credit financing, and also avoid large financial, especially systemic, risks.

Most regulatory policies for shadow banking were issued after extensive public consultation. Communication and information disclosure by the market during the issue of the current policies was generally thorough and regular, so that the authority of regulatory policies, special features of the financial industry, the effectiveness of regulation, and popularization among the public were all accounted for, and the effects of these policies are favorable.

1.3.6.2 There Are Many Defects in Regulatory Policies and Measures

However, there are still flaws in the regulation of China's shadow banking system. These are due to the following three factors.

First, regulation lacks a systematic guiding thread combining the regulation of development with the prevention of risk, and actively regulating and guiding related financial innovations with the aim of serving the development of the real economy. Potential risks should be prevented by strengthened regulation. At present, the regulatory authorities publish various notices and regulatory documents to tackle specific problems in shadow banking. They are also busy fixing regulatory loopholes. However, theydo not provide an overall assessment of the innate defects of financial systems and mechanisms, such as whether rates of financial factors should be marketized, whether financial regulatory indexes are reasonable, and whether access to the financial market is fair. Therefore, these policies need to be improved in order to provide a more comprehensive understanding and prevent risks.

Second, regulatory agencies have underestimated the ability and speed of innovation of financial institutions that have a comprehensive understanding of the risks and contagion mechanism of shadow banking. The basic principle of regulation is "surround and destroy," after regulatory arbitrage and financial innovations. When regulatory policies or measures are issued, banks and other financial institutions are becoming tired of responding. They face enormous pressures when their business structures need to be adjusted to conform to regulation. This shows that regulatory competence and the construction of the regulatory system need to be improved.

Third, theoretical studies and policy investigations ahead of the publication of regulatory policies, and appropriate follow-ups, need to be improved.

1.4 Suggestions for the Regulation and Reform of China's Shadow Banking System

The Third Plenary Session of the 18th CPC Central Committee in 2013 discussed the general requirements of improving the financial system. It revealed the urgent need for stronger guidance and regulation. Major tasks that should be implemented to improve the system included bringing the decisive role of the market into play, catering to the developing trend of non-traditional credit financing, perfecting the diversified financial system, promoting the marketization reform of interest rates, and completing the macroprudential financial framework. It is the responsibility of financial institutions to explore various ways of transforming diversified financial services.

1.4.1 The Construction of a Diversified Financing System Is an Inevitable Choice to Adapt to the Development of the Shadow Banking System

The development of shadow banking and non-traditional credit financing is inevitable and reasonable; to guide, encourage, and regulate its development within a diversified financing system constitutes the basic principle of the regulatory authorities.

China's present financial structure has gradually transitioned from being bank dominated to market dominated. The over-rapid development of interbank finance has caused banks to rely heavily on the wholesale market and the apparent maturity mismatch during the fund allocation of traditional and non-traditional credit. However, interbank business plays a fundamental supporting role in improving the efficiency of fund allocation for banks and the interbank market. Reasonable regulatory measures need to be taken to encourage the development of interbank business and guide market entities to prevent maturity mismatch risks. The establishment of a multi-level financial market and diversified financial system is an inevitable requirement of diversified financing during economic development and transformation.

1.4.2 The Bottom Line of Regulation Is to Eradicate Systemic and Regional Risks

Regulatory authorities should carry out effective micro regulation to prevent systemic and regional risks in shadow banking. Regulations should incorporate the principle of total amount control, separate account operation, and classified management. A macroprudential management framework of finance based on systemic risk prevention should also be established. Looking from a macroprudential perspective, the excessively fast expansion of non-traditional credit services should be prevented by the active implementation of total amount control to prevent systemic risks. Separate account operation and classified management should occur in each field, to clarify the derivative and contagion mechanisms of risks in different businesses. Active efforts also need to be made to innovate regulation and prevent obvious regulatory loopholes. Finally, attention should be paid to potential systemic risks caused by internal relationships in the bank-dominated financial system. A macroprudential management system framework should be established to tackle this problem.

1.4.3 Non-Traditional Credit Creation Mechanisms within the Banking System is the Emphasis of Regulation

The banking system is a crucial part of China's financial system. Future regulation should therefore focus on the non-traditional credit creation link within the banking system.

First, the development of interbank business should be regulated and guided on the basis of strengthened risk management. Financial regulatory authorities need a theoretical understanding of the development trends and risks of the interbank business from the perspective of the development of financial systems and diversified financing. They should fully recognize the reasonability and inevitability of interbank business, and comprehensively regulate and guide the development of interbank business so as to improve the multi-level financial market and diversified financing system and promote the transformation of the financial structure from bank dominated system to market dominated system.

Second, the standardization and transparency of interbank business should be improved as soon as possible. High standardization and information transparency in intermediary and interbank lending businesses leads to relatively low risk . The high risks of disguised deposits, interbank payments and reverse repo are associated with their non-transparency. Regulatory authorities should not adopt a uniform prohibition of relevant businesses. Internal absorption and alleviation of risk through the improvement of information transparency may be more effective than external regulation. Regulatory authorities should incorporate standardization and transparency in order to regulate and strengthen interbank business administration, complete relevant assessments and regulatory mechanisms, and guide its steady development on the basis of regulation.

Third, interbank business should be included in the general credit granting system. Provision for capital and risk should be considered because of existing quasi-credit services within interbank business. However, this specific operation has raised a few questions, including whether to incorporate interbank business in the general credit granting system of the whole bank. Another question is whether to require provision for capital and risk according to the "penetration principle" in reference to general requirements for loans. The third is whether to apply the practice to all interbank business categories. We believe it is reasonable and feasible to include interbank business in the general credit granting system, and some banks have already done this. With regard to capital and risk provision, classified management should be adopted for interbank business, especially non-traditional credit financing. Different capital and risk provisions, which can be lower than those for regular loans, should be applied to different categories of non-standard credit assets. In fact, there have already been commercial banks that prepare risk provisions for interbank businesses, such as risk provisions ranging from 0.25–1%[21] for different non-standard asset categories. At the beginning of 2014, the State Council issued Document no. 104. It stated that "capital provision should be calculated and prepared according to the principle of substance over form so as to reasonably control the degree of maturity mismatch between assets and liabilities." That reflects regulatory authorities' strategy of including interbank business in the unified credit granting system.

Fourth, the financial statistics and accounting system should be further enhanced to more comprehensively and precisely reflect the credit expansion of commercial banks. Accounting methods in interbank business should also be upgraded. This would be advantageous for: (1) the breakdown management of balance sheets and maturity and liquidity management of banks; (2) the financial regulatory departments to accurately grasp the credit expansion mechanisms of the banking system; (3) reduced non-transparency of information within the banking system and financial system; and (4) more effective implementation of macro-economic policies, especially monetary policies.

1.4.4 Deepen the Reform of Financial System Mechanisms

Reform is an imperative task, which needs to be correctly executed in order to repair the cracks in the financial system. The risk generation and expansion mechanisms of non-traditional financing are in fact directly related to flaws in the financial system.

Reform of the financial regulatory system needs to be intensified. The macroprudential management framework should also be completed. The rapid development of shadow banking and other non-traditional credit services demonstrate that China's financial system has broken through the barrier of divided operations. The transition to integrated operations has introduced problems ranging from industry-wide to systemic risks. Under such circumstances, the system of separate regulation should be adjusted as soon as possible to establish a new regulatory system adapted to integrated operations. In particular, a comprehensive and flexible macroprudential management framework is urgently needed to react to systemic risks. Liquidity management and price adjustment mechanisms should be strengthened. Systemic risks need to be prevented from a macroprudential perspective. Shadow banking and non-traditional credit financing should be seen as the endogenous factors of systemic risk. Non-traditional credit creation activities should be included in the macroprudential policy framework. A clarification of the risk derivative and contagion mechanisms of various types of credit expansion is needed. Taking an innovative approach to regulation would help avoid regulatory loopholes in the integrated operations model. It would also stress the effectiveness of micro regulation of non-traditional credit financing. Finally, it is important to emphasize the systemic significant position of the banking system, and prevent on-balance-sheet and off-balance-sheet risks arising out of the development of shadow banking.

We recommend that the Chinese government improves the following aspects of the construction of the financial infrastructure and its related systems: one, improving risk pricing mechanisms in the financial market to fully reflect the credit spreads among different institutions in the market; two, completing market operation mechanisms, especially liquidity supply mechanisms and liquidity rescue mechanisms in an extreme market environment; three, actively promote the reform of interest rate marketization; four, break rigid cashing and set up effective marketized mechanism to cope with defaults; five, accelerate the completion of bank information disclosure systems and financial consumer protection mechanisms (such as the deposit insurance system); and six, vigorously promote the standard construction of underlying assets, such as the introduction of a large-denomination negotiable certificate of deposit (CD), and lower the proportion of non-standard credit assets by means of asset securitization.

It is crucial that the central government maintains the stability of financial policies. Some financial risks are derived from the government's policy adjustments. If government policies interfere too much with the financial system, risk pricing mechanisms in the financial market may be disordered, causing financial risks. If macro adjustment remains stable, on the basis of effective regulation, the financial market and financial system will bring their endogenous risk pricing and self-healing mechanisms into play to carry out marketized allocation of credit financing and non-traditional credit financing and enable effective deployment between the real economy and the financial sector.

Finally, financial institutions need to have a balanced risk-management approach and explore different ways of effectively transforming and upgrading their services in the context of interest rate marketization and finance disintermediation. Banks should be more innovative in diversified financing, in view of interest rate marketization conditions. Support for the real economy also needs to be strengthened with non-traditional credit financing. During the process of business innovation and non-credit capital expansion, financial institutions should prevent financial risks and make the transition from the simple credit-risk management model to the comprehensive risk management model incorporating credit risks, liquidity risks, market risks, etc.

Notes

1. Sinha, Anand. "Regulation of Shadow Banking-Issues and Challenges", presentation at an event organized by the Indian Merchants' Chamber, Mumbai, 7 January 2013.
2. Yang, Zaiping. "Understanding 'Shadow Banking'", speech at the Innovation Forum for Financial Sectors on January 14, 2013. Ba, Susong. "Misunderstandingthe Shadow Banking System", Speech at the 2013 China Economy Forum on January 20, 2013.
3. Liu, Yihui. "Risks of shadow banking in China's Style", December 11, 2012. http://www.ftchinese.com/story/001056812.
4. Zhu, Haibin. "China's shadow banking accounts 70% of GDP", *Securities Times*, June 17, 2013.
5. Li, Yang. Don't Regulate the Shadow Banking in a Rude Way (in Chinese), *China Securities Journal*, 19 July 2013. Hu, Bin and Liansheng Zheng. The shadow banking of China: From the perspective of non-traditional credit, *Shanghai Securities News*, 9 May 2014.
6. The initial definition given by the FSB uses being subject to regulation as the criterion defining the shadow banking system, but their statistics are gathered in the non-banking credit intermediaries sector based on the frequency of shadow banking business. The statistics do not therefore conform to the FSB's definition.
7. FSB, Global Shadow Banking Monitoring Report 2013, 14 November 2013.
8. *Securities Daily* published a report on December 13, 2011 about the PBOC's second investigation into private lending. It revealed that the scale of private lending was about 3.38 trillion yuan. The People's Bank itself did not release any official report or statistics.

9. The figure shows the scale at the end of 2012, collected by the office of the joint conference of regulatory departments of financing guarantee business.
10. Data source: China Trustee Association.
11. Data source: Wind Information.
12. Data source: The CBRC, cited from a report of Financial Times on November 29, 2013, http://www.financialnews.com.cn/gs/cw/201311/t20131129_45516.html.
13. Data source: China Trustee Association, cited from a second source of a report of International Finance News on December 4, 2013, http://www.yanglee.com/research/newsdetail.aspx?NodeCode=105022020&ID=100004722958162.
14. According to a report by China Securities Journal Online on August 27, 2013, the scale of fund subsidiaries was likely to reach 1 trillion yuan, http://www.cnstock.com/v_fortune/sft_jj/tjj_yndt/201308/2714879.htm.
15. Fitch Ratings, "China's money market funds hit a record", January 15, 2014.
16. Zhu, Haibin. "China's shadow banking accounts 70% of GDP", Securities Times, June 17, 2013.
17. The FSB calculated the scale of China's non-banking credit intermediaries at 2.1 trillion dollars, roughly 12.8 trillion yuan. That is much smaller than our statistics, due to the absence of some trust assets and other businesses in their statistics.
18. Statistics comes from banks' third-quarter reports.
19. Quoting from a speech made by Ben Bernanke, former Chairman of the FED at the Federal Reserve Bank of Atlanta Financial Markets Conference on April 9, 2012. It was published in *China Finance*, Issue 12, 2012.
20. The "Notice on Relevant Issues concerning the Regulation of the Investment Operation of Wealth Management Services of Commercial Banks", http://www.cbrc.gov.cn, March 25, 2013.
21. The data were from our surveys of some banks.

References

Ba, Susong. 2013. Misunderstanding to the shadow banking system. Speech at 2013 China Economy Forum on January 20, 2013.

Speech by Ben Bernanke, former Chairman of the FED at the Federal Reserve Bank of Atlanta Financial Markets Conference on April 9, 2012. It was published in China Finance issue 12, 2012.

CBRC. Cited from a report of Financial Times on November 29, 2013. http://www.financialnews.com.cn/gs/cw/201311/t20131129_45516.html.

China Securities Journal Online on August 27, 2013, the scale of fund subsidiaries was likely to reach 1 trillion yuan. http://www.cnstock.com/v_fortune/sft_jj/tjj_yndt/201308/2714879.htm.

China Trustee Association. Cited from a second source of a report of International Finance News on December 4, 2013. http://www.yanglee.com/research/newsdetail.aspx?NodeCode=105022020&ID=100004722958162.

Fitch Ratings. 15 January 2014. China's money market funds hit a record.

FSB. 14 November 2013. Global shadow banking monitoring report 2013.

Hu, Bin, and Liansheng Zheng. 2014. The shadow banking of China: In the perspective of non-traditional credit. *Shanghai Securities News*, May 9.

Li, Yang. 2013. Don't regulate the shadow banking in a rude way (in Chinese). *China Securities Journal*, July 19.

Liu, Yihui. 11 December 2012. Risks of shadow banking in China's style. http://www.ftchinese.com/story/001056812

Sinha, Anand. 7 January 2013. Regulation of shadow banking-issues and challenges. Presentation at an event organized by the Indian Merchants' Chamber, Mumbai.

The Notice on Relevant Issues concerning the Regulation of the Investment Operation of Wealth Management Services of Commercial Banks. 25 March 2013. http://www.cbrc.gov.cn

Yang, Zaiping. Correctly understand 'shadow banking'. Speech at Innovation Forum for Financial Sectors on 14 January 2013.

Zhu, Haibin. 2013. China's shadow banking accounts 70% of GDP. *Securities Times*, June 17.

CHAPTER 2

Digital Finance: Definition, Models, Risk, and Regulation

Bin Hu and Liansheng Zheng

China has the most prosperous digital financial system in the world. The country's economy is facing unprecedented historical development opportunities as it embraces tertiary and innovative sectors. Cross-over industrial financial innovation has become a new trend. The merge of Internet technologies and financial activities in China over the last few years makes digital finance a noteworthy phenomenon of the country's economy. The booming development of Digital financial products has quickly overtaken traditional savings and money fund avenues. Financial products like Yu'ebao, created by e-commerce giant Alibaba's online payment arm Alipay, have been instant hits. Despite its success, Digital finance has become a major financial concern in industrial, academic, and political circles. Experts are divided on its future development, potential impact, and effective regulation.[1]

Although China has seen the most rapid development of Digital finance in the world, there is no clear or widely accepted definition of the term. The concept does not even exist in developed economies. In the USA, there are similar products such as electronic finance, network finance, and online finance. Digital finance is different from indirect financing in the banking system and is distinct from direct financing. Some researchers call it 'the third financing mode'. The regulatory department should take into

B. Hu (✉) • L. Zheng
Institute of Finance and Banking, Chinese Academy of Social Science, Beijing, China

© The Editor(s) (if applicable) and The Author(s) 2016
B. Hu et al. (eds.), *Development of China's Financial Supervision and Regulation*, DOI 10.1057/978-1-137-52225-2_2

consideration the fundamental risks of Digital finance. Some researchers have recommended the so-called '12 rules'[2] of Digital financial regulation, which serve to boost innovation and prevent risks. Promoting the development of Digital finance on the basis of risk prevention and regulation has become a realistic policy issue for discussion.[3]

2.1 Digital Finance: Definition and Development

2.1.1 Definition of Digital Finance

The term Digital finance generally refers to any organization that offers its financial applications to the public over the Internet or any other IP network. It includes peer-to-peer (P2P) lending and crowd funding. Digital finance typically embodies the attributes of fairness and inclusiveness. It can be used by the general public online; its functions are user-friendly and it offers a range of personalized interactive services. Digital finance offers much more freedom than traditional finance. It embraces the idea of globalization, breaking boundaries and enabling users to be mobile, prompt and efficient.

The diverse range of services that have become available over the last few years in China are mainly due to the convenience and advanced technologies of the Internet. Most domestic Digital finance businesses maintain the essential characteristics of finance. Digital finance is the extension, upgrade, and innovation of finance using Internet technologies.[4] In developed economies such as the USA and the UK, Digital finance has not yet become an independent ecological system of finance. It does not have a subversive impact on the traditional financial system. Instead, it promotes innovation and, to some degree, the fusion of the financial sector with Internet technologies. China's system, institutions and markets during a time of transition have been the main driving factors in the success of Digital finance.

2.1.2 The Development of Domestic Digital Finance

The speed and scale of the development of Digital finance in China is greater than in developed economies. The size of the country's Internet credit business has exceeded that of the USA. Over the past three years, there has been explosive development with increasingly strong businesses such as Internet loans (P2P) and crowd funding. Even Internet wealth management businesses have experienced a period of high-speed development driven by Yu'ebao and its counterparts in the market. Within less than six months, the Internet money fund associated with Yu'ebao became the largest single fund in China. It exceeded the total size of assets under management of any other fund within a year and a half.

The fusion of Internet technology and the financial system was born alongside the development of information technologies (IT) in the early 1990s. The growing trend towards electronic, informational, and network-based development of the financial industry has steered China's financial system in the direction of gradual IT-based modernization. Over the years, Digital finance has acted as a kind of technological support for the financial industry. Emerging Digital financial products are changing the sector's role in the industry. Products such as third-party payment, P2P loans, crowd funding and Yu'ebao, are helping Digital finance become an independent force, rivalling the traditional financial industry and attracting considerable attention from various circles. In general terms, China's Digital finance has been through three major periods of development.

The first period is the Internetization of the traditional financial industry from the 1990s to 2005, similar to US and European trends. During this period technological support, infrastructure, and process re-engineering combined with the financial industry, technologies were upgraded, processes re-engineered, infrastructure and efficiency improved, and mutually connected financial informational networks formed. In this period, Internet technologies were basically auxiliary.

The second, prosperous, period saw the development of third-party payments around 2005–2011. During this time, it was the USA that mainly experienced the Internetization of traditional financial services, with the emergence of Digital financial services for banking, insurance, and wealth management networks. China's third-party payment system was associated with the rapid development of e-commerce, and the payment and settlement system was relatively backward. During this period, Digital finance began to penetrate the payment and settlement system, becoming a competitive counterpart of the traditional payment and settlement system.

The third period is the development of substantive financial services based on the Internet from 2011 to the present. The development of China's Digital finance during this period is equivalent to that of the second and third periods in the USA. Digital finance has entered substantive financial services, particularly network loans, crowd funding and Internet money funds.[5] Network loans were developed after 2005, but substantive Internet-based financial services were mostly started after 2012. The introduction of Yu'ebao in 2013 rapidly accelerated this development.

2.2 Main Business Models of Digital Finance in China

Although the history of Digital finance in China has been short, its business models and ecological systems are relatively complete, with rapid exponential growth. Since virtual currency has not become a major area of attention at home, the focus of domestic Digital finance is mostly on Internet credit services and Internet money funds in addition to the payment and settlement system. Over the last three years, domestic Digital finance has been developing prosperously and has gradually adopted varied business models and operating mechanisms.

The Digital finance business model has always been a major concern in both academic and industrial circles. In the academic realm, there is still no agreement reached on the business division of Digital finance. Xie Ping et al. believe the three backbones of Digital finance are payment methods, information processing, and resource allocation.[6] Based on these, eight types of innovative models can be identified: Internetization of traditional finance; mobile payment and third-party payment; Internet money; credit investigation and network loans based on big data; insurance based on big data; P2P; crowd funding; and big data applications in securities investment.[7] Consulting agencies that focus on actual business group domestic Digital finance into five business categories: payment and settlement; online financing; virtual currency; intermediary business; and information services.[8] Some believe that third-party payment, P2P, crowd funding, big data finance, Digital finance portal web, and IT promotion of financial institutions constitute the six major business modules of Digital finance.[9] The country's short but rapid development has involved mixed models and numerous innovations, which is why no consensus has been reached on the classification of Digital finance. Based on the experience of other countries and the current state of Digital financial services in China, there are five types of Digital finance business model.

2.2.1 Internetization of Traditional Financial Services

Internetization of traditional financial services, also known as the Financial Internet, mainly includes new forms of business operated via the Internet by commercial banks, securities, insurance, private wealth management, and asset management, and has three main aspects. First, the fusion of Internet technologies and traditional financial services is the informational upgrade of the original financial services. This includes network banks, ATM services, financial IC cards, etc. The second is the innovative development of traditional financial services relying on Internet technologies, such as Internet money funds (e.g.,Yu'ebao). The third includes institutions or platforms that serve traditional financial services and emerging Digital financial services, such as fund websites or supply-chain finance.[10]

The developing Internetization of traditional financial services mainly caters to their need for convenience, efficiency, and safety. In this business model, traditional financial services depend on Internet technologies to upgrade or even rebuild the business process, optimize service, and strengthen professional management of the risk module for wider coverage, higher convenience, and better guarantees of the efficiency and safety of financial services. During operations, financial institutions use informational, intensified, and process-based management, while the Internet becomes the infrastructure of an improved financial service.[11]

The most popular Internet money fund in China, Yu'ebao, typifies the explosive growth of Digital finance and the Internetization of traditional financial services. Yu'ebao, founded in June 2013, has attracted more than 80 million investors. By the end of the first quarter of 2014, the size of its related fund—Tianhong Zenglibao money fund—had reached 541.275 billion yuan.[12] At the end of 2014, at 578.935 billion yuan,[13] its size far exceeded that of any other single domestic fund was bigger than any other fund company.

2.2.2 Third-Party Payment

In the narrow sense, third-party payment means that non-banking institutions of a certain size and credit guarantee establish connections between users and banking payment and settlement systems by signing agreements with each big bank. . Internet third-party payment systems, such as Alipay and 99bill, rely on information technologies. In its Administrative

Measures for Payment Service of Non-financial Institutions, the Central Bank defined third-party payments as network payment, prepaid cards, acceptance of payments via bank cards, and other payment services prescribed by the People's Bank of China (PBOC), in which non-financial institutions act as the payment intermediaries between payees and payers. The extensive range includes Internet payments and off-line payments, comprehensive payments, and related services.[14] The definition of third-party payments given by the Central Bank is a broad one, and includes Union Pay. In this paper, the discussion focuses on its narrower meaning.

Third-party payment—the payment and settlement system of finance—is a measure of Digital finance's penetration of the financial infrastructure Representative examples are 99bill, YeePay, Alipay, and Tenpay. In July 2013, the PBOC issued a second batch of third-party payment licenses. The number of license holders is currently 250.[15]

At present, third-party payment services are of two types.[16] Comprehensive third-party payment is based on its own e-commerce website and provides a credit guarantee as added value, which guarantees the interests of buyers and sellers on the e-commerce website. The consumer is the main customer.Examples are Alipay and Tenpay. Independent third-party payment carries no guarantee and only provides a payment service for users. This model mostly depends on businesses as their main customers. 99bill and YeePay are examples.

2.2.3 Peer to Peer (P2P)

Peer to peer, also known as "person to person" in the USA, is usually translated in China as network loans or everyone loans. Network loans originated with Zopa, the first network loan platform in the world, founded in the UK in March 2005. It spread to the USA, Germany, Japan, and other countries, and became even more successful in the USA. Network loan companies in China have gradually developed since 2006 and experienced rapid development after 2011. In 2013, the number of domestic network loan platform companies exceeded 350, with annual transactions of over 60 billion yuan.[17] In 2014, network loans grew explosively. According to a report by Analysis, the scale of network loan transactions in 2014 was 201.26 billion yuan.[18] According to the *2014 Annual Report of China's Network Loan Industry,* jointly issued by Wangdaizhijia (Network Loan Family), the China Center for Financial Research Tsinghua University, and Yingcan Business Consulting Co., Ltd., the number of network loan platforms reached 367 in 2014. Cumulative network loan transactions for the whole year reached 252.8 billion yuan, and the loan balance was 103.6 billion yuan.[19] Data from P2P001, however, showed network loans in China as high as 329.194 billion yuan in 2014, far exceeding the statistics of Analysis and Wangdaizhijia.[20]

The typical P2P operational model consists of three main bodies: network loan company, fund demand side, and fund supply side. The traditional network loan platform provides loan demand informaton. It enables the debtor and creditor to make offers freely, and matches transactions. The lender gains interest income and bears the risk, the borrower repays the principal when it is due, and the network loan platform charges an information service fee. The greatest advantage of P2P network loans is to enable borrowers that cannot be covered by traditional banks to fully enjoy the efficiency and convenience of borrowing money in the virtual world. On the network loan platform, demand and supply fund sides overcome the information asymmetry and conduct direct, face-to-face transactions. In China, however, there is a rather weak credit foundation, insufficient risk awareness on the part of investors, and incomplete risk education, leading to a variety of network loan models. Credit information on both sides is seriously asymmetric, so the purely intermediary P2P model cannot grow and develop smoothly in China. Development of domestic network loan platforms has gone way beyond the information platform. Most network loan platforms have actually become bodies in their own right in substantive financial services.

2.2.4 Crowd Funding

Crowd funding is a way of financing in which the project initiator uses the power of the Internet to mobilize the public and centralize funds, capacity and channels to provide the necessary funding support for small enterprises, professionals, or individuals to undertake certain activities, or establish start-ups.[21] Compared to traditional methods of financing, the essence of crowd funding resides in its small size, large coverage, and convenience. It is has lower thresholds, and does not judge a project solely on its commercial value, thus opening up a new financing route for new types of start-up which are thus no longer limited to banks, securities, PE and VC.

There are many types of crowd-funding projects, including commercial projects such as new product R&D and the foundation of new companies but also scientific research, livelihood projects, disaster relief, art design, political campaigns, etc. Through years of rapid development, multiple operational models of crowd funding have gradually come into being, such as reward-based crowd funding, equity-based crowd funding, donation-based crowd funding, and debt-based crowd funding. Typical platforms include Demohour, Dajiatou, and JEEMOO. However, the most typical Digital finance crowd funding model is equity-based crowd funding, or equity crowd funding, a new concept also known as "network investment banking". In other countries, regulatory agencies have basically defined equity crowd-funding platforms as securities brokers.

2.2.5   Internet Virtual Currency

The fifth kind is Internet virtual currency. American companies such as eBay, Facebook, and Google all provide virtual currencies, which can also be exchanged for real currencies.[22] For example, the American supermarket chain Target sells a Facebook virtual currency card. Bitcoin, a new type of electronic currency, does not even require the involvement of the banking system and is not connected to the Central Bank. However, due to strict controls over virtual currency, similar businesses have limited its development potential.

2.2.6   Dissimilated Digital Finance Businesses

It is also worth noting that some Digital finance businesses (especially Internet credit services) in China use the Internet to dissimulate regular financial services. In dissimulated Digital finance businesses, Digital finance becomes a cover for traditional credit services.[23]

In the case of P2P, the traditional P2P platform is actually an information platform; for example, the two big platforms in the USA, Lending Club and Prosper, are mainly "information intermediaries".[24] However, many P2P services in China operate under other disguises, even illegal fund-raising.[25] Currently, P2P models in China include the following: pure platform; deposit; credit assignment; and credit asset securitization.[26] The pure platform mode should be dominant but it has actually become a rare breed, while the other models have actually disguised the "information intermediary" as a "credit intermediary". This relies on the Internet platform providing a cover for traditional credit business. There are also many cases of dissimulation in crowd funding. The main model should be equity based, but there is now a trend towards project-based and debt-based crowd funding. "Internet usury" is the illegal accumulation of personal savings to issue loans at extremely high interest rates.[27]

2.3 THE DEVELOPMENT TREND OF DIGITAL FINANCE AND ITS INFLUENCES

2.3.1 Development Trend of Domestic Digital Finance

The scale of Digital finance in China has surpassed that of the USA to become the most prosperous Digital financial market around the world. Despite the USA having the most developed financial market in the world, Digital finance has only developed to a moderate extent, similar to other developed nations such as the UK, Europe and Japan. The prosperity of Digital finance in China is therefore rooted in the intrinsic systems and mechanics of the Chinese market.

2.3.1.1 Case Study: Paypal in the USA
Yu'ebao was the prelude to the explosive growth of China's Digital finance, and domestic money funds of a similar kind to Yu'ebao have become the dominant model for Internet money funds. Founded in June 2013, Yu'ebao attracted over 80 million investors in a short period of time. Its related money fund exceeded 500 billion yuan after nine months and reached 578.935 billion yuan by the end of 2014. The total of domestic money funds hit 2100 billion yuan by the end of 2014,[28] of which 1500 billion yuan were from Yu'ebao and similar sources.

Yu'ebao's businesss model is not an original Chinese creation. Paypal's money market fund, the first Internet money fund in the world, was founded in 1999 by Paypal, the subsidiary of eBay. Paypal's history and its results provide a major insight into the future of Digital finance in China. Once, the fund was favored by investors for its liquidity and reached one billion USD by 2007, but the financial crisis destroyed Paypal's fortune. The zero-interest-rate and quantitative easing policies in the USA sealed the fate of Paypal's money fund. The constantly declining rate of return caused a stream of investors to redeem their investments, bringing Paypal's money fund to an end in July 2011. The fate of Paypal forced experts to analyze the model and discover its weaknesses. First, its rate of return was not competitive. The fund's main assets were bonds, and a wide variety of bond funds in the USA could be substituted for it. Its rate of return was also normally lower than stocks. All these factors made it clear that it did not have the necessary interest foundation for explosive growth. Second, the innovative advantage of Paypal was its liquidity, but credit, payment and settlement in developed markets, and financial services in the USA reduced the competitiveness of liquidity, so Paypal lacked the market driver for constant expansion. Third, the final liquidation of Paypal was subject to the restraint of the real economy and macro-economic policy, causing the rates of return to fall until they became negative. Paypal lost the foundations of the economic policy, which it had depended on.[29]

2.3.1.2 The "Special" Foundation for the Development of Digital Finance in China[30]

The history of Paypal demonstrates that the long-term development of financial innovations like Internet money funds depends on multiple factors, from the foundations of the financial system to the degree of development of the financial market, to macro financial policies. Products like Yu'ebao develop extremely fast. By the end of 2014, there were 79 of this type of wealth management products like Yu'ebao, with a total size of over 1500 billion yuan.[2] The rapid growth of Yu'ebao and similar wealth management products has its specific foundation.[31]

The high yield and high growth of wealth management products like Yu'ebao are based on special system foundations, such as interest rate control. Since the interest rate in China is not marketized, and especially because the deposit interest rate is still controlled, and the interest margin is rather large and institutionalized, deposit is the best way for liabilities to create profits and the most important resource for the banking system. The regulation system is another factor. Domestic regulatory authorities use micro regulatory indicators like loan-to-deposit ratio, which banking institutions must strictly abide by in their asset and liability management. Especially at supervision occasions or regulation dead lines, deposits are hard to come by.

The successful growth of Yu'ebao and similar wealth management products is also based on the particular features of the market structure. In China's financial structure, banks occupy an absolutely dominant position in the mechanism of capital supply and allocation, and restrict capital holders' returns. However, Yu'ebao and similar products enable the public to be the real supplier in the capital market and receive their due returns as capital holders. By February 28, 2015, Yu'ebao's rate of return was approximately 4.475%, higher than the interest rate on a 1-year term deposit (2.5%), and ten times that of a deposit on demand. Yu'ebao and similar products provide a higher-return option in wealth management for the general public, and represent a breakthrough of marketization for the control of fixed deposit interest rates.

Yu'ebao and similar wealth management products have specific competitive advantages in the financial products market. The range and depth of the Chinese financial market is modest, and it lacks steady fixed-income products, while Yu'ebao and similar wealth management products offer quasi-fixed income financial products with good liquidity and return. On the other hand, such products can be tied into third-party payment methods such as Alipay, 99Bill, WeChat Payment, etc., making it a really convenient and inclusive way for most smart-phone users to invest. At the same time, when tied to third-party payment platforms, these products basically have the same liquidity as cash. Deposits on demand with third-party payment platforms like Alipay can easily be transferred to a money fund and then to cash, without much affecting the liquidity of cash. The rate of return, however, improves tenfold, fulfilling the huge market demand.

2.3.1.3 Analysis of the Development Trend of Digital Finance in China

The prosperous development of Digital finance has counterbalanced problems of insufficient financial development in depth and financial restraint and helped establish a mechanism by which the demand and supply sides of funds allocate capital based on the marketized price. Before the in-depth reform of its financial system, China represented fertile ground for the development of Digital finance. The regulatory authorities, however, are also tolerant of Digital finance, as it promotes marketization and breaks through financial restraint. Its development follows a reforming trend, in that it allows the market to play a decisive role in resource allocation. Digital finance also gives more equal rights to participants. This is reflected in a relatively high rate of return for capital ownership and provides a convenient source of finance for small and micro enterprises. On the whole, Digital finance has the infrastructure for continuous development in the future.

However, in respect of the development scope, normative development, risk prevention, and internal competition of Digital finance, no consensus has yet been reached in China. An objective assessment should enable us to clearly see the future development of Digital finance.

First, the scope for development of China's Digital finance is determined by the speed and depth of the marketization reform of China's financial system. The development of Digital finance in China is supported by specific systems and institutions, therefore this development may be slowly undermined as the marketization reform deepens and the financial market system gradually improves. For example, if China realizes the marketization of deposit interest rates in the short term, then the high rate of return of Yu'ebao and similar wealth management products will lose its institutional and market foundations, and return to the general level of a money fund. In the long run, Yu'ebao and similar products are the type of money fund that will approach medium rates of return. Where there is no marketization of interest rates, holders of large capital have strong bargaining power to gain a relatively high rate of return with their deposit agreement. There is littleadvantage over the rate of return of general money funds.

Second, the degree of financial disintermediation is subject not only to the demands of the real economy, but also to the adjustment of the risk–return relation. Additionally, the future development of Digital finance should match that of the real economy. According to the history and experience of Digital finance in the USA, Digital finance and the real economy have actually adapted to each other. In the real economy, great changes in the output rate of industries and microeconomic entities will occur during periodic fluctuations, policy changes, and structural adjustment. For example, in an economic cycle the ROE level of enterprises will often experience fluctuations in which the financing cost of enterprises changes with the benchmark interest rate, and the rate of return for investment will also be adjusted as the risk-free return rate (e.g., the return rate of the national debt) fluctuates. Digital finance is tied to the nature of finance, while the long-term rate of return of the financial sector in most cases matches the condition of the real economy.

Third, the development of Digital finance is closely related to its regulation. At present, no regulatory framework for Digital finance has taken shape in China. As the government or relevant regulatory authorities have begun to issue guidance on Internet regulation and associated rules, the difficulty and costs of regulatory arbitrage or regulation avoidance for Digital finance will be greatly increased. This will undoubtedly limit the speed and scale of the development of Digital finance. For example, the network loans will gradually be regulated, and regulatory indicators like capital fund, risk provision, etc. may also be published, which will greatly restrict the development of disguised credit businesses under the umbrella of Digital finance.

Fourth, there is a process of mutual competition between Digital finance and traditional finance, which will also influence the future development of the former. Digital finance, as a typical disintermediated business, is in competition with traditional finance, especially the banking service. For example, the development of Yu'ebao has undoubtedly had a considerate impact on the banking industry's demand deposit business, forcing the banking sector to develop more similar products. By 2014, there were as many banking sector wealth management products as non-banking Internet money funds like Yu'ebao in the market. The response of traditional finance will also affect the institutional, market, and customer foundations that Digital finance has relied on. In March 2014, some banks even made a joint decision to reject agreement deposits from Internet money funds like Yu'ebao, and some banks sharply reduced daily and monthly upper limits for money transfers from debit card to Internet money fund accounts. Under the traditional system, the banking sector benefits from dividends like interest margins and so is not internally motivated to innovate. However, under the impact of innovative businesses, traditional finance, with its powerful advantages in terms of clients, channels, capital, and risk control, can also quickly satisfy the demand of individuals and enterprises for financial services and wealth appreciation.

Fifth, there will be survival of the fittest in Digital finance. Online enterprises cannot expand the scope of their deposits, common funds, and securities, like traditional financial institutions. Such businesses can hardly support demands for larger-scale multi-level financial services with only their own capital and limited entities.[32] For example, in the competition between Didi Taxi and Kuaidadi for third-party payments, both use subsidies for passengers and taxi drivers as effective ways of expanding their customer group and coverage. However, profitability of third-party payment services is relatively low, so high subsidies of over 20 yuan a time (about 7 yuan higher than that of kuaidadi), as in the Didi Taxi operational model, are hardly sustainable. The passenger subsidy gradually decreased to 10, 5, and then 3 yuan. In the end, some companies would be unable to afford this and would be forced to quit the competitive market or face acquisition and restructuring.[33] The same problem is also faced by the network loan market. Most network loans require guarantees, so the size of the market is in fact determined by the guarantee capacity and risk tolerance of the bonding company. Loans with an interest rate as high as 20% and even higher produce a high default rate that most bonding companies cannot afford in the end, leading to the closure or default of related network loan platforms. In 2014, over 275 P2P platforms were closed.[34]

Finally, the development of Digital finance requires solutions to its risks and technologies. The development of Digital finance cannot be separated from the physical platform of the Internet; with ongoing in-depth development, risks will also gradually emerge, and market entities will increasingly demand safer and more convenient technologies. At the same time, the advancement of Internet technologies and the deepening integration of the Internet with the financial system will surely provide more diversified and safer payment and financing methods for the market, which will also have a substantial impact on current business models.[35]

2.3.2 Analysis of the Influence of Digital Finance

2.3.2.1 The Influence of Digital Finance on Traditional Finance

Along with the prosperous development of Digital finance, so far five typical business models have come into existence, including the Internetization of traditional financial services, third-party payments, network loans, crowd funding, and virtual currency. This section focuses on the different business models, their size and their impact on corresponding areas of traditional finance, and asks whether Digital finance can substitute for or subvert the traditional realm.

2.3.2.2 Analysis of the Influence of the Main Business Models of Digital Finance

The various business models of Digital finance have relatively limited influence in relevant fields, but the cross-over issue of Digital money funds is clearly influential. First, in the area of Internetization of traditional financial services, Internet technologies play the role of supporting, merging, and complementing rather than substituting. Internet technologies basically enhance the basis of the development of traditional finance and favor the sustainable development and continuous competitiveness of traditional finance, so Digital finance is still a kind of improvement to and complement for traditional finance. Only innovative businesses, such as Yu'ebao, have the potential to substitute for traditional finance or produce cross-over effects.[36]

Second, in the area of payment and settlement, Internet third-party payment is gradually expanding its influence to become a major player in the payment and settlement system. In 2014, third-party payments amounted to approximately 23 trillion yuan.[37] This accounts for 1.3% of the total volume of non-cash payment services (1817.38 trillion yuan) and 1.6% of all electronic payments (1404.65 trillion) in 2014. Internet third-party payments reached 8 trillion yuan, an increase of 2.6 trillion yuan or 48% on a year-on-year basis, accounting for 0.44% of all non-cash payment services, 0.57% of electronic payments, and 32.4% of network payments (24.72 trillion yuan) in 2014.[38] Internet third-party payments have the potential to substitute for certain parts of the traditional payment system, but, from the perspective of a diversified and improved financial infrastructure, third-party payments are simply an excellent complement to the whole payment and settlement system.

Third, the rapid growth of network loans (P2P) exceeded 60 billion yuan in 2013, surpassing the USA and quickly becoming the country with the largest network loan business in the world. In 2014, network loans continued to grow sharply. According to the *2014 Annual Report of China's Network Loan Industry*, the number of network loan platforms in 2014 was 367, only a slight increase on 2013 (350). However, network loan transactions for the whole year reached 252.8 billion yuan, with a loan balance of 103.6 billion yuan. In the social financing system, network loans made up 1.54% of the total (16.46 trillion yuan), which was lower than the 0.35% of 2013. Network loans also accounted for 2.58% of the total scale of RMB credit financing (9.78 trillion yuan), an increase of nearly 2 percentage points over 2013. The rapid growth in network loans makes them an emerging force in the social financing system, but in the bigger picture their role in social financing is still relatively limited. Especially in 2014, network loan platforms went into liquidation one after another, restricting the momentum of high-speed growth and its role in the social financing system.

Fourth, crowd funding is on an extremely limited scale and as a concept is something of a "hype". "Network investment banking" crowd funding is developing rapidly, but its overall size is very limited. In 2013, global crowd funding was estimated at five billion US dollars, in which Asia accounted for 3–5%. Project financing on domestic crowd funding platforms currently amounts to tens of thousands to hundred thousands of yuan, and cases of over a million yuan are quite rare. Similarly, crowd funding has also experienced a period of swift development in China. In 2014, the number of crowd funding platforms increased from about 30 in 2013 to nearly 120, of which 27 are equity-based crowd funding. Funds raised through crowd funding platforms in 2014 exceeded 900 million yuan, of which 700 million yuan represented equity-based financing.[39] Crowd funding prospers in China as part of "network investment banking", but it is still at a fairly early stage of development and has hardly any influence on the direct financing system, judging by its position and role.

Fifth, virtual currency basically has no influence on China's financial system. Due to strict control by domestic monetary and financial regulatory authorities over the development and use of Internet virtual currency, domestic Internet virtual currency has extremely limited influence.

Finally, the most influential area of Digital financial services is Internet money funds such as Yu'ebao and similar wealth management products, mostly because the cross-over operation has influenced demand deposit and agreement deposit businesses in the banking sector. Demand deposits on a bank's balance sheets are transferred to money fund assets outside the banking system, and again enter the bank's balance sheet by way of agreement deposits. The costs to the bank are ten times higher than demand deposits and its interest margin is drastically reduced.[40]

2.3.2.3 Digital Finance's Influence on the Banking System

Digital finance has a relatively limited direct impact on the banking sector, but its long-term potential influence may be quite profound. As a cross-over financial innovation, Digital finance is also a typical method of financial disintermediation and breakthrough from traditional mechanisms. In China's bank-dominated financial system, the entity most directly influenced by Digital finance will be the banking system, with the most substantive influence in the short term being Internet money funds and third-party payments, which cause a decrease in banks' demand deposit reserves, weaken deposit absorption ability, and increase the cost of liabilities. Of course, because the third-party payment system is still related to the traditional banking sector, apart from some retained funds mainly in provision accounts, the two parties to most third-party payments are still banks. Meanwhile, the scale of Internet money funds is only 1.5 trillion yuan, and network loan balance stands at s approximately 100 billion yuan. In contrast, by the end of 2014, the deposit balance of banks had reached 117.4 trillion yuan, and the loan balance stood at 86.8 trillion yuan. So far, banks have not suffered much direct impact from the development of Digital financial services.

However, in the long term, if the reform of the domestic financial market system does not proceed smoothly, Digital finance may influence the banking sector comprehensively. First, as its business expands, third-party payment institutions may ultimately undertake mainstream and substantive financial services, and become direct competitors to banks in the areas of credit creation and financing services. Second, the banking industry faces the dual impacts of "capital" disintermediation of the financial system and "technological" disintermediation of the Internet. Due to the continuous influence of disintermediation, the banking system will lose the initiative in asset and liability management. Finally, Digital finance may cause a profound change in the banks' attitude to service operation modes. The relatively self-centered service and operation mode of banks will be greatly affected by the convenience, inclusiveness and cheapness of Digital finance.

2.3.2.4 Digital Finance's Influence on the Whole Financial System

As an emerging method of financial services, Digital finance has even been described as the third financial format. Its business models and mechanisms are still based on general financial system rules but with expanded channels and methods. As an organic component of the financial system, if Digital finance maintains strong growth and development, it will exert a comprehensive influence on the financial system. First, the cross-over quality of Digital finance will inevitably cause major changes in entities, structure, market, products, risk distribution, etc. of the whole financial system. Second, the increasing development of Digital finance will have a significant effect on innovation, operating mechanisms, and attitudes in financial services, and the marketization of financial factors. Third, the macro-economic effect of Digital finance will gradually emerge, and when it becomes a major force in financial systems, substantive changes in money policy and its transmission mechanisms may occur. However, because the present scale of Digital finance is still limited, these diverse and comprehensive influences are only in their preliminary stages.

Besides, Digital finance actually favors the comprehensive, deepening reform of the financial system. As a cross-over innovation, Digital finance will be an internal force within the financial system, promoting innovation and development. Digital finance faces the traditional financial industry with new competition and favors its accelerated transition. Digital finance breaks through the existing system and mechanisms in areas like interest rate control, which in effect favors the acceleration of interest rate marketization and promotes financial factor marketization. The cross-over development of Digital finance speeds up integration between different industries and sectors of the financial system and furthers the cross-over development of finance and other industries.

2.4 Investigation of Risks of Digital Finance

As an emerging cross-over mode of finance, the risks of Digital finance have two major characteristics. As an organic component of both the Digital and finance, it is at risk from both Internet technologies and financial services. Significant risks also arise from cross-over practices. Financial risks accompanying the financial innovation of Digital finance are not only included in the business, but also closely related to the blurred lines between business, regulation avoidance, and regulation arbitrage.[41]

2.4.1 *The Dual Character of the Risk of Digital Finance*

Digital finance, with its improved combination of technology and financial services, and its cross-over characteristics, carries its own specific risks.[42] The regulatory authorities believe there are three major risks in Digital finance: (1) lack of clarity around the legal position of institutions may result in illegal activities; (2) the lack of third-party deposit systems is a potential safety hazard; (3) inadequate internal control systems may cause operational risks.[43]

In a sense, there are two sides to Digital finance risk. On the one hand, the introduction of advanced big-data technology and cloud computing helps strengthen data analysis, partially overcoming the problem of information asymmetry, increasing the effectiveness of financial risk management, and spreading related financial risks. On the other hand, Digital finance by its nature does not eliminate or reduce risk; it merely transfers it. It is a type of financial innovation that carries the triple risks of the Digital, finance, and the combination of the two. In particular, the fact that it is fragmented, cross-over, and potentially infectious in nature may generate new kinds of financial risk.[44]

2.4.2 *Risk Analysis of Digital Finance*

The risks of Digital finance are related to those of the Internet industry. As most Digital financial services have certain "technical" features, Digital finance carries with it related risks at a technical level.[45] Risks include information leakage, identity recognition, and information control and processing. Third-party capital deposits and potential capital safety issues are another risk factor. System failures can lead to risk to the financial infrastructure. Finally, potential operational risks, and those based on manual or electronic technologies are more prominent;[46] these include problems of the protection of consumer rights and benefits in Internet retailing.

Since Digital finance shares the characteristics of finance, the possibility of serious financial risks remains.[47] The first is the risk of information asymmetry. The virtual nature of Digital finance produces distinct information asymmetry in respect of identity recognition, capital flow direction, credit evaluation, and so on, and big-data analysis may even cause serious information noise.[48]

Second, the degree of credit risk caused by Internet credit services is even higher, because these services are not at present comprehensively and effectively regulated in China and lack adequate consumer protection mechanisms. For example, the "run-away" of P2P network loan companies is a typical credit risk. In 2014, there were as many as 275 bankrupt P2P network loan companies.

The third risk is liquidity. The technical, interactive, and cross-over properties and the high-speed capital operation of Digital finance can lead to a break in the fund chain and liquidity risk. For example, Internet money funds allocate 90% of their funds to deposit agreements. Some banks use funds acquired through deposit agreements for trust usufruct resale, which carries higher risks, and the trust project then allocates the fund to a local financing platform or the real-estate sector. If just one of these links fails, the liquidity risk will become dominant and even lead to systematic risk.[49] Finally, Digital finance will face increasingly serious legal and policy risks.[50] Some businesses are outside the existing policy, legal, and regulatory framework, and policy adjustment. In particular, traditional finance businesses operating under the "cloak" of the Internet will suffer from more prominent policy, legal, and financial risks.[51]

2.4.3 Overall Risk Evaluation of Digital Finance

Of the five typical Digital finance business models that are currently in operation, the risks are mainly concentrated in two areas: network loans (P2P) and Internet money funds such as Yu'ebao. Third-party payment has been included in the regulation of the payment and settlement system. Virtual currency carries extremely limited risk with strict control by regulatory authorities, and crowd funding is an even smaller risk because of its limited scale. The potential for fraud and counterfeit loans, and information safety problems are significant aspects of P2P private lending. Yu'ebao and similar products carry certain risks of deposit absorption, assets and liabilities, term and liquidity management, and so on, for banks.

On the whole, the risks of Digital finance are controllable and will not cause systemic risks. Digital finance introduces new concepts and attitudes rather than changing the actual business model or nature of finance. Digital finance is still in the early stages of development and is operating on an extremely limited general scale. The five typical business models do not so far exert a substantial influence. The regulation of of Digital finance is basically effective; for example, third-party payments on a relatively large scale have already been included in the regulatory system. Finally, the development of Digital finance has specific foundations, which will be undermined with the continuation of comprehensive reform.[52]

2.5 Digital Finance Regulation: Current Position, Problems, and Suggestions

2.5.1 The Current Position of Digital Finance Regulation

According to other countries' experience of Digital finance regulation, the sustainable development of Digital finance can only proceed with standards, guidance, and appropriate regulation.[53] The issue has received much attention from the regulatory authorities, who have conducted research and put forward twelve principles for the regulation of Digital finance. These principles provide a relatively comprehensive regulatory framework for Digital finance, covering specific initiatives in respect of principles, mechanisms, measures, guarantees, etc.

More importantly, the regulation of Digital financial services has become more specific and substantive. The regulatory authority has issued measures for the regulation of third-party payments, two-dimensional code payments, virtual credit cards, etc., which generally speaking have solved the problem of risk prevention as related to third-party payments. Meanwhile, thanks to strict currency regulation, virtual currency does not present major risks in China.

However, network loans and crowd funding (especially equity-based crowd funding) lack effective regulatory measures and risk response mechanisms. More importantly, risk prevention and the regulatory framework of the whole Digital finance industry lack top-level design and national guidelines.

2.5.2 The Challenges of Digital Finance to the Regulatory System

Digital finance poses various challenges to the regulatory system, which need to be dealt with. Digital finance is deepening financial industry trends towards integration and mixed operation, whereas the existing regulatory system regulates institutionally different businesses separately. This may cause a systematic mismatch between the trend towards mixed operations and the separate regulation systems. There may also be outstanding regulation loopholes because of the high level of innovation. Furthermore, high levels of informationization technology together with the prominent cross-over features of Digital finance pose challenges to the timeliness, adequacy and effectiveness of the existing regulatory system. Finally, the virtual environment of Digital finance creates technological problems with investigation and evidence search. The absence of regulation should be dealt with to encourage the development of Digital finance.[54]

2.5.3 Suggestions for Digital Finance Regulation

Digital finance is developing quickly, while its various business models are also changing dynamically, requiring attention to problems such as whether or not regulation is required, who should be responsible, what should be brought under regulation, and coordination between regulatory departments. The following areas require attention.

The basic principles of Digital finance regulation need to be established. Digital finance is developing alongside the trend towards building diversified financing systems and multi-tier capital markets, and improving financial market systems. Digital finance contributes to improved efficiency in stock money allocation services to individuals and business sectors, the development of direct financing systems, innovationa in traditional finance, and so on Proper would encourage the development of Digital finance, provide guidance in the market to prevent technical, legal and financial risks, and strengthen consumer protection and information disclosure. The development of Digital finance will see the establishment of a multi-tier financial market and diversified financing system, which will diversify financing demands and the need for convenient, cheap financial services on the part of individuals and businesses.[55] The fundamental principle of Digital finance regulation is "to tolerate, encourage, guide, and standardize", in such a way as to encourage development and at the same time prevent risks. Regulation should also be sufficiently "comprehensive, timely, professional, and effective" to prevent systemic and regional risks, and strengthen consumer protection and information disclosure.

The regulatory framework also requires improvement. National laws are needed specifying the framework, principles and objectives of Digital finance regulation. Relevant departments should also issue appropriate standards to regulate Digital finance. Systems should be established to ensure coordination between functional regulation and institutional regulation, and coordination between the China Banking Regulatory Commission and the Ministry for Industry and Information Technology. Finally, the off-site regulation of information technology should be strengthened to establish effective risk monitoring, warning and emergency.[56]

To prevent the regulation of different types of Digital finance from becoming generalized, some clarification of the dividing lines is required. Regulators, the subjects and range of their regulation should be clarified, and the applicability of principle-based or restrictive regulation to various Digital finance business models also needs to be distinguished.[57] Specifically, it is important to discover which types have generated substantive unregulated financial activities (or institutions) by utilizing the Internet and avoiding the existing regulatory system, so that these activities (or institutions) can be included in the existing regulatory system. It should be specified, for example, which network loans are information platforms and which are using the Internet to connect online with offline to absorb savings and issue disguised loans. In the case of the former, the emphasis of regulation is to standardize information disclosure, strengthen information safety, and prevent fraud. For the latter, the focus is to include such financial activities in the existing regulatory system, and to issue and improve rules as appropriate to fill gaps in the regulations and close loopholes. As for crowd funding, if it involves equity financing that is covered by existing laws and regulations, securities regulatory departments should take responsibility for regulating such behavior by issuing or improving fraud prevention regulations in accordance with the law.

Digital finance carries various risks including operational risk, technical risk, legal risk, and regulation failure; these risks require regulatory agencies to publish policies and introduce measures to close regulation loopholes and prevent regulation failure. Attention should be paid to systems to prevent the spillover effects of Digital finance in traditional finance and systemic mismatches between mixed operations and separate regulation.[58] Little attention has been paid by regulatory departments to Digital finance as a catalyst to the mixed operations of traditional finance. For example, when Yu'ebao became popular, banking institutions followed suit and established similar wealth management products, expanding the range of mixed operations in the banking industry, and causing banks and other financial institutions to place greater reliance on the short-term capital market and accept a higher risk of maturity mismatch and management pressure. However, as the existing regulatory system is separate, deficiencies and loopholes with regard to regulation of Digital financial products may appear in multiple business areas, acting as a potential trigger for Digital financial risk. Digital finance has strong internal cohesion but its infectiousness may act as a trigger for the "butterfly effect."[59] The regulatory authorities need to set up mechanisms for monitoring, obstruction and the fusion of risk for different sub-industries and markets, bringing the role of the regulatory system as a firewall into play.

At its core, Digital finance regulation should combine consumer protection and information security. Principal–agent problems or moral hazard issues between the demand and the supply parties may become more pronounced in Digital finance. Customer benefits can only be protected if the compulsory information disclosure mechanism is improved. For example, if such a disclosure mechanism reveals problems like illegal deposit absorption, on-lending, or unethical network loans, the consequences of a platform's bankruptcy, the seriousness of suspects avoiding prosecution and the loss of customers would all be greatly reduced. Compulsory information disclosure mechanisms and consumer protection mechanisms are among the most urgent tasks of the regulatory authorities to strengthen Digital finance regulation.[60]

Finally, the reason why China's Digital finance has received so much attention is mostly because of the significant level of financial repression in China which is closely related to defects in parts of China's financial system and mechanisms. The prosperity of Digital finance in China reflects deep-rooted systemic deficiencies in the country's financial system, including: non-marketization of prices of financial factors; an incomplete credit system, especially lack of market credit; the dominance of banks in capital supply and allocation mechanisms; unsatisfied demands of small and micro enterprises and individual businesses at a time of limited capital availability;

limited steady, fixed-income investment tools; a lack of effective investment channels; and arbitrary charges and poor service on the part of the banks, and so on. Financial regulatory agencies should deepen the reform of China's financial system with special attention to improved marketization of financial factor price, financial infrastructure, marketization of exit mechanisms for financial institutions, financial regulation, and consumer protection.[61]

Notes

1. Zheng, Liansheng. "Digital Finance in China: Nature, Mode, Impact and Risk", *International Economic Review*, Issue 4, 2014.
2. Xie, Ping & Chuanwei Zou."A Research on the Mode of Digital Finance", *Journal of Financial Research*, Issue 12, 2012.
3. Chen, Jingmin. "Some Thoughts on Digital Finance", *Financial Perspectives Journal*, Issue 9, 2013.
4. Hu, Bin & Liansheng Zheng. "Digital Finance is not a Subverter", *Shanghai Securities News*, July 3, 2014.
5. Zheng, Liansheng. "Digital Finance in China: Nature, Mode, Impact and Risk", *International Economic Review*, Issue 4, 2014.
6. Xie, Ping & Chuanwei Zou. 'A Research on the Mode of Digital Finance', *Journal of Financial Research*, Issue 12, 2012.
7. Xie, Ping. 'The Reality and Future of Digital Finance', *New Finance*, Issue 4, 2014.
8. iResearch. Research on Modes of Innovative Digital Finance, July 2013.
9. Luo, Mingxiong. "Analysis of Six Modes of Digital Finance", *High-Technology & Industrialization*, Issue 3, 2014.
10. Zheng, Liansheng. "Digital Finance in China: Nature, Mode, Impact and Risk", *International Economic Review*, Issue 4, 2014.
11. Zheng, Liansheng. "Developing Trend and Regulatory Framework of China's Digital Finance", in 2014 Annual Development Report of China's Finance edited by Zhang Zhonghua, Subject 9, Peking University, Version 1, September 2014.
12. Data source: 2014 the 1st Quarterly Report of Tianhong Zenglibao Money Fund.
13. Data source: 2014 the 4th Quarterly Report of Tianhong Zenglibao Money Fund.
14. People's Bank of China. "Administrative Measures for Payment Service of Non-financial Institutions", June 15, 2010.
15. http://www.pbc.gov.cn/publish/zhengwugongkai/3580/index_2.html.

16. Chen, Mingzhao. "Main Modes of Digital Finance and Analysis of its Impact upon the Development of Commercial Banks", *Economic Research Guide*, Issue 11, 2013.
17. PBOC. 2013. Annual Report of People's Bank of China, June 11, 2014.
18. Analysys. "Quarterly Monitoring Report of China's P2P Network Loan Market", March 5, 2015.
19. Wangdaizhijia. "2014 Annual Report of China's Network Loan Industry", January 7, 2015.
20. P2P001. "2014 P2P Network Loan Data Report", February 5, 2015.
21. Luo, Mingxiong. "Analysis of Six Modes of Digital Finance", *High-Technology & Industrialization*, Issue 3, 2014.
22. Yang, Xiaochen & Ming Zhang. "Bitcoin: Principles of Operation, Typical Features, and Prospects", *Financial Review*, Issue 1, 2014.
23. Zheng, Liansheng. "Digital Finance in China: Nature, Mode, Impact and Risk", *International Economic Review*, Issue 4, 2014.
24. Wang, Pengyue & Jun Li. "The Development of American P2P Platform: History, Current Situation, and Prospect", *Financial Regulation Research*, Issue 4, 2014.
25. Peng, Bing. "P2P Internet Loans and Illegal Fund-raising", *Financial Regulation Research*, Issue 6, 2014.
26. Ye, Xiangrong. "A Research of Mode Risks and Regulation of P2P Loans", *Financial Regulation Research*, Issue 3, 2014.
27. Zheng, Liansheng. "Digital Finance in China: Nature, Mode, Impact and Risk", *International Economic Review*, Issue 4, 2014.
28. Data source: WIND, by March 1, 2015.
29. Zheng, Liansheng. "Why the US doesn't Have a Yu'ebao Fever", *China Securities Journal*, March 31, 2014.
30. The same as the last footnote.
31. RONG 360, "2014 Digital Finance Report", February 4, 2015.
32. Zhu, Jinchuan. "A Research of the Background, Current Situation, and Trend of Digital Finance", *Rural Finance Research*, Issue 10, 2013.
33. Didi Taxi canceled taxi subsidy on the passenger client on May 16, 2014, and canceled order subsidy for the driver client on August 13, 2014; at the same time, to avoid cutthroat competition, Didi Taxi and Kuaidadi announced their merger on February 15, 2015.
34. Wangdaizhijia. "2014 Annual Operation Report of China's P2P Network Loan Industry", January 3, 2015.
35. Zhu, Jinchuan. "A Research of the Background, Current Situation, and Trend of Digital Finance", *Rural Finance Research*, Issue 10, 2013.
36. Hu, Bin & Liansheng Zheng. "Digital Finance is not a Subverter", *Shanghai Securities News*, July 3, 2014.

37. China Electronic Commerce Research Center: "The Scale of Third-party Payment in China in 2014 was 23.3 Trillion Yuan", January 20, 2015.
38. Data source of non-cash payment, electronic payment and network payment: PBC, 2014 General Condition of the Payment System Operation, February 12, 2015.
39. RONG 360, "2014 Digital Finance Report", February 4, 2015.
40. Hu, Bin & Liansheng Zheng. "Digital Finance is not a Subverter", *Shanghai Securities News*, July 3, 2014.
41. Zheng, Liansheng. "Digital Finance in China: Nature, Mode, Impact and Risk", *International Economic Review*, Issue 4, 2014.
42. Wu, Xiaoqiu. "Deep Financial Reform and Digital Finance in China", 2014 China Capital Market Forum Report.
43. Liu, Shiyu. "Carrying forward the Philosophy of Tolerance and Innovation, Dealing Right with the Relation between Development and Regulation of Digital Finance", *Tsinghua Financial Review*, Issue 2, 2014.
44. Wang, Hanjun. "Risk Challenge of Digital Finance", *China Finance*, Issue 24, 2013.
45. Zheng, Liansheng. "Digital Finance in China: Nature, Mode, Impact and Risk", *International Economic Review*, Issue 4, 2014.
46. Shang, Jiangang et al. "A Review of the Seminar on Legal Risks and its Prevention in Digital Finance Innovation", *Shanghai Lawyer*, Issue 9, 2013.
47. Zheng, Liansheng. "Digital Finance in China: Nature, Mode, Impact and Risk", *International Economic Review*, Issue 4, 2014.
48. Xu, Rong et al. "A Research of Potential Risks of Digital Finance", *Financial Regulation Research*, Issue 3, 2014.
49. Gong, Minghua. "Digital Finance: Characteristics, Influence, and Risk Prevention", *New Finance*, Issue 2, 2014.
50. Feng, Juanjuan. "A Research of the Regulation of Digital Finance in China", *Times Finance*, Issue 10, 2013.
51. Peng, Bing. "P2P Network Loans and Illegal Fundraising", *Financial Regulation Review*, Issue 6, 2014.
52. Zheng, Liansheng. "Digital Finance in China: Nature, Mode, Impact and Risk", *International Economic Review*, Issue 4, 2014.
53. Zheng, Liansheng. "Digital Finance in China: Nature, Mode, Impact and Risk", *International Economic Review*, Issue 4, 2014.
54. An, Bangkun & Jinyang Ruan. "Digital Finance: Regulation and Legal Principles", *Financial Regulation Research*, Issue 3, 2014.
55. Zheng, Liansheng, Jin Zhu & Jiyue Sun. "Digital Finance Regulation should Emphasize Five Aspects", *Securities Daily*, May 31, 2014.
56. Zheng, Liansheng. "Digital Finance in China: Nature, Mode, Impact and Risk", *International Economic Review*, Issue 4, 2014.

57. Chen, Guang. "Digital Finance: Vampire or Catfish?", *China Business Times*, March 11, 2014.
58. Hu, Bin & Liansheng Zheng. "Digital Finance is not a Subverter", *Shanghai Securities News*, July 3, 2014.
59. Zheng, Liansheng, Jin Zhu & Jiyue Sun. "Digital Finance Regulation should Emphasize Five Aspects", *Securities Daily*, May 31, 2014.
60. Zheng, Liansheng, Jin Zhu & Jiyue Sun. "Digital Finance Regulation should Emphasize Five Aspects", *Securities Daily*, May 31, 2014.
61. Hu, Bin & Liansheng Zheng. "Digital Finance Is Not a Subverter", *Shanghai Securities News*, July 3, 2014.

REFERENCES

Analysys. March 5, 2015. Quarterly monitoring report of China's P2P network loan market.

Chen, Guang. 2014. Digital finance: Vampire or Catfish? *China Business Times*, March 11.

Chen, Jingmin. 2013. Some thoughts on Digital finance. *Financial Perspectives Journal*, Issue 9. pp 13–15.

Chen, Mingzhao. 2013. Main modes of Digital finance and analysis of its impact upon the development of commercial banks. *Economic Research Guide*, Issue 11. pp 119–120.

China Electronic Commerce Research Center. January 20, 2015. The scale of third-party payment in China in 2014 was 23.3 Trillion Yuan.

Feng, Juanjuan. 2013. A research of the regulation of Digital finance in China. *Times Finance*, Issue 10. pp 20–24.

Gong, Minghua. 2014. Digital finance: characteristics, influence, and risk prevention. *New Finance*, Issue 2. pp 08-10.

Hu, Bin, and Liansheng Zheng. 2014. Digital finance is not a subverter, *Shanghai Securities News*, July 3.

iResearch. July 2013. Research on Modes of Innovative Digital Finance.

Liu, Shiyu. 2014. Carrying forward the philosophy of tolerance and innovation, dealing right with the relation between development and regulation of Digital finance. *Tsinghua Financial Review*, Issue 2. pp 06–09.

Luo, Mingxiong. 2014. Analysis of six modes of Digital finance. *High-Technology & Industrialization*, Issue 3. pp 56–59.

P2P001. February 5, 2015. 2014 P2P network loan data report.

PBC. February 12, 2015. 2014 general condition of the payment system operation.

PBOC. June 11, 2014. 2013 annual report of people's bank of China.

Peng, Bing. 2014. P2P internet loans and illegal fund-raising. *Financial Regulation Research*, Issue 6. pp13–25.

People's Bank of China. June 15, 2010. Administrative measures for payment service of non-financial institutions. http://www.pbc.gov.cn/publish/zhengwugongkai/3580/index_2.html

RONG 360. February 4, 2015. 2014 Digital finance report.

Shang, Jiangang and Han Zheng. 2013. A review of the seminar on legal risks and its prevention in digital finance innovation. *Shanghai Lawyer*, Issue 9. pp 23–26.

Wang, Hanjun. 2013. Risk challenge of digital finance. *China Finance*, Issue 24. pp 19–21.

Wang, Pengyue, and Li Jun. 2014. The development of American P2P platform: history, current situation, and prospect. *Financial Regulation Research*, Issue 4. pp39–44.

Wangdaizhijia. January 3, 2015. "2014 annual operation report of China's P2P network loan industry.

Wangdaizhijia. January 7, 2015. 2014 annual report of China's network loan industry.

Zheng, Liansheng. March 31, 2014. Why the US doesn't have a Yu'ebao fever. *China Securities Journal*.

WIND. March 1, 2015.

Wu, Xiaoqiu. 2015. Deep financial reform and digital finance in China. 2014 China Capital Market Forum Report.

Xie, Ping. 2014. The reality and future of digital finance. *New Finance*, Issue 4.

Xie, Ping, and Chuanwei Zou. 2012. A research on the mode of digital finance. *Journal of Financial Research*, Issue 12. pp 11–22.

Xu, Rong, Liu Yang, and Wen Wujian. 2014. A research of potential risks of digital finance. *Financial Regulation Research*, Issue 3. pp 21–24.

Yang, Xiaochen, and Ming Zhang. 2014. Bitcoin: principles of operation, typical features, and prospects. *Financial Review*, Issue 1. pp 38–53.

Ye, Xiangrong. 2014. A research of mode risks and regulation of P2P loans. *Financial Regulation Research*, Issue 3. pp 33–37.

Zheng, Liansheng. 2014. Digital finance in China: nature, mode, impact and risk. *International Economic Review*, Issue 4. pp 103–118.

Zheng, Liansheng. September 2014. Developing trend and regulatory framework of China's digital finance. In *Annual development report of China's finance*, ed. Zhang Zhonghua, Subject 9, Peking University, Version 1. pp 1–16.

Zheng, Liansheng, Jin Zhu, and Jiyue Sun. 2014. Digital finance regulation should emphasize five aspects. *Securities Daily*, May 31.

Zhu, Jinchuan. 2013. A research of the background, current situation, and trend of Digital finance. *Rural Finance Research*, Issue 10. pp 43–47.

CHAPTER 3

Annual Developments in Banking Regulation

Gang Wang and Zhuqing Mao

3.1 A Review of the Regulation and Operation of the Banking Industry

3.1.1 Banking Regulation Policies in the Last Three Years: A Review and Summary

In recent years, in the face of a grim and complex economic and financial situation abroad and the downward pressure of the transition to the "new normal" economic growth at home, banking regulation has fulfilled the following functions: risk prevention and urging banking institutions to do a good job of risk elimination, formulate response plans, and take strict precautions against risks in key areas; directing regulation aimed at promoting development of the real economy, and leading the transition of

---

Gang Wang is a postdoctoral researcher at the Institute of Finance and Banking CASS and an associate researcher the Financial Institute of the Development Research Center of the State Council; Zhuqing Mao is a postdoctoral researcher at the CASS Institute of Finance and Banking.

G. Wang
Institute of Finance, Development Research Center of the State Council, Beijing, China

Z. Mao
China Banking Regulatory Commission, Beijing, China

© The Editor(s) (if applicable) and The Author(s) 2016
B. Hu et al. (eds.), *Development of China's Financial Supervision and Regulation*, DOI 10.1057/978-1-137-52225-2_3

the banking industry; continuously regulating the development of shadow banking to effectively control potential risks; and making an overall plan to promote deeper reforms and further open up the banking industry to provide greater market access. Regulation has, on the whole, achieved the steady operation of the banking industry and maintained as its bottom line no systematic and regional risks.

3.1.1.1 Capital Rules for Commercial Banks (Provisional) Issued and Put into Effect; Basel II and Basel III Implemented in China

In July 2012, the CBRC issued the "Capital Rules for Commercial Banks (Provisional)" (hereinafter referred to as "Capital Rules"). To act in concert with the implementation of the new capital system, the CBRC released a series of supporting regulatory rules and guidelines. The first was the "Notice of the CBRC on Transition Arrangements for the Implementation of the Capital Rules for Commercial Banks" which promoted the implementation of capital methods.

Second, it issued four documents in support of policies of capital regulation, including the "Supplemental Regulatory Provisions for the Internal Rating System of Commercial Banks," designed to adapt to new changes in international rules of capital regulation.

Third, to support commercial banks' capital instrument initiatives and expand capital supplement channels, it released the "Supervisory Guidance on Capital Instruments Innovation for Commercial Banks" and "Guidelines on Corporate Bond Issue by Commercial Banks as a Means of Capital Supplement." Fourth, it released the "Provisional Rules on Advanced Approach of Capital Management for Commercial Banks," specifying standards, procedures, and subsequently the regulatory framework for approving advanced approaches, and laying the foundation and direction of the implementation of advanced approaches to capital management. At this point, the CBRC has established a capital regulation system centering on capital rules and complemented by transitional arrangements, implementation rules for advanced approaches, and capital instrument innovation. In October 2013, the 149th session of the Basel Committee officially approved an assessment report on China's capital regulation system. The report awarded the system the highest grade, "compliant," revealing the compliance of China's capital regulation with prevailing international rules and its progressiveness.

In April 2014, the CBRC and the CSRC (China Securities Regulation Committee) jointly published the "Guidelines on Preferred Stock Issuance of Commercial Banks as a Means of Tier-1 Capital Supplement" as an auxiliary policy document to support commercial banks to carry out pilot work on preferred stocks. The Guidelines lay down detailed rules on preferred stock issue by commercial banks to supplement Tier-1 capital. Its aim is to regulate application and approval procedure for preferred stock issue by commercial banks, maintain the capital quality of commercial banks, and protect the legal rights and benefits of stakeholders. In April 2014, the CBRC approved the five big banks—Industrial and Commercial Bank of China, Agricultural Bank of China, Bank of China, China Construction Bank, and Bank of Communications—and China Merchants Bank to implement advanced approaches to capital management.

3.1.1.2 *Continuously Strengthened Regulation of Shadow Banking*
In recent years, the CBRC has taken a series of measures to continuously strengthen shadow banking regulation. First, it clarified that six kinds of non-banking financial institutions and businesses are subject to appropriate regulatory laws and daily regulation: banks' wealth management services, trust companies, finance companies, financial leasing companies, auto finance companies, consumer finance companies, and money brokerage companies. These companies do not belong in the category of shadow banking, and so the CBRC will continuously strengthen the regulation of these financial institutions. Second, it has strengthened the comprehensive risk management of banking institutions, and has conducted strict consolidated regulation. Third, it has implemented list management of financing guarantee companies and small loan companies, strictly controlling their financing from banking institutions. Fourth, it severely combats illegal activities such as illegal fund raising. The general direction of the CBRC is based on the development level of the financial industry and the architecture of the regulatory system at China's current stage so as to actively bring out the complementary and innovative role of the shadow banking system in the financial system on the one hand, and strengthen identification and supervision of its risks, enhancing standardization and transparency for its sustained, healthy and stable development on the other.

3.1.1.3 *Finance Directed Towards Serving the Real Economy*
Banking regulation has always stressed the real economy as the foundation of finance. Without nourishment from the real economy, the financial industry will become a tree with no roots. In February 2012, the CBRC formulated the Green Credit Guidelines, which provided specific requirements for banking institutions to effectively implement green credit and

vigorously promote energy conservation, reduction of CO_2 emissions and environmental protection. After the release of "the State Council's Ten Articles for Finance" in 2013, the CBRC further defined finance's relation with the adjustment, transformation and upgrading of the economic structure, stressing that finance should lead and promote the transformation and adjustment of key areas and industries, and play its role in market resource allocation by directing credit flow. In recent years, to give financial support for the development of small and micro enterprises and to strengthen credit support for agriculture, the CBRC has issued a series of regulatory measures, including: the issue of special financial bonds; appropriately increasing the tolerance of non-performing loans lent to small and micro enterprises; and keeping the growth of small and micro business loans and agriculture-related loans at a level at least equal to the average growth rate of that year, and the loan increment at least equal to that during the same period of the previous year.

3.1.1.4 Enhanced Protection for Financial Consumers

The 2012 National Work Conference on Finance had a clearly-stated objective "to strengthen the protection of financial consumers' rights and benefits." The top level of financial consumer protection, which gave greater prominence to the protection of financial consumers' rights and benefits, was designed. In the same year, the CBRC Banking Industry Consumer Protection Bureau was founded; the establishment of regulatory consumer protection systems showed that financial consumer protection had really been put into action, and the content of consumer protection been officially included in the comprehensive risk regulation framework. As to specific measures, first, the "Planning Outline for Consumer Protection in the Banking Industry (2012–2015)" covers the aims, principles, and framework of consumer protection in the banking industry. Second, a series of rules and regulations concerning consumer protection in the banking industry have been established including Consumer Complaint Handling Procedure for the Banking Industry; the consumer complaint response mechanisms of the CBRC and its agencies have also been improved. Third, a joint conference system for consumer protection in the banking industry has been set up, which improves cooperation between the CBRC and relevant departments on consumer protection in the banking industry in accordance with the principle "unified action, coordinated orderliness, specific boundaries, and pursuit of high efficiency."

3.1.2 A Review of Banking Regulation in 2014

In 2014, in the face of complicated and changeable economic and financial conditions both at home and abroad, the China Banking Regulatory Committee devised an overall plan to promote reform and opening up, used multiple means to eliminate financial risks, took various measures to serve the real economy, and set various regulatory tasks in motion. The main measures are as follows. First, breakthroughs have been made in the reform and opening up of the banking industry: the first batch of five private banks has been approved and is under construction; commercial banks have made progresses in setting up special departments for interbank services and wealth management; a security fund for the trust industry has been founded; China Development Bank has established a housing finance business unit; opening up to the outside world has also continued to deepen as the regulation of the administration of foreign-funded banks was revised and foreign banks' market access adjusted. Second, there have been benefits to the real economy. Objectives for small and micro enterprise loans and agriculture-related loans have been reached; consumer protection in the banking industry has been enhanced; and basic financial services have achieved 100% coverage across the country. Third, risks in main areas have been relieved. Business risks in steel trading, guarantee circles, etc. have been eased gradually, shadow banking risk and excess capacity have been controlled, and the principal of no systematic and regional risks has been well maintained. Fourth, the effectiveness of banking regulation has been strengthened continuously: a set of administrative examination and approval items has been abolished or delegated, separate regulation been improved, consolidated regulation enhanced, a series of regulation rules issued, and on-site examination with targets carried out.

A large number of relevant rules and regulations were issued, which was different from the previous year. These include not only fundamental regulations such as "Internal Control Guidelines," "Rules on Liquidity Risk Management of Commercial Banks (trial)," and "Rules on the Administration of Service Prices of Commercial Banks," but also business-specific rules on factoring, interbank services, etc.

3.1.3 Development of the Banking Industry in 2014

3.1.3.1 Development of Banking Services
The operation and development of the banking industry in 2014 have maintained a steady trend, with various indicators of operational manage-

ment and risk monitoring appearing positive and remaining at a good level in international terms.

The scale of assets and liabilities increased. By the end of December 2014, the total assets in home currency and foreign currencies of China's banking institutions at home and abroad had reached 172.3 trillion yuan, a year-on-year increase of 13.87%; the total liabilities in home currency and foreign currencies of banking institutions at home and abroad reached 160.0 trillion yuan, a year-on-year increase of 13.35%.[1]

The capital adequacy ratio remained stable. By the end of December 2014, the weighted average capital adequacy ratio of commercial banks (branches of foreign-funded banks excluded) was 13.18%, an increase of 0.99 percentage points compared with the beginning of 2014.[2]

Credit risks continued to rise, while the quality of credit assets was generally controllable. By the end of December 2014, the non-performing loan balance of commercial banks (according to the statistical standard for corporations) was 842.6 billion yuan, an increase of 250.6 billion yuan compared with the beginning of the year; the ratio of non-performing loans hit 1.25%, a rise of 0.25% over the beginning of the year.[3]

The level of reserve funds continued to increase steadily. By the end of December 2014, the balance of commercial banks' loan loss reserves was 1.96 trillion yuan, an increase of 281.2 billion yuan compared with the beginning of the year; the provision coverage was 232.06%, a decline of 50.64% compared with the beginning of the year; the loan provision rate was 2.90%, an increase of 0.07% compared with the beginning of the year.[4]

3.1.3.2 Risk Status

By the end of 2014, the non-performing loan balance of commercial banks (according to the statistical standard for corporations) was 842.6 billion yuan, an increase of 250.6 billion yuan compared with the beginning of the year; the ratio of non-performing loans hit 1.25%, a rise of 0.25% over the beginning of the year, but still lower than major economies of the world.[5] Non-performing loans rebounded to some extent mostly because of the global economic downturn and cyclical and structural factors in the domestic economy which caused aggravated adjustment, declining benefits, and outstanding problems of overcapacity in some companies and industries, and exacerbated problems with joint guarantees and mutual guarantees. Generally speaking, however, since China's banking industry has a high risk tolerance, the possibility of systemic risks resulting from the continuously deteriorating credit quality of the banking industry is small.

The CBRC urges banking institutions to conduct a timely and thorough investigation of the real risks, arrange and improve risk prevention systems as soon as possible, and cooperate with other departments on risk prevention. For loans to industries with excess capacity, the CBRC has set up and improved industry risk-monitoring and pre-warning mechanisms, carried out an in-depth credit preventative risk investigation, and implemented differentiated credit policies to eliminate and dispose of risks in an orderly fashion. For loans by local government financing platforms, strict control over the total amount of loans has optimized loan structure, completed the statistical information system, and strengthened overall risk management. For real-estate loans, it is continuing the strict implementation of list management and applies differentiated credit policies to effectively prevent and eliminate relevant risks. It regulates wealth management investment operations, and the proportion of wealth management funds' investments in non-standard credit assets has declined as a result. For liquidity risks, it urges banking institutions to carry out a trial of "Commercial Bank Liquidity Risk Management Measures." Through strengthened active liability management, cash flow calculations, and pressure testing and detailed follow-up and analysis of liquidity risk conditions, the liquidity of the banking industry over the whole year remained generally stable.

3.2 IMPORTANT BANKING REGULATION MEASURES IN 2014

3.2.1 *Banking Reform in 2014*

Against the general background of deepening reform, the 2014 banking reform took place according to the logic of marketization, during which the focus is mainly on pilot projects by private financial institutions. The construction of the first five private banks was approved, and one has already been approved to start trading; fourteen new privately funded non-banking financial institutions were established, and 108 new village banks dominated by private capital were opened. Regulatory policies also supported the participation of private capital in rural credit cooperatives' property rights reform, capital and share increases for rural commercial banks, the merger and reorganization of problematic institutions, and so on. The categories and qualifications required of investors were specified in the revised "Measures for the Implementation of Administrative Licensing Matters of Small and Medium Rural Financial Institutions" and the "Notice on Encouraging and Directing Private Capital to Participate in Property Rights Reform of Rural Credit Cooperatives" was issued. These initiatives help to promote the diversity of equity and stimulate financial institutions to become main market players.

In addition to reforms that established new institutions, in 2014 the banking regulatory department attempted to deepen banking and regulatory reform, aiming to enhance the competitiveness of the banking industry on the one hand and improve regulatory efficiency on the other. First, it promoted deepening organizational system reform with the topic "improving the corporate governance systems of commercial banks" to promote operational and management efficiency and risk management abilities and to build a complete, balanced, effective, and compatible operational mechanism. Second, it promoted the reform of wealth management and interbank business governance systems s by establishing rules and regulations including "Guiding Opinion on the Regulation of Wealth Management Business of Commercial Banks in 2014," "Notice on Relevant Matters of Improving the Organization and Management System of Bank's Wealth Management Business," "Notice on Regulating Interbank Business of Financial Institutions," and "Notice on Regulating the Governance of Interbank Business of Commercial Banks." Third, it achieved a prudential regulation policy system that combines microprudential and macroprudential regulation, and issued the "Notice on Adjusting the Calculation Standard of Commercial Banks' Loan-to-deposit Ratio" to optimize calculation methods for loan-to-deposit ratios; it also made further progresses in other areas such as the regulation of systemically important banks and countercyclical regulation.

3.2.2 Comment on the Construction of Supervisory Laws and Regulations in 2014

3.2.2.1 Main Contents and Significance of Internal Guidelines on Regulatory Rating for Commercial Banks

In 2014, the CBRC devised the "Internal Guidelines on Regulatory Rating for Commercial Banks," which aimed to improve the accuracy and precision of regulatory rating by completing its indicator systems, updating rating standards, improving the priority setting of each indicator, optimizing rating procedures, etc. The rating has taken advantage of the most recent experience of liquidity and information risk regulation, which is not only in line with the latest international regulatory rules but also takes risk characteristics of commercial banks in China into account, a milestone in the whole-system off-site regulation of the CBRC.

*3.2.2.2 Main Contents and Significance of Internal Guidelines
on Internal Control for Commercial Banks*

On September 28, 2014, the CBRC issued the revised "Internal Guidelines of Internal Control for Commercial Banks" (hereinafter referred to as the Guidelines) in the form of normative document no. 40. The Guidelines were formulated in 2002 and revised in 2007, the 2014 version is the subject of public consultation. Parts of the 2007 version gradually broke down with the rapidly developing banking business. For example, the 2007 version required on-site investigation during the pre-loan investigation and post-loan inspection of commercial banks, but current practice for most commercial banks is to adopt batch approval for credit card and small consumption loan business. Second, as banking is introducing new innovations with each passing day, many new businesses such as Internet finance and online banking are not covered by the 2007 version. Third, a series of the newly issued regulatory systems conflict with the previous guidelines. For example, Article 53 of the old guidelines provided that "commercial banks should confirm responsibilities for each deal of credit risk and loss caused by violation of laws and regulations," whereas Article 17 in the 2013 version of "Bad Debt Write-off Management Methods for Financial Enterprises" requires "financial enterprises [to] confirm responsibilities and call relevant persons to account for losses caused by subjective reasons." Fourth, some internal control requirements did not match the status quo of banking operations. Commercial banks in China have gone through considerable changes in their complex organizational structure in recent years and now face increasingly diversified risks, increasing the importance of internal controls and requiring timely revision of the Guidelines in the hope of encouraging banks to improve their internal control systems.

During the revision process, the internal controls in various kinds of banks in China were examined with particular attention to the variety of risks they face. At the same time, relevant regulations at home and abroad were collected and summarized. Regulations have been published in recent years on six aspects of domestic banking: bank credit, capital, deposit and counter business, debit cards, wealth management, and information technology. The "Basic Norm of Enterprise Internal Control" was published jointly by five ministries/commissions, including the Ministry of Finance, in 2008. As for international regulations, the Guidelines consulted the "Framework for Internal Control Systems in Banking Organizations" issued by the Basel Committee in 1998 and the revised "Internal Control Integrated Framework" published by the Committee of Sponsoring Organization of Treadway Commission (COSO) in May 2013.

The revised Guidelines have the following features: first, they are oriented toward principle-based regulation such as international counterparty regulation and no longer include detailed internal control requirements for specific businesses; second, internal control review is added in order for commercial banks to continuously improve their internal control systems; third, supervision of internal controls are strengthened to encourage banks to implement various requirements of the Guidelines; fourth, punitive measures are added to enhance regulation and restriction.

The revised Guidelines consist of seven chapters and 51 articles and took effect on the day of issue; financial institutions other than banks under CBRC regulation can use them as reference. it's the first chapter mainly provides definition, objectives, and the basic principles of internal control; the second chapter lays down the governance and organizational structure of banks and the assignment of internal control responsibilities; the third chapter concerns internal control measures, specifying requirements in terms of institutions, procedures, systems, responsibilities, positions, delegation, etc.; the fourth chapter is on internal control guarantee, including information management, personnel management, assessment management, and internal control culture systems; the fifth chapter concerns the review of internal control, specifying requirements regarding the organization and implementation of an internal control review, its scope and frequency, application of review results, etc.; the sixth chapter describes internal control supervision, clarifying internal supervision responsibility, external supervision measures, and penalties; the seventh chapter consists of supplementary articles on the powers of interpretation and date of implementation of the Guidelines.

Thanks to this revision, the content of the Guidelines has become more systematic and comprehensive and embodies the requirements of principle-based, orientation-based regulation, which helps guide commercial banks and other financial institutions to uphold the concept of stable operation, determine their internal control emphasis, rationally allocate limited resources, and truly improve the efficiency of their internal control management.

3.2.2.3 Main Contents and Significance of the Revision of "Regulation of People's Republic of China on Administration of Foreign-Funded Banks" and "Measures for the Implementation of Administrative Licensing Matters of Foreign Banks"

In recent years, the State Council has accelerated the reform of the administrative licensing system and announced several decisions abolishing and adjusting certain administrative approval items. Meanwhile, as the opening up of the financial industry deepens, market access standards for Chinese and foreign banks are brought further into line. To reflect developments in regulatory policies, the CBRC revised the "Measures for the Implementation of Administrative Licensing Matters of Foreign Financial Institutions" and changed its name to "Measures for the Implementation of Administrative Licensing Matters of Foreign Banks", which was issued and took effect in September 2014. The revised version has abolished eleven administrative licensing items for foreign banks, including the establishment of electronic banking and debit cards, operating agencies and changes to the working capital of branches, changes of business address, the establishment of self-service banking, deferring constructionand opening for business of foreign banks and their branches, temporary suspension of business, resumption of business, etc.; it has simplified application and approval procedures for foreign-funded banks setting up branches and acceptance inspection procedures for RMB business, narrowed the range of examination and approval, further specified enhanced in-process and follow-up regulation requirements, and unified regulatory standards.

The "Decision of the State Council on Revising the Regulation of People's Republic of China on Administration of Foreign-funded Banks" was issued by CBRC in December 2014. The revision was a proactive measure for China's banking industry to further open up against a background of comprehensive and deepening reform. To ensure effective regulation, it appropriately relaxed restrictions on foreign banks setting up branches and starting RMB business and provided more convenient ways for foreign banks to extend their business. The main opening-up measures are: cancelling the requirement for minimum working capital for domestic branches of foreign-funded banks; cancelling the requirement for foreign-funded banks to establish representative offices before setting up operating agencies; and greatly relaxing the conditions for foreign-funded banks' operating agencies to apply to run RMB business.

The revised "Regulation of People's Republic of China on Administration of Foreign-funded Banks" and "Measures for the Implementation of Administrative Licensing Matters of Foreign Banks" fully reflect the thorough implementation of the State Council's guiding ideology of transforming government functions, streamlining administration and delegating power to lower levels, further expanding the scope of opening up.

3.2.2.4 The Establishment and Significance of the Commercial Bank Deposit Deviation System

Deposit rush has been a long-standing problem for commercial banks at certain times. The deposit rush phenomenon, featuring sudden increases at ends of seasons and falls at beginnings of seasons has been quite outstanding. It occurs because some commercial banks absorb deposits in breach of regulations, or falsely declare increased deposits at key moments like the end of season or end of year.

To impose restrictions on such behavior by commercial banks, in September 2014 the CBRC published the "Notice on Relevant Matters concerning Strengthening the Administration of Commercial Bank Deposit Deviation" (hereinafter referred to as the Notice). The Notice is divided into seven sections: the first urges commercial banks to improve their performance appraisal systems, strengthen the administration of branch organization performance appraisal, and assign tasks rationally so as to restrict grassroots "deposit rush"; the second prohibits commercial banks from attracting high-interest deposits, or offering illegal rebates, the third urges commercial banks to strengthen their management of deposit stability and control the deposit deviation rate at ends of months within a rational range of no higher than 3%, and, meanwhile, to add restrictions on the calculable sum of monthly and daily average deposits at ends of seasons in order to prevent commercial banks from increasing their average monthly and daily deposits through deposit rush at ends of seasons to evade restrictions on the deposit deviation rate the fourth section asks regulatory departments at each level to establish a monitoring system for deposit fluctuation statistics, and to adopt rectifying or punitive measures for banks with problems of significant abnormal fluctuations, deposit absorption in breach of regulations, fake deposit increases, etc. according to their degree of severity.

The issue of the Notice will further standardize the operation of commercial banks, maintain healthy financial order, ease the deposit fluctuations at ends of months and seasons, and promote the stable operation of commercial banks. At the same time, it helps decrease the cost of debt to the banks and thus reduces finance costs for enterprises.

3.2.2.5 *The Revised Version of the "Guidelines on Consolidated Management and Supervision of Commercial Banks" and Its Significance*

The 2008 CBRC "Guidelines on Consolidated Supervision of Banks (trial)" preliminarily set up the institutional framework for consolidated supervision of banks in China. While various countries have continued to reflect on and improve their systems and approaches to consolidated supervision since the global financial crisis, and there have been great changes in the financial market structure and the organizational and business structure of banks in China, the CBRC totally revised the existing Guidelines in 2014 and planned to change the title to "Guidelines on the Consolidated Management and Supervision of Commercial Banks."

The revision has borrowed the from the latest experience of international financial regulation reform, considered the combination of principles with operability, highlighted consolidated risk features, rebuilt the consolidated management framework, and enhanced the applicability and foresight of the Guidelines. The main contents of the revision are as follows. First, it clarifies three aspects of consolidation: accounting consolidation, capital consolidation, and risk consolidation. Second, it considers demands by the banking forum for business collaboration, and provides requirements based on multiple collaborative mechanism perspectives: strategic collaboration, operational collaboration, resource collaboration, etc. to prevent risks while at the same time promoting further logical development of banking groups. Third, it adds appropriate corporate governance requirements to help banking groups relate to the corporate governance of the parent company, the overall governance structure of the group, and the corporate governance of affiliated companies. Fourth, it adds the requirement of overall risk management, proposing specific requirements on the structure and responsibilities of overall risk management, unified risk preference and policies, unified credit management, unified risk classification, unified risk view, etc. Fifth, it expands the scope of concentration management, covering multi-dimensional concentration management requirements for concentration ratios of business areas, asset distribution, counterparties, liability composition, and earnings. Sixth, it adds the overall requirements for supervision of insider trading to aspects of the supervisory structure.

Seventh, it specifies firewall systems in respect of supervision isolation, business isolation, separation of self-operation and agent risks, notoriety isolation, personnel isolation, information isolation, and isolation by exit. Eighth, it adds risk recovery and disposal plan requirements.

Public consultation on the Guidelines has now closed, and on this basis the CBRC will revise and issue improved Guidelines.

3.2.2.6 Main Contents of the "Interim Measures for the Administration of Factoring Business of Commercial Banks"

To further prevent and control the risks of factoring and promote the healthy development of factoring by commercial banks, the CBRC carried out extensive industry-wide consultation before issuing the supervisory rules "Interim Measures for the Administration of Factoring Business of Commercial Banks" as the CBRC Decree 2014 No. 5. They took effect on the date of issue, April 3, 2014.

Factoring is a comprehensive financial service based on the creditor's transfer of his receivables; it combines receivables collection, management, bad-debt protection, and financing in one kind of business. Factoring began in China in 1993; with the recent transformation of the global economy from a seller's to a buyer's market, factoring is just the kind of financial services product that fits the transformation of business credit sale methods and awards win–win to bank and enterprise. Unlike general loan financing, factoring adopts comprehensive evaluation methods and is easier to access. Small and micro enterprises can effectively improve their credit by relying on their upstream and downstream relationships with powerful core enterprises. Through factoring finance, banks can spread their services from core enterprises to small and micro supplier enterprises and help the latter to transform receivables into cash income, which not only expands the finance channel for small and micro enterprises and helps solve their financing difficulties, but also extends the depth of the bank's service, again a win–win solution for both banks and enterprises. At the same time, enterprises can request banks to investigate the credit standing of their counterparty, which can effectively reduce default risks arising out of information asymmetry between buyer and seller, shorten the payment collection cycle, and improve collection efficiency.

For these reasons, factoring has been growing rapidly in recent years and has meanwhile created problems such as the unsatisfactory examination of the authenticity of receivables and trade, general business transactions in the name of factoring financing, and increasing potential risks to banks' factoring businesses. In response to this the CBRC drew up the "Interim Measures for the Administration of Factoring Business of Commercial Banks" on the in-depth investigation of relevant risks associated with factoring.

The Measures contain six chapters and 38 articles; they define and classify the factoring business, factoring finance, receivables and assignments, and the standard of qualified receivables. The Measures provide standards for the procedure and key aspects of factoring finance including access for clients and cooperative agencies, business examination, special account management, finance ratio and term, etc. They also specify corporate governance, institutional improvement, and internal control requirements for commercial bank factoring, and stipulate regulatory measures and penalties for breaches of the Measures. The Measures set up standards in the following main areas.

1. Definition and classification of the business

    The Measures define factoring in accordance with the "General Principles of International Factoring" by the Factors Chain International, "Factoring Business Norms for Chinese Banking Industry" by the Professional Committee of Factoring, China Banking Association, specify that the assignment of all rights and benefits of receivables is the basis of factoring, and classify factoring from different perspectives. The Measures also define receivables in accordance with the PBC's "Measures for the Registration of Receivables Pledges." Strict standards are established in respect of qualified receivables and several unqualified receivables are clarified, including future receivables, receivables with unclear ownership, and claims for payment of negotiable securities.

2. Factoring Finance Business procedures

    Currently, the highest risk in factoring lies in factoring finance. In light of this, the Measures regulate business processes in factoring finance, including products, client access, cooperative agency access, business examination, special account management, financing ratio and term, information disclosure, etc. They propose specific prudential management requirements for single factoring finance, that is, the management of whole-term credit extension for sellers or buyers based on true trade.

3. Risk management framework for factoring
   The Measures regulate corporate governance, institutional improvement, and so on, stressing that banks should develop prudent business strategies, set up and regularly examine relevant systems. The management framework also involves team building, delegation, separation of front, middle, and back offices, system construction, risk monitoring and disposal. The aim is for banks to establish a professional, independent management framework for their factoring business.

3.2.2.7 Main Content and Significance of the "Rules on the Administration of Service Charges by Commercial Banks"

In 2003, the CBRC and the National Development and Reform Commission (NDRC) jointly issued the "Provisional Rules on the Administration of Service Charges by Commercial Banks" (hereinafter referred to as the Provisional Rules) and classified service charges made by commercial banks as official government charges or market-adjusted charges in accordance with the Price Law. With a continuing demand for finance, the financial products and value-added services provided by China's banking institutions have also become increasingly plentiful in recent years. At the same time, commercial bank diversification and processing channels have created complexity both for bank disclosure of charges and consumer understanding and choice. With legal provisions mostly taking the form of scattered guiding principles, the growing problems of bank service charges urgently require regulation. Against this background, the CBRC and the NDRC held discussions to revise the Provisional Rules and formulated "Rules on the Administration of Service Charges by Commercial Banks" (hereinafter referred to as the Rules) which were issued and took effect at the beginning of 2014.

To protect the legal rights of consumers, the Rules promote the marketization of bank service charges as far as possible and propose independent pricing mechanisms based on the market principles. Bank service charges are therefore systematically regulated in terms of charging principles, government reference charges and official charges, market-adjusted charges, price information disclosure, internal management, supervision and administration, etc.

The Rules include general principles, formulation and adjustment of government reference and official charges, formulation and adjustment of market-adjusted charges, service charge information disclosure, internal management, supervision and administration of service charges, and supplementary articles—seven chapters and 38 articles in all. Its main contents are as follows.

First, according to the relevant provision of the Price Law, the Rules divide bank service charges into government reference charges, official government charges, and market-adjusted charges for separate management. Basic banking services, which are widely used by clients of banks and are of great significance both to people's lives and to national economic development, are included under government reference charges or official government charges, and are formulated and adjusted by the appropriate authorities according to such factors as commercial banks' service costs, the effect of service charges on individuals or organizations, and market conditions. At the same time, the Rules define the range of banking services where market-adjusted charges are appropriate, emphasize that formulation and adjustment of market-adjusted charges should by law be carried out by headquarters of commercial banks and branches of foreign banks and in accordance with the; procedures specified in the Rules.

Second, to counter problems with handling charges for withholding payment services and third-party payment services, which have caused a lot of complaints, the Rules require relevant handling fees to be charged according to the principle of "consignors are payers" and no charges arise for organizations and individuals other than the consignor.

Third, to deal with the problem of deductions made in the absence of service termination mechanisms, the Rules provide that banks should adopt effective measures to terminate related services at an appropriate time according to customer requirements. The Rules prohibit banks from obliging clients to accept charges for services and payments. Most complaints have been covered.

Fourth, the Rules contain strict requirements on service charge information disclosure by commercial banks, astipulating that commercial banks should publicly display accurate information on individual service charges, and on how government reference charges, official government charges, and market-adjusted charges are applied in all kinds of places of business and on website home pages. It also requires commercial banks to display notifications at least three months before increasing market-adjusted service charges.

Fifth, to protect clients' rights to have full information and to choose, the Rules provide that banks should strictly obey relevant service charge information disclosure rules and offer services only after clients have confirmed and accepted the charges. For clients who clearly express unwillingness to accept relevant service charges, banks should terminate services promptly and should not oblige clients to accept, whether openly or covertly.

Sixth, the Rules strengthen the internal management of commercial bank service charges. They stipulate that commercial banks should identify the department responsible for service charge management, set up management systems and strictly adhere to them, improve complaint-handling procedures, and specify the management procedure, the department in charge, and time limits for registration, investigation, handling, and reporting back of customer complaints.

Seventh, it specifies penalties for breaches of laws and regulations on banking service charges. The Rules provide a specific legal basis for penalizing commercial banks for arbitrary pricing in violation of relevant provisions on: government reference charges and official government charges; formulation and adjustment of market-adjusted charges; service charge information disclosure; and internal management.

The Rules also encourage social supervision and industry self-regulation to jointly promote normative service charging behavior by commercial banks and make banking service charges more open and transparent.

In general, the publication of the Rules lays the foundation for the sustainable development of financial products and services by commercial banks on the basis of norms.

3.2.2.8 Main Content and Significance of the "Rules on Liquidity Risk Management of Commercial Banks"

To promote strengthening of liquidity risk management in China's banking industry and maintain the steady operation of the banking system, in February 2014 the CBRC issued "Rules on Liquidity Risk Management of Commercial Banks" in the form of Chairman's Decree No. 2 (hereinafter referred to as the Rules), establishing the legal framework for liquidity management and supervision of commercial banks in China. The release of the Rules also marks the final implementation of the four regulatory tools established by the CBRC's Chinese version of Basel III.

Liquidity risk is the risk that commercial banks cannot acquire adequate funds in time and at a reasonable cost to pay maturing bonds, fulfill other payment obligations, or satisfy the demand for funds of normal business operations. This round of global financial crises, starting with the sub-prime crisis in the USA is in essence a liquidity crisis. In June 2013,

China's interbank market showed tight liquidity and a steep increase in interest rates, attracting extensive attention both at home and abroad and exposing the fact that liquidity risk management of domestic commercial banks had failed to catch up with the developments and changes in business methods and risk conditions that have occurred in recent years. Therefore, the implementation of international banking liquidity risk management and regulatory standards such as Basel III and a real improvement in the efficiency of liquidity risk management and regulation of commercial banks are essential for the safe and stable operation of the banking industry.

The Rules follow the principle of "three combinations"— qualitative and quantitative approaches, microprudential and macroprudential regulation and regulatory requirements of Chinese banks and foreign banks— to build a liquidity risk regulatory framework with full horizontal and vertical coverage for commercial banks in China.

The Rules contain four chapters, 66 articles, and four attachments. The first chapter "General Principles" clarifies the range of application of the Rules and defines liquidity risk, and the general requirements of liquidity risk management and regulation. The second chapter "Liquidity Risk Management" sets out the overall qualitative requirements for banks' liquidity risk management systems, and is divided into separate sections to regulate key elements including: governance structure; strategies, policies and procedures;; identification, calculation, monitoring and control of liquidity risk; and management information systems.

The third chapter "Liquidity Risk Regulation" provides three regulatory indicators for liquidity risk, namely liquidity coverage ratio, deposit-to-loan ratio, and liquidity ratio, proposes a multi-dimensional framework and instruments for the monitoring and analysis of liquidity risks, and stipulates liquidity risk regulation procedures. The Rules temporarily exclude the Net Stable Funding Ratio, since the Basel Committee has not completed the relevant technical details.. The Rules include deposit-to-loan ratio as a regulatory indicator, regarding it as a legal regulatory indicator determined by the Commercial Bank Law. This topic has received universal attention from the industry, and the Rules will continue to improve regulation of the deposit-to-loan ratio with a view to establishing a legislative body to revise relevant provisions of the Commercial Bank Law.

The fourth chapter, "Supplementary Articles," clarifies the implementation timetable for the Rules, the range of applications of the liquidity coverage ratio, and transitional arrangements. The Rules apply to commercial banks set up in China, including Chinese commercial banks, wholly foreign-funded banks, and Sino-foreign joint venture banks. Rural cooperative banks, village banks, rural credit cooperatives, and branches of foreign banks can use the Rules as reference. The liquidity coverage ratio requirements do not apply to rural cooperative banks, village banks, rural credit cooperatives, branches of foreign banks, and commercial banks with assets of less than 200 billion yuan.

Column 1: The Implementation of New International Financial Regulatory Standards in China

Since the latest global financial crisis, there has been frequent international financial regulation reform and a constant issue of new regulatory standards and rules, the most outstanding of which is a series of new standards on capital, leverage ratio, liquidity, etc. issued by the Basel Committee on Banking Supervision. These new rules keep evolving and are still in the process of revision and improvement. Reform of international financial regulatory rules continues to expand in content, from the principal concern of improving the quality and level of capital to the calculation of risk-weighted assets, from capital regulation to liquidity regulation. As regards objectives, the regulatory rules tend to seek a balance which will maintain risk sensitivity on the one hand, and lower complexity, and improve comparability and consistency on the other. As to orientation, it pays more attention to dynamic microprudential regulation and the effective implementation of international regulatory standards.

As a member state of the Basel Committee of Banking Supervision, China has given consideration to its international obligations and national conditions during the implementation of new standards of international financial regulation, and has played an active role in promoting the positive value of international financial regulation.

1. *New standards of international regulation transformed into domestic legislation comprehensively and promptly*

    In 2011, the "Guiding Opinions of the CBRC on the Implementation of New Regulatory Standards in China's Banking Industry" (CBRC Issue 2011 No. 44) were issued, specifying regulatory standards for capital adequacy ratios, leverage ratios, liquidity, and loan loss reserves, based on Basel III together with the actual condition of banking operations and regulation in China, according to the principle of organic combination of macroprudential and microprudential regulation. It is a key document setting out the plan for China's regulatory department to transform international regulatory standards to domestic regulatory standards.

In 2011, the "Rules for the Leverage Ratio Management of Commercial Banks" were published; they were revised in February 2015 following revision of international rules of leverage ratio in the "Basel III Leverage Ratio Framework and Disclosure Requirements" issued by the Basel Committee in January 2014, which improved regulatory indicators of leverage ratios.

In 2012, the "Capital Rules for Commercial Banks (provisional)" (CBRC Order 2012 No. 1) was released, which integrated the calculation methods of Basel II and standards of Basel III and set up a framework of three pillars and overall risk management. The Basel Committee's general assessment of China's capital regulatory rules and their consistency with international capital regulatory rules was "compliant".

In 2012, the "Guidance on Innovation of Capital Instruments by Commercial Banks" (CBRC Issue 2012 No. 56) was issued, establishing the legal position of capital instruments with write-down clauses and share-conversion clauses as capital in China. In 2013, the "Guiding Opinions of the State Council on Carrying out a Preferred Shares Pilot Project" was released, which established the legal position of preference shares.

In 2014, the "Rules on Liquidity Risk Management of Commercial Banks (provisional)" (CBRC Order 2014 No. 2) were issued, marking the implementation of the 2010 Basel III International Framework for Liquidity Risk Measurement, Standards, and Monitoring, and the 2013 Basel III Liquidity Coverage Ratio and Liquidity Risk Monitoring Tools, and introducing regulatory indicators for liquidity and risks such as liquidity coverage ratio.

2. *Attention paid to the implementation of new international regulatory standards*

The capital rules apply to all commercial banks. The "Capital Rules for Commercial Banks (provisional)" clearly stipulates that it applies to all commercial banks set up in the territory of the People's Republic of China and does not exclude small banks. All commercial banks should calculate their capital adequacy ratio according the rules. The implementation of advanced approaches to capital management is also promoted in China.

In April 2014, the CBRC examined and approved six banks (ICBC, ABC, BOC, CCB, Bank of Communications, and CMB) implementing advanced approaches to capital management. China's banking industry had reached a new level in its ability to build risk governance, and Basel II and Basel III had been comprehensive implemented in China.

Innovative capital instruments were issued. Chinese commercial banks have issued innovative capital instruments such as tier II capital bonds and preferred shares, and have achieved diversification of their capital.

3. *Emphasis on the value and active role of new international regulatory standards*

New standards set up by international regulation reform represent the latest concepts and latest trends in international financial development and international financial regulation. This not only reflectsinternational regulation but also provides a summary of the risk management experience of the international banking industry—not only supervisory rules but also laws which banking operations should comply with, and China's banking regulation can learn a great deal from them. At the same time, the adaptability of new international regulatory standards in China and the whole of Asia does present an issue. The new standards are based on European and American markets and originate from advanced banking business models and capital structures, but fail to give due consideration to the unbalanced development of the global banking industry; the new standards are prescriptions for European and American crises and are thus of limited applicability in the Asian banking industry.

In implementing these new standards, China has regard to their positive effects. While performing its international obligations, China is considering the applicability of these standards to its national conditions, transferring international regulatory rules to domestic risk management practices to bring out their positive effects and maximize their value, strengthening the concept of comprehensive risk management for commercial banks, promoting the reform of commercial banks in respect of capital management and risk management, internalizing these standards in the risk culture, systems, and procedures of commercial banks, and achieving transformational development.

3.2.3 Comment on Regulatory Measures in 2014

3.2.3.1 Reform of Business Governance Systems

Interbank Business Governance

In recent years, reverse repurchase assets have been growing rapidly in interbank business. Supernormal growth mainly occurred in trust beneficiary rights, directional asset management plans, and wealth management products of other banks. New methods of joining interbank deposits to non-standard assets like commissioned directional investments come up constantly.

The rapid and disorderly development of interbank business may accumulate systemic risks. One is liquidity risk. Large quantities of short-term interbank capital circulation are joined to medium- and long-term non-standard credit assets with serious problems of maturity mismatch, which can easily cause liquidity risks. The second is high leverage risk. Fund accumulation and borrowing with large quantities of interbank transactions between different financial institutions are likely to promote excessive leverage and pro-cyclical fluctuations in the financial system. The third is correlation risks. Non-standard credit assets have rather a long business chain, a complicated financing structure and transaction process, and poor transparency, which mask financial risk more effectively and increase its infectivity in interbank business.

Since 2014, the CBRC has implemented the requirements of the Notice of the State Council on strengthening the regulation of shadow banking, has encouraged commercial banks to enhance normative development and risk prevention in their interbank business, and has helped interbank business to return to liquidity management. First, it requires commercial banks to design interbank business development strategies scientifically, effectively control the scale and proportion of interbank business, and let interbank business return to liquidity management. Second, banks should go ahead with setting up special interbank business departments one stage at a time, first establishing special departments at corporate headquarters to operate interbank business separately and to replace other departments and branches where interbank accounts that are already opened should be settled and closed on maturity. Third, commercial banks should do a good job of due diligence investigation, examination and approval, duration management, and internal supervision of the interbank financing business to ensure the counterpart financial institution has an appropriate credit rating, fully disclosed trading background, legal use of its funds, and controllable business risks.

In May 2014, PBC, CBRC, CSRC (China Securities Regulatory Commission), CIRC (China Insurance Regulatory Commission) and SAFE (State Administration of Foreign Exchange) jointly issued the "Notice on Regulating Interbank Business of Financial Institutions" (CBRC Issue 2014 No. 127, hereinafter referred to as the Notice). To encourage financial innovation and maintain the independent operation of financial institutions, the Notice gave eighteen normative opinions on regulating interbank business operations, strengthening and improving internal and external management of interbank business, promoting regulated innovation of asset and liability business and so on. The general premise is to "prevent malpractice, introduce good practice, strengthen management, and promote development." At the same time, to implement the Notice issued by the five commissions, the CBRC General Office published a supporting document, the "Notice on Regulating the Governance of Interbank Business of Commercial Banks" (CBRC Office Issue 2014 No. 140), which laid down ten specific requirements for the governance of interbank business by commercial banks. By the end of 2014, major commercial banks had all established special interbank business department as required, bringing the risks of interbank business under effective control.

Governance of the Wealth Management Business

Since the release of the CBRC's document No. 8 in 2013, the quantity of non-standard credit assets in the wealth management business of banking institutions has decreased, but risks are still hidden in the investment area of some wealth management products. To counter these problems, since 2014 the CBRC has been encouraging commercial banks to pay close attention to the reform of their wealth management business units according to the principles of "separation of wealth management from credit business, one-to-one correspondence between product and project, independent account management, and open and transparent information," thus promoting the return of the wealth management business to investment management on the customer's behalf, as well as its regulated and healthy development.

First, it requires each wealth management product, both on and off balance sheet, to be independently accounted for, with detailed accounts set up for each independent accounting subject; banks should calculate each item of income and wealth management fees comprehensively to achieve independent accounting.

Second, it requires effective risk isolation by separating wealth management from the credit business, self-operated business from commissioned business, the bank's own wealth management business from third-party wealth management, different kinds of wealth management product from each other, and the operation of wealth management from that of other kinds of business.

Third, it requires normative behavior by banks in their wealth management business, including normative sales, normative investment, and normative operation. Fourth, it requires specific centralized management. The headquarters of a bank should set up an independent management department with systems for centralized management of the wealth management business and responsibility for drafting relevant rules and regulations, including R&D of wealth management products, investment operations, cost accounting, risk management, compliance investigation, product release, sales management, data systems, reporting and so on. Fifth, separate operations should be adhered to, and the bank's wealth management business unit should run its wealth management business within the scope approved by the CBRC.

In July 2014, the CBRC issued the "Notice on Relevant Matters of Improving the Organization and Management System of Bank's Wealth Management Business" (CBRC Issue 2014 No. 35), which requires banking institutions to improve the internal organization and management systems of their wealth management business, set up special wealth management business departments to be in charge of centralized operation and management of the whole bank's wealth management business, and conduct their wealth management business according to the four basic principles of "independent accounting, risk isolation, normative behavior, and centralized management," so as to prevent the accumulation of risk in their wealth management business. By the end of 2014, over 400 banks had set up wealth management business units, the reform of wealth management governance systems had gone smoothly, and business risks had been brought under effective control.

Security Funds Founded in the Trust Industry
To establish market-oriented risk disposal mechanisms that can effectively prevent risks in the trust industry, the CBRC and the Ministry of Finance have jointly drafted and issued the "Administrative Measures on Security Funds of the Trust Industry" (hereinafter referred to as the Measures) based on the experience of risk disposal in the securities and insurance industries. On December 19, on the approval of the State Council, the China Trust Industry's Security Funds Company, designed in accordance with the Measures, was founded.

Along with the increasing pressures of economic downturn and the problems of excess production capacity, plus changing trends in the real-estate market, risks in the trust industry have become increasingly prominent in recent years and may become the trigger for industry risks which can develop into regional and systemic risks. For this reason, there is an urgent need to set up long-term mechanisms to effectively resolve risks in the trust industry. The timely release of the Measures has contributed to the steady advance of single-risk disposal in the trust industry.

The Measures are divided into seven chapters of 36 articles, the general rules of which stipulate the property, fund manager, and principal decision maker of the security fund, and set out the basic principles of risk disposal in the trust industry. The Measures also contain specific provisions on the responsibilities and objectives of the security fund company and its board of directors, security fund raising and management, use, allocation, and liquidation of the security fund, and the supervision and administration of regulatory departments.

The Measures define the security fund as the important infrastructure of the trust industry—a non-governmental mutual fund commonly raised by market participants in the trust industry to resolve and dispose of risk in the trust industry. Its objective is to set up market-oriented risk disposal mechanisms and protect the legal rights of parties involved. It operates by the security fund intervening to provide a "time window" for risk mitigation to first control and absorb single and institutional risks within the trust industry, and then gradually release accumulated risks so as to reduce the negative impact on the financial market and wider society. In view of the pressing need for security fund companies to take responsibility for risk disposal in the trust industry, the Measures provide the company with market-oriented operating systems to operate their own funds in order to provide the trust company with liquidity relief and resolve the liquidity risk of trust products, and act in concert with the security fund to effectively resolve and dispose risks of the trust industry.

3.2.3.2 Reform of Capital Regulation

Reforms of international regulation represented by Basel III are still on the increase, while international standards and rules will continue to be issued. In 2014, China made major progress in promoting capital regulation.

First, advanced approaches to capital management in the form of an internal rating-based system were introduced. In April 2014, the CBRC approved six banks (ICBC, ABC, BC, CCB, Bank of Communications, and CMB) to implement advanced capital management approaches; this marked the application of the international regulatory rules and risk management systems represented by Basel II and Basel III to the Chinese banking industry, and the industry passed a significant milestone in its risk management history.

Second, commercial banks issued new capital instruments to not only expand channels of capital supplement but also provide new investment tools for investors. The regulatory department issued the "Guidelines on Preferred Stock Issue by Commercial Banks as a Means of Tier-1 Capital Supplement" as the institutional foundation for the issue of new capital instruments. In 2014, the issue of new capital instruments was very active: in December 2014, the ICBC issued preference shares in three currencies—USD, euro, and RMB—through private placement on a scale of 2.94 billion USD, 0.6 billion Euros, and 12 billion RMB. The BC successfully issued 30 billion yuan of tier II capital bonds and 32 billion yuan of preference shares in succession in the domestic market, and 6.5 billion USD of preference shares and 3 billion USD tier II bonds in the overseas market. The ABC issued 30 billion yuan of write-down tier II capital bonds and 40 billion yuan preference shares. Hua Xia Bank issued 10 billion yuan of tier II capital bonds.[6]

3.2.3.3 *Regulatory Measures for Major Risks*

Credit Risk

The quality of financial assets is the weathervane for the operation of the real economy, and credit risk is a major risk in the banking industry. Since 2014, some pressures accumulated during the three superimposed periods—growth-rate shift period, structural adjustment period with growing pains, and stimulus policy digestion period—have started to be reflected in the quality of banking credit, mainly in the continuous increase of both the balance and ratio of non-performing loans. According to CBRC statistics, by the end of November 2014 the balance of non-performing loans of China's commercial banks was 843.6 billion yuan, which had been increasing for 12 quarters in a row, and the non-performing loan ratio was 1.31%, an increase of 0.28% compared with the beginning of the year.[7]

From this year, the CBRC is encouraging banking institutions to implement the "Guidance on Non-performing Loan Prevention and Control in 2014" in order to enhance management of the balance and ratio of non-performing loans on the basis of accurate classification of assets and full disclosure of risks, to attempt to identify the existing quantity, control the incremental quantity, and relieve the total quantity, and actively to prevent and resolve credit risks. First, strengthen risk prevention and control in key areas. Credit risk investigation and prevention and control are carried out in key areas of industries with excess production capacity, financing platforms, real estate and bulk commodity trade, and monitoring of the risk transmission of on- and off-balance-sheet businesses is strengthened. Headquarters of commercial banks are required to adhere to a differentiated credit granting policy, which will avoid the capital chain rupture of enterprises caused by banks uniformly drawing back, stopping, and delaying loans and prevent new non-performing loans being formed.

Second, prevent and resolve the risks of excessive credit granting, mutual guarantees, and guarantee circles. For well-functioning enterprises with a stable income but in financial difficulties caused by mutual guarantees, effective risk disposal and coordination mechanisms should be established to mitigate and resolve risks and avoid extensive spread of risks. In credit granting contracts, borrowing customers should be strictly restricted as to subsequent financing and guarantee behavior to avoid excessive debt. The banking association should take the lead in investigations to establish a "blacklist" system for enterprises in key industries such as the steel trade that deliberately avoid debts, and to improve information sharing among banks to prevent dishonest business owners getting further bank loans from other lenders.

Third, strengthen the risk disposal of non-performing loans and the management of bad-debt write-offs. During the process of liquidating non-performing loans, banks should actively communicate with local government, lay legal claim to group rights in compliance with regulations, and firmly prevent and combat debt avoidance by enterprises. Banks should cooperate with the local judiciary to promote the construction of "green passageways" for financial claim disposals. The system for preservation and collection of written-off debts should be based on the principle of "writing off debts, saving files, withholding rights, and keeping confidentiality." Fourth, further enhance and improve credit risk management. Headquarters of commercial banks are required to carry out macro-economic pressure tests to analyze the impact of adverse situations on banks in order to formulate response plans in advance. At the same time, to counter the fact that large quantities of small and micro enterprise loans and personal loans are mainly actually approved and issued by frontline branches, commercial bank headquarters are urged to strengthen their risk management ability and improve internal branch auditing systems with targets in key areas.

Operational Risk

Due to the unsatisfactory implementation of internal control system, the incidence of banking operational risks has been on the rise since 2014; information technology risks in particular are affecting the safe and steady operation of the system. For this reason, the CBRC will be ruthless in its mission to prevent risk incidents, carry out risk prevention assessment, and identify and dispose of hidden risks promptly through risk investigation. Administrative penalties, delayed access, downgrading, and so on are used to strengthen the investigation and deal with major breaches of laws and regulations. Second, the CBRC is improving practitioner management. A personnel management system of banking institutions has been established, and the strict responsibility and punishment mechanism put in place. Third, it has strengthened supervision of information technology risks. The CBRC has paid close attention to the management of information systems security and business continuity and has guided banking institutions to accelerate improvement and upgrading of their IT systems, carry out risk investigations and emergency exercises, and ensure the safe operation of their information systems.

Non-Credit Business and Off-Balance-Sheet Business

In recent years, some banking institutions have shown little awareness of compliance and have continued to design various non-standard credit business models to avoid the requirements of credit scale management, administrative policy restrictions and regulation. In addition to wealth management and interbank business, one channel they rely on is trust, as trust assets include considerable channel services involving various kinds of financial institutions such as banks, securities, insurance, funds, and so on, where there is an inherent problem of undefined division of final risk responsibilities and unclarified risks. The second channel is investment. As regulation of wealth management and interbank business is strengthened, some banks are continuing related businesses under the description of self-operating capital. The third is off-balance-sheet business such as entrusted loans. Since 2013, entrusted loans have kept grown rather fast. Some banks go out of their way to provide guarantees for entrusted loans, while, in other cases, the funds in entrusted loans actually come from bank loans and go to local government financing platforms and real estate.

On the micro level, risk management of non-standard credit business is rather weak. First, levels of normativity and prudence in pre-loan, in-process, and follow-up management are generally much lower than those of on-balance-sheet loans. In some cases, due diligence investigation is insufficient, risk investigation and post-loan fund management unsatisfactory, and the problem of banks providing implicit guarantees remains. Second, the problem of defective risk capital and risk provision is universal, causing banks' credit risk exposure to be underestimated. On the macro level, if non-standard credit business develops in a disorderly way, it may accumulate systemic financial risks. For one, it represents a concentration risk. Large quantities of non-standard credit capital are invested to restricted or speculative areas such as local government financing platforms, real estate, and mining, which actually increases the bank's concentration of risk in these areas. For another, it represents speculative risks. In the non-standard credit business chain, through several levels of channel charges, the overall rate is significantly higher than that of general loans, which not only increases the financing cost for the real economy, but also forces these funds to invest in projects and enterprises of higher risks for higher return, making the risk chain more fragile.

To counter this problem, the CBRC has adopted effective regulatory measures. For trust services, it first urges trust companies to strengthen compliance management, maintain trust products as private placements, set up strict investor qualifications, and fully disclose risks. Second, trust companies should do a good job of risk investigation for existing projects, carry out pressure tests of key risk areas on a regular basis, and formulate response plans. They should also actively and steadily promote liquidation of businesses with shadow banking characteristics such as non-standard wealth management capital pools. Third, the CBRC is promoting the establishment of long-term risk-prevention systems and control mechanisms for trust services, regulating existing business models, and actively promoting the transformational development of trust companies' business. With respect to entrusted loans, the CBRC first urges banking institutions to thoroughly understand the nature of loans entrusted to them as intermediaries, clarify their management responsibilities, clearly separate risks of their own loans from those of entrusted loans, and set up fixed standards of not providing funds for the consignor, not providing guarantees or implicit guarantees for the safety of the principal and interest of entrusted loans, and not replacing entrusted loans with their own loans. Second, the CBRC has given thought to the issue of management measures to regulate the entrusted loan business. For the healthy and orderly development of other kinds of off-balance-sheet business, the CBRC will consider revising the "Guideline on Risk Management of Off-balance-sheet Activities of Commercial Banks" to include off-balance-sheet services with credit-substitutable properties such as finance-based wealth management, asset management plans, etc. in unified credit granting and approval of off-balance-sheet loans, and will prepare standard provisions prohibiting banks from hiding risks under the cover of off-balance-sheet business.

Adjusted Calculation Standards for Loan-to-Deposit Ratio of Commercial Banks

To adapt to the changing asset and liability structure of the banking industry in China and reduce the rigidity of the loan-to-deposit ratio as a regulatory indicator, at the end of June 2014, the CBRC issued the "Notice on Adjusting the Calculation Standard of Loan-to-deposit Ratio of Commercial Banks", which took effect on July 1, 2014.

The adjustment mainly covers the following aspects. One, it adjusts the calculation currency of loan-to-deposit ratios. Assessment is no longer according to the total of domestic and foreign currencies; the object of regulatory assessment is solely RMB business, while the total of domestic and foreign currencies and the loan-to-deposit ratio of the foreign currency business are changed to monitoring indicators. Two, it adjusts the calculation standard for the numerator (loan) in the loan-to-deposit ratio. On the basis of previous adjustments and deductions from the numerator (deducting re-loans to support agriculture, special financial bonds for small and micro enterprise loans, loans corresponding to agriculture/farmer/rural area-related special financial bonds, and farmer and small and micro enterprise loans issued by village banks with deposits from the initiating bank), the following three further deductions are allowed: loans corresponding to other kinds of bonds issued by commercial banks, with residual maturity of more than a year, which the creditor has no right to ask the bank to pay ahead of time; small and micro enterprise loans corresponding to re-lending to support small enterprises; loans issued by commercial banks with loan capital from international financial institutions or foreign governments. Three, it adjusts the calculation standard of the denominator in the loan-to-deposit ratio. Two items are added: negotiable certificates of deposit issued by banks to enterprises and individuals; net amount of deposits with more than a year's maturity absorbed by foreign-funded banks from their parent banks abroad.

The market generally holds that, in the adjustment of the loan-to-deposit ratio, the adjustment of the numerator has a greater impact while the adjustment of denominator barely has any effect on domestic commercial banks. From a dynamic point of view, the improvement of the denominator should survey the market scale of certificates of deposits of non-financial companies and residents in the future. Looking at all the adjusted items, the market predicates that the influence of the Notice on the loan-to-deposit ratio of the whole industry will be around 1.3–2 percentage points and may release credit on a scale of 2 trillion yuan.

Judging by its effects, the relaxation of the loan-to-deposit ratio regulation will marginally improve the liability costs of banks, especially those banks with scope for improvement in their credit limit and rather great pressure to attract deposits. As to whether the adjustment can in effect improve the level of credit availability, the differentiated deposit reserve ratio formula and credit limit regulation by the central bank remain constraints.

3.2.3.4 Regulation of Global Systemically Important Banks

Increase of Global Systemically Important Banks in China

On November 8, 2014, the Financial Stability Board published an updated list of global systemically important banks (G-SIBs) according to data from the end of 2013. Following the Bank of China's inclusion in the 2011 list and the ICBC in 2013, this year the Agricultural Bank of China became the third global systemically important bank in China. According to the FSB announcement, the three Chinese banks are allocated to bucket 1, which are required to meet the requirement of 1% additional capital surcharge with core capital on the basis of Basel III's capital adequacy ratio supervision requirements.

Supervisory Measures

The general policy framework for the supervision of global systemically important financial institutions, approved by the G20 summit in Cannes, mainly includes the following supervisory measures. First, implement higher additional capital surcharge requirement. G-SIBs are classified in five buckets according to their systemic importance, and for each bucket of banks 1–3.5% of additional capital surcharge is required. Second, strengthen the supervision of G-SIBs in respect of frequency, range and depth of supervision and examination, and require one country's regulatory authorities to carry out continuous, comprehensive risk assessment of G-SIBs jointly with the host country through a supervisory joint conference. Third, the regulatory authorities of each country should establish comprehensive disposal mechanisms to deal with the potential bankruptcy of systemic important banks The home country's regulatory authorities are required to establish a crisis management team for each G-SIB jointly with the host country's regulatory authorities; all G-SIBs should make recovery plans, assist regulatory authorities in making plans and receive reports of joint investigations by regulatory authorities of the home and host countries.

In accordance with these requirements, China has continued to strengthen the regulation of G-SIBs and has improved the effectiveness of its regulation. First, in accordance with the Capital Rules, five big banks including BC, ICBC, and ABC have all prepared 1% of additional capital surcharge with core tier I capital for systemic importance. Second, supervision of systemically important banks has been continuously improved with comprehensive risk assessment and improved frequency, range, and depth of examination. Third, five big banks are required to make recovery plans and cooperate with the regulatory authorities in their disposal plans. Currently, the CBRC, together with the PBC, is considering draft regulatory rules for systemically important banks in an effort to strengthen supervision of systemically important banks and improve their risk resistance.

The Guidance on Disclosure of Evaluation Indicators of Global Systemic Importance of Commercial Banks

To implement relevant requirements of the Basel Committee and continue to improve supervision of G-SIBs, the CBRC issued the "Guidance on Evaluation Indicator Disclosure of the Global Systemic Importance of Commercial Banks" (hereinafter referred to as the Guidance) in January 2014, requiring commercial banks whose balance of on- and off-balance-sheet assets after adjustment at the end of the previous year exceeds 1.6 trillion yuan or which have been recognized as G-SIBs in the last year (hereinafter referred to as information disclosing banks) to disclose evaluation indicators of global systemic importance as of 2014. The Guidance, which consists of four chapters containing 26 articles and two attachments, specifies bank disclosures as regards contents, time, and means of disclosure.

According to this Guidance, thirteen banks need to disclose these indicators at present, including the five big state-owned commercial banks and eight joint-equity commercial banks in China, excluding Evergrowing Bank, Zheshang Bank, Bohai Bank, and Guangfa Bank. The disclosure list may vary each year with future changes in assets and other indicators.

3.3 Outlook for Regulation

3.3.1 Analysis of Major Factors That Influence the Development of Banking Regulation

The environment for the development of the banking industry in China is undergoing profound changes, which includes both changes in the external environment of banks and internal financial changes.

With respect to the external environment of banks, first, there is the transformation of the economic development model. Economic growth led by external demand has moved to growth led by domestic demand; economic growth driven by the investment of labor and production factors has changed to growth where the driving forces are the improvement of labor productivity and technological progress; and growth that relies more on investment of resources has been transformed into growth relying more on technological progress. Reliance on export of products with low added value and high pollution has reduced, while domestic demand and domestic consumption and service industries have expanded. The changes in economic development in China require banks to change their existing business development models in terms of customer selection, production design, and risk control methods. Financial strategies are changing from mobilizing financial resources to support development and growth as the main targets, to targets of domestic demand, efficiency of production factors, and technologies in order to achieve internal development and fine management.

Second, there is the transformation of the international and domestic economic situations. On the international scene, the world economy will continue its slow recovery; in the domestic sphere, our economy faces three superimposed periods: growth-rate shift, structural adjustment with growing pains, and stimulus policy digestion. These exert varying degrees of influence on different regions, industries, and fields and greatly affect the development strategy and business model transformation of our banking industry. The direct manifestation of economic slowdown is aggravated credit risk, which will also change banks' operating strategies and profit growth from high-speed growth to medium- to high-speed growth.

First, the progress of interest rate marketization has sped up. Currently, the PBC only controls the RMB deposit interest upper limit for financial institutions. Interest rate marketization makes it more difficult to supervise bank pricing; it also causes continuous narrowing of the interest margin at certain times and impacts the foundation of banks' profitability, which will increase interest rate risk and liquidity risk, challenge the traditional business development model that relies on interest margin, and test banks' risk pricing ability.

Second, there is a trend towards financial disintermediation. The proportion of traditional bank credit in total social financing is decreasing year by year from 80.76% in 2006 to 59.20% in 2013, which will affect the source and use of banks' funds.[8]

Third, there is the emergence of Internet finance. Internet finance can be defined on two levels: in its narrow sense, it refers to innovative financial services carried out on the Internet platform; in the broad sense, it is a general term for all kinds of financial services achieved via Internet and mobile communication technologies, including traditional financial services through the Internet provided by banks as well as new types of Internet financial services initiated by banks and non-financial institutions.

Fourth, capital constraint has tightened. On the one hand, channels of capital supplement need to be expanded not only to strengthen the ability to accumulate endogenous capital but also to complete the capital structure with new capital supplement tools such as preference shares and tier II capital instruments. On the other hand, capital constraint should also be enhanced by improving long-term capital management systems and setting up and finalizing balance mechanisms between capital supplement and capital occupation so as to transform business development models and pursue a low capital consumption path.

3.3.2 Development Trends in Banking Regulation and Improvement of Regulation Effectiveness

In 2016 the CBRC will continue to promote the reform of banking service management structures in order to further improve the professionalism of operational management and the effectiveness of risk control. First, it will continue deepening the reform of business unit systems to promote the transformation of "department-based banking" to "process-oriented banking" and gradually separate the processes of accounting, risk management, and performance assessment. Second, it will continue with the reform of specific departments. To improve and promote the experiences of running particular departments in interbank business, the CBRC will encourage banking institutions to try out the "special department" model in areas such as investment and derivatives trading, with a view to achieving reasonable business integration, shortening chains of operations, reducing the breadth of management, and effectively separating risks while promoting business development. Third, it will explore reforms of the subsidiary system in some business sectors. The CBRC will encourage banks in mature positions to carry out pilot reforms of subsidiary systems in business sectors such as credit cards, wealth management and private banking, and to realize independent management of corporations.

To improve the effectiveness of banking regulation, the CBRC should pay due attention to two matters. On the one hand, it should promote separate regulation to break homogeneous competition. In recent years, the homogeneous competition of China's banking institutions has caused the assimilation of businesses from different institutions that tend to pursue "all trades" regardless of their size, operating condition, and level of risk management. This does not conform to the operating rules of the financial industry, nor does it contribute to the healthy development of the institution. Management and supervision of different classes and levels of financial institutions should be improved through reform. International experience can be drawn upon to design feasible classification standards based on China's national situation, according to asset size, complexity of business, systemic importance, management abilities, and so on, and to implement a limited license system to promote the differentiated positioning and individual development of financial institutions.

On the other hand, the reform of banking regulation system should accord with continuous changes in the business models and risk characteristics of banking institutions. First, the CBRC should make a bigger effort to streamline administration and delegate powers to lower levels. Classification of regulatory powers should be improved. Under the principle of local regulation and efficiency, part of the market access approval function will be delegated to local regulatory agencies at the place where the banking institution has been registered, regulatory service websites listing supervisory powers and duties, and providing negative lists, will be established on different levels, and examination and approval procedures will be made public to improve transparency of supervision.

Second, regulatory rules need to be improved. Standardized operating rules and regulatory standards should be established for each kind of business to promote fair competition between different institutions. Third, the CBRC will actively attempt to improve regulation methods. With respect to off-site regulation, it should make good use of existing off-site regulatory systems and risk precaution systems, improve regulatory rating standards, promote data quality, identify risks accurately, strengthen the monitoring of systemic risks, and improve the level of off-site regulation. As to on-site examination, the CBRC should stick to the principle of scientific establishment of projects, stress key points, raise the importance of special inspections, explore the possibility of setting up a professional inspection team through integration, further popularize the application of electronic inspection systems, enhance accountability and penalty systems, and improve the effectiveness of on-site inspection. Finally, it will steadily push forward the reform of the regulatory organization and system, exploring the establishment of a regulatory governance framework that would separate enactment of regulatory rules from their implementation, prudential regulation from behavior regulation, administrative matters from regulatory items, off-site supervision and on-site examination from regulatory penalties, integrate and concentrate regulatory resources at the frontier of implementation, and truly emancipate the productive force of regulation.

3.3.3 Improvement of Regulatory Legal Systems and Regulation According to Law

The Fourth Plenary Session of the 18th Communist Party of China Central Committee clearly laid down the guiding principles and general objectives of comprehensively advancing the rule of law. Focusing on comprehensive implementation of the spirit of the Fourth Plenary Session, in 2016 the CBRC will promote the legal construction of the banking industry in respect of legislation and law enforcement. First, it will finalize the banking industry legal system by revising basic laws including the Commercial Bank Law, Law on Banking Regulation and Supervision, and Trust Law, and gradually improving the level of laws relating to policy banks, trust companies, and finance guarantee companies to fill legislative loopholes in areas such as commercial banks, inclusive finance and private financing. Second, it will improve the process of regulatory law-making in accordance with the requirement of scientific and democratic legislation, expand the participation of the industry and the public, and improve the quality of legislation. Third, it will improve supervision and law enforcement. The CBRC will promote the standardization and legalization of banking regulation powers and authorities, drive forward the transformation of government functions, continue the work of streamlining administration and delegating power to lower levels while combining delegation and regulation, accelerate the process of setting up power lists, duty lists, and negative lists, divide regulatory powers and responsibilities appropriately, and further define the responsibilities of local regulatory authorities. It will regulate law enforcement, ensuring that lawful evidence, appropriate laws, and strict enforcement are applied during the process. The work of administrative review will be enhanced to rectify negative acts, malpractice, and violations of the law during regulation. It will also strengthen the construction and training of the law enforcement team to improve the skills and professional ethics of supervisory personnel.

3.3.4 Outlook for Banking Regulation in the Next Three Years

In the next few years, the CBRC will promote the reform and opening up of the banking industry with an emphasis on the following aspects in order to improve regulation effectiveness and maintain the absence of systemic and regional risks.

(a) Further improvements to the banking system

First, accelerate the reform of policy banks. Increase operating transparency, improve corporate governance, further clarify the boundary between policy service and commercial service, consider capital supplement channels, and improve the effectiveness of support for the real economy. Second, improve the system of community financial services. Encourage small and medium banks to set up sub-branches in communities to provide a convenient service for small and micro enterprises and community residents and to improve the coverage and convenience of rural financial services. Third, complete the rural financial service system. Carry on in-depth system reform in agriculture-related financial institutions, enrich rural financial services, and develop village banks.

(b) Actively expand access to the banking industry for private capital

First, to enhance regulation, accelerate the promotion of qualified private capital to legally initiate private banks. Meanwhile, uphold the principle of "assumption of risk" and set strict rules for market access and exit according to the law so that the banking industry can achieve "survival of the fittest." Second, expand consumer finance company pilot projects and encourage organizations with consumer finance resources under different types of ownership to found consumer finance companies. All kinds of qualified initiators are allowed to found financial leasing companies. Third, support private capital participating in the establishment of village banks, and encourage qualified village banks to increase their proportion of private capital. Fourth, encourage private capital to participate in the restructuring and transformation of high-risk urban commercial banks, rural credit cooperatives, and non-banking financial institutions.

(c) Transform the banking industry's mode of development

First, promote the transformation of strategy development. Guide banking institutions to find their place in the market, realize differentiated development, carry out business model transformation and rebuilding, and truly improve the quality of development. Second, drive forward the transformation of the profit model. Enhance close management, rebuild business procedures, optimize structure of assets and liabilities, and improve product pricing and risk management. Third, deepen the reform of the business management structure. Continue the in-depth reform of the business unit system, actively carry forward the reform of special departments, and explore the reform of subsidiary systems in certain business sectors.

(d) Improve corporate governance and internal risk control

First, strengthen shareholders' responsibilities and the board's ability to perform its duties. Second, improve the independence and professionalism of the board of directors, achieving a balanced corporate governance structure consisting of shareholders' meeting, board of directors, board of supervisors, and senior management. Third, guide banks to set scientific and reasonable operating objectives and assessment standards, and establish performance evaluation mechanisms that relate to long-term risk responsibilities. Fourth, further improve internal control and compliance systems, and fully bring out the roles of the three lines of defence: internal control, risk and compliance management, and internal audit.

(e) Improve the quality and efficiency of banking financial services

First, guide banks to actively support national strategies, increase financial support for economic structural adjustment and industry upgrades, and actively support the development of strategic emerging industries. Second, vigorously promote inclusive finance, improve and complete the construction of financial services in weak areas such as small and micro enterprises, and agriculture-related areas, guide banking institutions to establish a proper distribution at basic levels, and base their service at lower levels. Third, encourage financial innovation, enrich levels and products of the financial market, enhance innovation in liability business, credit business, non-credit business, and off-balance-sheet business. Fourth, guide banking institutions to carry out comprehensive pilot projects prudentially, improve risk isolation mechanisms, and promote the abilities of consolidated management.

(f) Strengthen regulatory capacity building

First, comprehensively advance the construction of the legal system in the banking industry. Strengthen the overall planning of legislation, improve normativity and public trust in supervision and law enforcement, and promote the modernization of the governance systems and governance abilities of the banking industry. Second, continuously enhance the work of streamlining administration and delegating power to lower levels, and at the same time strengthen in-process and follow-up supervision, and improve the effectiveness of regulation. Third, prudentially carry forward the construction of separate regulation, establish differentiated regulatory policy according to the different characteristics of banks, and determine varying degrees of strength and frequency of regulation. Fourth, improve the regulatory framework to organically combine microprudential and macroprudential regulation and promote the ability to identify, evaluate, and respond to systemic risks. Fifth, optimize the allocation of regulatory resources, continuously improve regulatory technologies and methods, and enhance the quality of off-site regulation information and on-site examination. Sixth, complete market-oriented exit mechanisms for financial institutions, and maintain the safe and steady operation of the banking industry. Seventh, complete coordination mechanisms for financial regulation to prevent repetitive supervision, regulation loopholes, regulatory arbitrage, and regulatory conflict.

Notes

1. BCRC: "China Banking Regulatory Commission 2014 Annual Report", 2015.5. http://www.cbrc.gov.cn/chinese/home/docView/7E0CF3C51001425E919F739562C350BA.html.

2. BCRC: "China Banking Regulatory Commission 2014 Annual Report", 2015.5. http://www.cbrc.gov.cn/chinese/home/docView/7E0CF3C510 01425E919F739562C350BA.html.
3. BCRC: "China Banking Regulatory Commission 2014 Annual Report", 2015.5. http://www.cbrc.gov.cn/chinese/home/docView/7E0CF3C510 01425E919F739562C350BA.html.
4. BCRC: "China Banking Regulatory Commission 2014 Annual Report", 2015.5. http://www.cbrc.gov.cn/chinese/home/docView/7E0CF3C510 01425E919F739562C350BA.html.
5. Data from BCRC: "China Banking Regulatory Commission 2014 Annual Report", 2015.5. http://www.cbrc.gov.cn/chinese/home/docView/7E0 CF3C51001425E919F739562C350BA.html.
6. Data from BCRC: "China Banking Regulatory Commission 2014 Annual Report", 2015.5. http://www.cbrc.gov.cn/chinese/home/docView/7E0 CF3C51001425E919F739562C350BA.html.
7. Data from BCRC: "China Banking Regulatory Commission 2014 Annual Report", 2015.5. http://www.cbrc.gov.cn/chinese/home/docView/7E0 CF3C51001425E919F739562C350BA.html.
8. BCRC: "China Banking Regulatory Commission 2014 Annual Report", 2015.5. http://www.cbrc.gov.cn/chinese/home/docView/7E0CF3C510 01425E919F739562C350BA.html.

Reference

BCRC. 2015. China banking regulatory commission 2014 annual report. 5. http://www.cbrc.gov.cn/chinese/home/docView/7E0CF3C51001425E91 9F739562C350BA.html.

CHAPTER 4

Annual Developments in Securities Regulation

Xiaochuan Zhang and Yongdong Pan

4.1 A Review of Securities Regulation and the State of Development of the Securities Industry

4.1.1 *A Review of Regulatory Policies for the Securities Industry over the Last Three Years*

Since 2012, China's economic growth rate has been decreasing year on year and the country is faced with the increasing pressure of economic transition and upgrade. Against this background, the securities market is facing great challenges and a rare historic opportunity for reform and development. In the last three years, the securities regulatory department has risen to the challenge and grasped the opportunity to promote reform and innovation, and strengthen market regulation, with significant success and considerable appreciation in various sectors of society. There are three aspects to these changes. First, securities regulation seeks to to con-

---

Xiaochuan Zhang and Yongdong Pan are special researchers at RCFLR, CASS.

X. Zhang
Boshi Fund Management, Beijing, China

Y. Pan
China Securities Regulatory Commission, Beijing, China

© The Editor(s) (if applicable) and The Author(s) 2016
B. Hu et al. (eds.), *Development of China's Financial Supervision and Regulation*, DOI 10.1057/978-1-137-52225-2_4

tinuously improve market systems and mechanisms, and enhance the efficiency of resource allocation in the capital market through marketization, legalization, and internationalization. Second, it focuses closely on serving the real economy, strives to expand market service coverage, and plays a significant role in alleviating enterprises' financing difficulties, promoting steady economic growth and transition. Third, regulation looks to the future, combines initiatives in the short term with top-level design in the long term, and maintains a balance between reform, development, and stability.

The first stage has been the simplification of administrative examination and approval. Since 2012, in accordance with the general requirements of the State Council on transforming government functions, streamlining administration and delegating powers, the China Securities Regulatory Commission (CSRC) has made great efforts to promote the reform of the administrative examination and approval system, has cancelled and delegated a great deal of work in this area, and has rationalized non-administrative tasks. In the past three years, nearly 150 administrative approval requirements in terms of professional qualification, institutional management, and personnel management have been deleted. These are strong reform measures which have greatly facilitated the marketization of securities, enhanced the attractiveness of the market, improved its efficiency, and won recognition from both society and the market.

Second, the CSRC has accelerated the construction of a multi-level market system. Reform has been carried out in the GEM (growth enterprise market) board system to relax the access requirements on finance for first issue in the GEM and refinancing systems suitable for GEM companies have been set up. On the basis of a pilot share transfer program in Zhongguancun Park that allows unlisted incorporated companies to enter the National Equities Exchange and Quotations(NEEQ), a national share transfer system for small and medium enterprises has been established, providing a favorable platform for share transfer and financing for unlisted companies and building up a multi-level captial market. The CSRC has worked with relevant departments and local government to clarify the development mechanism for the regional equity transaction market, and actively promote the normative development of regional equity markets. Progress has been made in the integration between the interbank bond market and the exchange bond market, while innovative types of bond have emerged and the scale of the market has been increasing significantly. A regulatory system has been established for the private market and a number of functions implemented including registration of privately offered funds, industrial data collection, and risk monitoring.

Third, the CSRC has driven forward reform and innovation in key areas. In 2012 and 2013, there were two rounds of reform of share-issue systems aimed at improving market-oriented mechanisms in new share issues, centering on information disclosure, strengthening supervision of new share issues, increasing relevant parties' sense of responsibility, and realizing the balanced, coordinated, and healthy development of a two-tier market. The two rounds of reform have laid a solid foundation for the transition to a new share-issue registration system. In 2012, the delisting system came into effect for the boards of GEM and SMEs : delisting indicators were added, and the delisting procedure completed, to produce a market-oriented, diversified standard delisting system. In 2014, the delisting system for listed companies was further improved, the active delisting system completed, companies which had committed major violations were compulsorily delisted, and market transactions and financial indicators for compulsory delisting strengthened. Investor return mechanisms were established and improved by issuing guidance documents for listed companies to set up continuous, clear, and transparent cash dividend and decision-making policies that clearly require the board of directors of a listed company to ensure a minimum proportion of cash dividend in profit distributions according to the phase of the company's development.

Fourth, financial products and trading mechanisms were enhanced. June 2012 saw the release of privately raised company bonds for SMEs that require no administrative approval and satisfy SME financing requirements. In September 2013, treasury bond futures were officially listed in China's Financial Futures Exchange for the first time in seventeen years, which was another major breakthrough for the futures derivative market following stock index futures. In the past three years, a dozen commercial futures varieties have been newly listed in the market, including silver futures, glass futures, rapeseed, , coal, iron ore, plywood, etc., while the variety of commercial futures in China has increased sharply to around 40. In 2014, a new financing tool for enterprises was launched in the form of a preferred stock system. In February 2015, the Shanghai Stock Exchange 50 ETF share option was successfully released, a landmark in the history of no-share option products in China.

Fifth, the CSRC strengthened regulation and law enforcement in relation to violations of laws and regulations in the securities industry. Since 2012, the regulatory department has upgraded the task of inspection and law enforcement to a principal activity and core task of the CSRC. To strengthen inspection and law enforcement, the CSRC issued rules and regulations in the areas of case registration, investigation, and closure, penalties, law enforcement team building, etc., substantially increased the manpower of the inspection and law enforcement division, increased investment in inspection and law enforcement infrastructure and technology, condemned violations of laws and regulations in securities and futures, penalized illegal behavior by fund managers such as rat trading, new type of information manipulation, etc., imposing severe penalties on Wanfu Biotechnology, Xindadi, Everbright Securities, and many others for their violations of laws and regulations, and effectively keeping the market in order.

Finally, the CSRC has widened the opening up of the capital market to the outside world. The Qualified Foreign Institutional Investors (QFII) investment quota has been increased to 150 billion USD, while RMB Qualified Foreign Institutional Investor (RQFII) pilot projects have been exptended to several countries and regions including Singapore, London, and Germany, with the RQFII total increased to 820 billion yuan,[1] further opening up the capital market. In 2014, Shanghai–Hong Kong Stock Connect was successfully launched, starting up a new method of cross-border securities investment that is easy to operate and risk controllable.

4.1.2 A Review of Securities Regulation in 2014

In 2014, the momentum of global economic recovery was weaker than expected, while economic growth rates of the principal economies were very different: the US economy grew rapidly after the second quarter, the Eurozone was going through a very slow process of economic recovery, and the Japanese economy was volatile. Different economic trends in the developed economies obviously led to discrepancies in monetary policies: the USA gradually abandoned its quantitative easing monetary policy, while Europe and Japan continued with quantitative easing policies to stimulate their economies, causing continuing appreciation of the US dollar and depreciation of the euro and the yen. The growth of emerging economies slowed down, and some countries entered stagflation and outstanding structural contradictions. Affected by weakening demand and USD appreciation, prices of international commodities mostly declined, including large falls in the oil and iron ore price. China faced the major pressures of economic downturn, a bottleneck in the impetus for economic growth transition, looming currency deflation in the area of industrial production, and the onerous task of tackling major difficulties with reforms. Generally speaking, the internal and external conditions of the securities market in 2014 were very complex, creating great challenges for securities regulation and the steady operation of the market. In the face of this complex situation, the regulatory department has focused closely on serving the real economy, made great efforts to promote the transformation of regulation, strengthened market regulation, driven forward reform and innovation, and made significant achievements.

Securities regulation in 2014 had a number of characteristics. First, it centered on regulation transition. At the 2014 national securities and futures regulation work conference, Xiao Gang, the President of the CSRC, gave an important speech "vigorously promoting regulation transition," in which he expounded on the significance of regulation transition, proposed the objective of realizing "six transitions", and specified nine main tasks for regulation transition. Over the past year, the concept of regulation transition has been widely recognized by the securities regulation system and the market. The regulatory department has determinedly driven forward reform and innovation in accordance with this concept and has made great progresses in all nine tasks.

The second feature is comprehensive framework documentation. On May 9, 2014, the State Council issued "Several Opinions on Further Promoting the Healthy Development of the Capital Market," specifying overall requirements and policy measures for accelerating the development of a multi-tier capital market, referred to by the market as the "new nine articles of the state." This is the second framework document issued by the State Council for the capital market, coming ten years after the "nine articles of the state" in 2004. It has had a profound influence on improving market expectations, solving major problems that will affect the capital market as a whole, and reinforcing the developing foundations of the market. For a year, the main work of securities regulation has been implementing specific policies and measures relating to the "new nine articles."

Third, regulation acted in close cooperation with comprehensively deepening reform. The Third Plenary Session of the 18th CPC Central Committee began the process of comprehensivereform, while reforms in such areas as administrative examination and approval, state-owned assets, investment and financing systems, the mixed-ownership economy, the free trade zone, the "One Belt, One Road" initiative, and the social security system have continued to advance. While reform increases expectations of dividend release, it also faces greater resistance as it goes deeper. As a highly marketized platform of resource allocation, the securities market is expected to "let the market play a decisive role in resource allocation." The securities market not only provides an experimental platform for reforms in some key areas, such as the opening up of investment and financing in the free trade zone, but also alleviates the economic impact of reform on society by socialized mechanisms to spread the "reform risk." Therefore, shares related to reform have been quite popular and led the increase in the market.

Fourth, it strived to serve the development of the real economy. Since 2014, economic development has entered a "new normal" state, with great pressure from the economic downturn, demanding economic transition and upgrade tasks, outstanding problems of difficult and expensive financing for industrial enterprises, emerging economic high-leverage risk and structural foam, and decreasing marginal utility of traditional "free flooding" monetary credit policy. Under such circumstances, the regulatory department has accelerated the construction of a multi-tier capital market system as determined by the State Council, genuinely lowered access requirements in the capital market, continued to enrich instruments and products in the capital market, and vigorously developed direct financing in order to support the development of the real economy.

The work of securities regulation in 2014 included the following specific tasks. First, the CSRC further streamlined administration and delegated powers. In 2014, following the State Council's requirements on deepening reform of the administrative examination and approval system and the CSRC's general guidelines on regulation transition, the CSRC further simplified administrative approval and delegated more issues to the market. In the whole year, the CSRC deleted thirteen entire administrative licensing requirements and some conditions in another four administrative licensing matters; a further set of administrative licensing matters are in the process of being deleted. These include abolition of the examination of listed companies' acquisition reports and of the approval of purchase, sale and swap of major assets not constituting back-door listing. These measures have been fully recognized by the market, which has freed over 90% of acquisition and reorganization deals by listed companies from CSRC approval. The verification system for publicly offered funds has also changed to a registration system, which has greatly improved efficiency in the issue of publicly offered fund products. For new areas such as privately offered funds and asset securitization, the industry association will be subject to self-regulation rather than advance approval procedures. In addition, the integration and restructuring of functions, agencies, and personnel of nine CSRC departments have been completed.

Second, the CSRC has strengthened the construction of the multi-level market system. In May 2014, the CSRC issued the revised "Measures on Administration of Initial Public Offering and Listing on Growth Enterprise Board," which formally relaxes access restrictions in terms of finance, removes the limitation whereby enterprise applicants were required to be in nine strategic emerging industries, and provides for more innovative companies to be listed on the GEM board; at the same time, it issued the "Interim Measures for the Administration of Securities Issuance of Listed Companies on the GEM Board" which sets up an appropriate refinancing system for the GEM board and meets the continuously increasing demand for finance by listed companies on the GEM board. The national share transfer system pilot project for SMEs (hereinafter referred to as the "new third board") was officially promoted on a national scale, allowing enterprises to be listed regardless of their size, industry, and region. By the end of 2014, the number of listed companies reached 1,572, an increase of 4.4 times over the 356 listed at the end of 2013.[2] In August, the CSRC launched the market-maker system, which has greatly ameliorated market liquidity and pricing mechanisms. On December 5, the CSRC launched a public consultation on the revised "Administrative Measures for Corporate Bond Issue and Exchange" which plans to establish public and private offering systems for corporate bonds covering all corporations. It established a pilot project for exchangeable corporate bonds issued by listed companies' shareholders; the first pilot company, Baosteel, has finished issuing 4 billion yuan of exchangeable bonds. The CSRC also approved the listing of crude oil futures, SSE 50 ETF option equity, and ten-year treasury bond futures.

Third, the CSRC promoted reform and innovation in key areas. At the beginning of the year, it further improved new share-issue systems in accordance with the operation of the new share market. In January, it released the "Measures on Strengthening Regulation of New Share Issues" to comprehensively strengthen supervision of quotation and pricing behavior in new share issues and conduct spot checks and on-site inspection of the quality of information disclosed by IPO enterprises. In March, to counter cashing-out phenomena in new share issues, such as in the case of Aosaikang Pharmaceutical, it revised the "Interim Regulations on Company Shareholders' Public Offering of Shares in IPOs" to regulate the selling of old shares. It took the lead in drafting plans for the reform of share-issue registration systems and explored ways of setting up more marketized share-issue systems. It published "Administrative Measures on Pilot Projects for Preferred Shares" and rules on pilot securities exchange services, issued documents jointly with the CBRC to specify relevant matters concerning the issue of preferred stock by commercial banks and formulated rules on information disclosure for the issue of preferred stocks by listed and unlisted companies. By the end of 2014, the quantity of issued preferred shares had reached 103 billion yuan, 100 billion yuan[3] of which were by listed banks which effectively supplemented their capital funds. On the basis of wide public consultation, in November 2014 the CSRC published several opinions on reforming, improving, and strictly implementing the delisting of listed companies, completed the active delisting of listed companies, compulsorily delistedcompanies committing major violations of the law, and further clarified delisting indicators in respect of market transactions and finance so as to protect the legal rights of small and medium investors.

Fourth, the CSRC promoted the innovative development of the securities, futures and fund industry. It released guidelines relating to securities institutions, the securities investment fund industry, and futures institutions, clarifying general principles, main tasks, and specific measures to enhance the development of securities and futures services. It published administrative measures for the operation of publicly offered funds and established the registration system for publicly offered fund products. It promoted the license system for publicly offered fund business, allowing securities companies and their asset management subsidiaries to obtain licenses for publicly offered funds. It drove forward the reform of shareholder diversification in fund management companies, permitting sole-shareholder fund management companies to be set up, private equity investment institutions to found fund management companies, and professionals to hold shares in fund management companies. It deliberated on draft measures for the administration of private investment funds and launched a system for private offered fund statistics and information reporting. By the end of 2014, the number of registered privately offered fund managers reached 4,955, while registered privately offered funds reached 7,654, with a scale of 2.12 trillion yuan.[4] It revised measures on the supervision and administration of futures companies, expanded the scope of futures company business, extended the range of futures companies' shareholders to private individuals, and optimized qualification requirements for corporate shareholders.

Fifth, it expanded the bilateral opening up of the capital market. In early April 2014, with the approval of the State Council, the CSRC and the Securities and Futures Commission of Hong Kong jointly announced the implementation of a pilot program connecting the Shanghai and Hong Kong stock exchanges; on November 17, the Shanghai–Hong Kong Stock Connect was officially launched, truly opening the channel between the domestic capital market and the overseas market. By the end of 2014, total transactions in the Shanghai–Hong Kong Stock Connect were 188.1 billion yuan, of which Shanghai Stock Connect accounted for 167.5 billion yuan and Hong Kong Stock Connect for 20.6 billion.[5] It cancelled financial verification for overseas listing applications to encourage domestic enterprises to obtain finance from overseas markets; in the whole year, the number of overseas listing applications filed by domestic enterprises was 49, and financing from overseas stock markets amounted to 36.5 billion USD. It increased the total RQFII quota to 820 billion yuan and expanded the scope of the pilot program. It approved establishment by SSE of a financial assets exchange platform in Shanghai Free Trade Zone, and supported securities and futures institutions setting up professional subsidiaries and branches in the free trade zone.

Sixth, it strengthened regulation and law enforcement. In 2014, following the trend towards regulation transition, the regulatory department attached greater importance to in-process and follow-up supervision and strengthened the inspection and law enforcement regime. Relevant law enforcement departments in six securities and futures exchanges, China Securities Depository and Clearing Co., Ltd., and Shanghai and Shenzhen detachments were expanded, the functions of specialist inspection and law enforcement offices in Shanghai and Shenzhen were expanded, agencies were empowered to impose administrative penalties, and law enforcement departments set up at the Shanghai and Shenzhen stock exchanges to enhance inspection, law enforcement, and specialist examination. It took a severe view of infringements of laws and regulations and severely penalized rat trading by fund managers, exposing over 15 fund managers suspected of rat trading[6]; it imposed strict penalties on new types of information manipulation, exposing dozens of cases of market manipulation; and it made great efforts to eliminate illegal securities investment consulting activities being carried on under the name of stock recommendation software. Law enforcement data significantly exceeded those of the previous year; hence market order was effectively maintained. In the whole year, 678 items of information were received, a year-on-year increase of

11%; the number of new cases registered for investigation reached 205, an increase of 8%; 74 cases were referred to public security authorities, an increase of 76%.[7]

4.1.3 Development of the Securities Industry in 2014

In the primary market of stocks, financing has increased greatly on a year-on-year basis. In 2014, new share issues recommenced after a year; despite some unexpected setbacks, new shares steadily began to be issued in the second half of the year with strengthened regulation and verification and complete systems and rules. In the whole year, a total of 125 new shareswere issued, of which 43 were offered on the Shanghai Stock Exchange and 82 on the Shenzhen Stock Exchange (31 on SME boards and 51 on GEM boards); funds raised from IPOs amounted to 66.9 billion yuan, each averaging 535 million yuan. Together with 665.8 billion yuan raised through directional addition issues by listed companies (cash and non-cash asset subscriptions), 13.8 billion yuan raised through rationed shares, and 13.2 billion yuan through the new third board, the amount of domestic equity financing in the whole year reached 76.01 billion yuan, an increase of 344.3 billion yuan on the previous year.[8] By the end of 2014, the number of listed companies on the Shanghai and Shenzhen stock markets was 2,613, an increase of 124 (with one delisted company).

On the secondary market, in the first half there were great fluctuations on the stock market index. The Shanghai Composite Index declined by 3.2%, and the Shenzhen Composite Index went up by 3.7%. In the second half, main stock indexes rose in both price and transaction volume; especially influenced by the PBC's first interest-rate reduction in two years, blue-chip stocks rose rapidly. In the whole of 2014, the Shanghai Composite Index increased by 52.87%, the Shenzhen Composite Index by 33.8%, and the Shanghai and Shenzhen 300 Index by 51.66%. SSE 50 and SSE 180 showed increases of 63.93% and 59.6% respectively, SME and GEM increased by 9.67% and 12.83% respectively, and blue-chip shares showed a significantly higher amount of increase compared with shares of small and medium market value. Nearly 90% of individual shares on the Shanghai and Shenzhen stock markets went up, and over 10% of individual shares had doubled in price or went even higher. According to industry categories classified by the CSRC, architecture, finance, and real estate had larger increases than others at 119%, 82%, and 72% respectively; agriculture, forestry and fishing, sports and the entertainment industry went up by 17% and 18%, following behind other industries. Transactions on the stock market were active throughout the year, while daily transactions on the Shanghai and Shenzhen stock markets averaged 303.6 billion yuan, showing an increase of 54% over the previous year; daily transactions in the first, second, third, and fourth quarters averaged 210.6 billion, 155.8 billion, 293.9 billion, and 550.4 billion yuan respectively, with particularly rapid growth after the third quarter. From November 24, 2014 to the year end, driven by the active trading activities of blue-chip stocks, the daily turnover of the whole market hit a historical high several times, reaching 1.25 trillion yuan on December 9.[9]

On the bond market, bond financing grew fast a large increase in bond values. According to statistics, in the 2014 bond market, a total of 11.92 trillion yuans' worth of bonds were issued, an increase of 35% on the year; among these, corporate credit bonds such as enterprise bonds, short-term financing bonds, medium-term notes, and corporate bonds to the value of 5.19 trillion yuan were issued, an increase of 41%, which significantly improved the proportion of direct financing and effectively alleviated the financing difficulties of small and medium enterprises.[10] In 2014, the exchange bond market issued a total of 384.7 billion yuans' worth of corporate bonds, convertible bonds, bonds with attached warrants, and SME bonds, a decrease of 3% on the year. By the end of 2014, interbank and exchange bond markets had been entrusted with a total of 35.6 trillion yuan, an increase of 5.9 trillion yuan compared with the end of year 2013; among these, the exchange market was entrusted with 2.57 trillion yuan.[11] Over the whole year, the bond market showed an upward trend: the China Securities Comprehensive Bond Index, which comprehensively reflects price trends in interbank and exchange bond markets increased by 9.74%, the SSE T-Bond Index and Corporate Bond Index went up by 4.42% and 8.73% respectively. In 2014, the spot turnover of the exchange bond market was 2.8 trillion yuan, a year-on-year increase of 62%; bond repurchase transactions hit 91 trillion yuan, an increase of 37%.[12]

On the futures market, futures varieties continued to increase, while prices of main futures varieties largely declined. In 2014, six kinds of commodity futures contracts, including hot rolled coil, late rice, silicon iron, manganese silicon, polypropylene, and corn starch were successfully offered to the market in succession, increasing the variety of commodity futures to 44.[13] Two financial futures, CSI 300 and 5-year treasury futures, also went public. The price trend in domestic futures was basically the same as the international market. Prices of most futures varieties went down, with iron ore, PTA, methyl alcohol, and cotton falling the furthest at 44.3%, 34.1%, 31.5%, and 31.5% respectively; CSI 300 futures went up by 53.2%, while 5-year treasury futures went down by 5.4%. In 2014, trading volume and turnover of futures were 2.5 billion deals and 292 trillion yuan, increasing by 22% and 9% year on year.[14]

4.2 Main Regulatory Reform Initiatives of 2014

4.2.1 The Launch of Shanghai–Hong Kong Stock Connect

On April 10, 2014, the CSRC and Securities & Futures Commission of Hong Kong made a joint announcement to approve in principle that the Shanghai Stock Exchange (SSE), Hong Kong Exchanges and Clearing Limited (HKEx), China Securities Depository and Clearing Co., Ltd. (CSDC), and the Hong Kong Securities Clearing Company Ltd. (HKSCC) could set up a pilot mechanism connecting the Shanghai and Hong Kong stock markets (hereinafter referred to as Shanghai–Hong Kong Stock Connect). After over six months' preparation, on November 17 the Shanghai–Hong Kong Stock Connect was officially launched—a significant event in the capital market and the entire economy of China.

4.2.1.1 The Significance of the Shanghai–Hong Kong Stock Connect Pilot Program

Put simply, the Shanghai–Hong Kong Stock Connect pilot program is an interconnection mechanism established between the SSE and the HKEx, enabling domestic investors to buy shares as prescribed by the HKEx, and Hong Kong investors to invest in stock prescribed by the SSE. The transaction is bidirectional and clearly differs from unidirectional transaction modes like the 1999 "Hong Kong Stock Thorough Train" system, which only allowed domestic investors to buy Hong Kong stocks, and QFII and RQFII, which only allow foreign investors to buy A shares. Because of its bidirectional transaction nature, the Shanghai–Hong Kong Stock Connect actually consists of two parts: the Shanghai Stock Connect and the Hong Kong Stock Connect. Shanghai Stock Connect is called the "northward transaction" by the market when referring to overseas investors commissioning HK securities companies or brokers to file a request to the SSE (order routing system) to buy or sell stocks in the Shanghai market within the prescribed limits through the securities transaction service set up by the HKEx; the Hong Kong Stock Connect is also known as the "southward transaction" when referring to domestic investors commissioning inland securities companies to file a request to the HKEx (order routing system) to buy or sell stocks in the HKEx within the prescribed limits through the securities transaction service established by the SSE.

The Chinese capital market has been in a relatively closed state. In spite of the establishment of QFII and RQFII, through which overseas investors can invest in A shares, these two systems are mainly targeted toward overseas institutional investors, impose relatively high qualification standards, and only allow individual investors to buy QFII and RQFII fund products to indirectly invest in A shares. Domestic investors can also invest in the overseas market indirectly through QDII, but the performance of QDII investment has not been satisfactory in recent years and is developing slowly. On the whole, our capital market is gradually opening up to both domestic and overseas investors, but the degree of opening is still limited, and in particular, cross-border direct securities investment mechanisms for individuals has not been established. Along with the development of the Chinese economy and finance, there has been a real demand from the market for cross-border direct securities investment. Especially from 2010 to 2013, main stock indexes overseas went up steadily, while domestic stock indexes largely declined; the blocked channel for cross-border direct securities investment prevented domestic investors from enjoying the growth and benefits of overseas markets. At the same time, many overseas investors are also optimistic about the prospects of the A share market and want efficient investment channels.

For this reason, promoting the bidirectional opening up of the capital market has become an important national strategy. The 12th Five-Year Plan for the Development and Reform of the Financial Industry stipulates that the country will further promote the opening of the capital market to the outside world, gradually expand cross-border RMB use, and deepen the country's cooperation with HK, Macau, and Taiwan in the financial realm. The decision of the Third Plenary Session of the 18th CPC Central Committee also proposes to "expand the opening up of the financial industry to both domestic and overseas investors," "push ahead the bidirectional opening of the capital market, and promote the convertibility of cross-border capital and financial transaction step by step." The launch of Shanghai–Hong Kong Stock Connect is a major part of promoting the opening up of the capital market, fitting in with market demand and reflecting the country's decision to deepen the opening up. On April 10, Premier Li Keqiang announced on the Boao Forum that Shanghai–

Hong Kong Stock Connect would be launched, revealing its significance in promoting the new round of high-level opening up.

In generalterms, Shanghai–Hong Kong Stock Connect represents a major breakthrough in the bidirectional opening up of our capital market and will exert a profound influence on both domestic and Hong Kong markets. First, it will comprehensively strengthen our capital market. The Chinese capital market has a lower proportion of foreign capital participation, with shares held by QFII and RQFII accounting for less than 2% of the circulation market value of A shares. The proportion of foreign investment in the Chinese stock market is far lower than average levels on the Asian market. The opening of Shanghai–Hong Kong Stock Connect makes it very easy for long-term overseas funds to invest in the A share market and will bring large quantities of new funds to the domestic capital market. In recent years, the valuation of China's blue-chip stocks has been lower than that of mature markets. For example, at the end of 2014, the constituent stocks of the SSE 50 index had an average PE ratio of only 12,[15] lower than that of world major stock indexes such as the Dow Jones Industrial Average and the UK's Financial Times Ordinary Shares Index. Bearing in mind that the Chinese economy will maintain medium- to high-speed growth in the long term, domestic blue-chip stocks are very attractive to foreign capital.

Moreover, for reasons of capital account control and QFII quota control, MSCI and other global main index providers have not included A shares in their global index systems, whereas the Shanghai–Hong Kong Stock Connect will eliminate the main concerns of overseas index providers, facilitate A shares' being included by the global index system, bring trillions of incremental funds to the Chinese capital market, and elevate the position of the Chinese capital market in the international market. Shanghai–Hong Kong Stock Connect will also gradually improve the investor structure of the Shanghai market, improve its international competitiveness, and further advance the construction of the Shanghai international financial center.

Second, it will elevate the position of the Hong Kong financial center. In recent years, Hong Kong has been in the throes of sluggish economic development, and its position as a financial center is also greatly challenged by regions like Singapore. Shanghai–Hong Kong Stock Connect provides an important platform for foreign capitals to invest in A shares and helps improve the attractiveness of the Hong Kong market to international investors. Hong Kong is a world-famous free market where capital can enter and exit freely. Overseas capital need to be attracted to Hong Kong first to invest in the A share market, which will strengthen the position of Hong Kong as a financial center. At the same time, domestic investors can invest in HKEx stocks through the stock connect, which also contributes to bracing the confidence of the Hong Kong stock market and reinforcing its international competitiveness.

Third, it will push forward RMB internationalization. Shanghai–Hong Kong Stock Connect uses RMB in settlement, which not only makes it convenient for domestic investors to use RMB to invest directly in the Hong Kong market, but also expands investment channels for overseas RMB funds, facilitating an orderly flow of RMB between the two sites. Currently, the RMB stock in Hong Kong has exceeded one trillion yuan,[16] though mostly in form of bank deposits with limited investment channels. Shanghai–Hong Kong Stock Connect provides new investment channels for RMB funds in Hong Kong and other countries, supports Hong Kong's development as an off-shore RMB business center, and contributes to RMB internationalization. In addition, Shanghai–Hong Kong Stock Connect benefits cross-border capital flow and financial transaction convertibility and will boost financial reforms such as capital account convertibility.

4.2.1.2 Main Features of Shanghai–Hong Kong Stock Connect Pilot Program

a. Investment objective. In the early stage of the pilot program, Shanghai Stock Connect covers constituent stocks of the SSE 180 and SSE 380 indexes and A + H stocks listed on the SSE, excluding stocks on the risk-warning board. According to this, the number of individual shares on Shanghai Stock Connect was approximately 568, accounting for nearly 60% of all listed companies on the Shanghai market, the market value of which forms 90%[17]—it can be said that these shares are highly representative. The scope of Hong Kong Stock Connect includes constituent stocks of HSLI and HSMI and A + H stocks listed on HKEx and SSE. According to this, the number of individual shares on Hong Kong Stock Connect is approximately 266, accounting for about 80% of the market value and trading volume of stocks listed on HKEx.[18] The investment objectives of Shanghai–Hong Kong Stock Connect are not fixed and allow both parties to make adjustments according to conditions in the pilot program.

b. Investment quota. Shanghai–Hong Kong Stock Connect is an unprecedented event in the bidirectional opening of the capital market and cannot afford to fail. During the pilot program, relevant parties had to stick to principles of steadiness and reliability and ensure controllability of risks. Therefore, like other policies of opening up to foreign capital such as QFII and RQFII, in the early stage of the pilot program, there was total quantity control of RMB cross-border investment quotas, with the total quota of Shanghai Stock Connect set at 300 billion yuan and that of Hong Kong Stock Connect at 250 billion yuan; at the same time, a daily quota limit was established and real-time monitoring carried out to control the daily limit of Shanghai Stock Connect to 13 billion yuan and that of Hong Kong Stock Connect to 10.5 billion yuan. In respect of total quota and daily quota, Shanghai Stock Connect had a higher limit than Hong Kong Stock Connect, showing that top-level designers (including perhaps the CSRC) expect Shanghai Stock Connect to heat up more than Kong Stock Connect. The writer believes the total quota of Shanghai Stock Connect is a conservative level; compared with QFII's 150 billion USD and RQFII's 800 billion yuan, the 300 billion yuan limit of Shanghai Stock Connect seems somewhat restrictive:[19] even when it is reached, it will not have much direct influence on the A share market. Of course, both markets can adjust investment quotas according to conditions on the pilot program.

c. Investors. In its purpose of attracting foreign capital, Shanghai Stock Connect does not have a clear threshold for foreign investors and allows investors to buy A shares through Shanghai Stock Connect as long as they can participate in stock trading on the HKEx. As an mature international market, the majority of the Hong Kong stock market's investors are institutional. For Hong Kong Stock Connect, investor eligibility is managed in the early stages, to ensure access to Hong Kong Stock Connect only to domestic institutional investors, or individual investors with a balance of more than 500,000 yuan in their securities account and capital account. In view of the fact that the domestic stock market is mainly dominated by retail investors with funds of less than 100,000 yuan, the 500,000-yuan investment threshold of Hong Kong Stock Connect is quite high and prohibits most domestic investors. This might be because a low threshold not only runs counter to investor protection but also impacts the operation of the Hong Kong stock market.

d. Rules for the settlement of transactions. With respect to system design, Shanghai–Hong Kong Stock Connect has fully considered the actual condition of both markets and has not changed any existing rules of the two markets; each fully respects the other's trading conventions, winning high recognition from both markets. In transaction settlement activities, the regulations and business rules of the market where the transaction settlement occurs should be obeyed, and Shanghai–Hong Kong Stock Connect only opens when both markets are trading and can meet settlement arrangements. Listed companies are still subject to the listing regulation and other provisions of their place of listing. As to the currency used in settlement of transactions, domestic investors use RMB directly in Hong Kong Stock Connect, Hong Kong investors can choose RMB or HKD when participating in Shanghai Stock Connect, but final settlements on Shanghai–Hong Kong Stock Connect are made in RMB. The CSDC and the HKSCC use direct cross-border settlement, in which the two parties become each other's settlement partners and provide a settlement service for Shanghai–Hong Kong Stock Connect. There are significant differences in the rules of the two markets, which should be noted by investors.

e. Limits on the domestic stock investment proportion of overseas investors. Investors in Shanghai Stock Connect by their nature are overseas investors; so, as with QFII and RQFII, the Shanghai Stock Connect introduces foreign capital. To act in concert with QFII and RQFII systems, the limit on the proportion of domestic stocks held by Shanghai Stock Connect investors is set at the same level as for QFII, i.e., shares in a single listed company held by a single overseas investor should not exceed 10% of the total shares of the listed company; the A shares of a single listed company held by all overseas investors should not exceed 30% of the total shares of the listed company.

f. Taxation issues. To clarify the taxation policy for the pilot program of Shanghai–Hong Kong Stock Connect, QFII and RQFII, on October 31, 2014, the Ministry of Finance, the State Taxation Administration and the CSRC jointly issued the "Notice on Taxation Policy of Shanghai–Hong Kong Stock Connect Pilot Program" and the "Notice on Temporary Exemption of Corporate Income Tax for QFII and RQFII Income Gained by Transferring Shares and Other Equity Investment Assets within the Chinese Territory," the main contents of which include the following. First, individual domestic investors are exempt from paying personal income tax on gains obtained through Hong Kong Stock Connect for three years from November 17, 2014. Bearing in mind that Shanghai–Hong Kong Stock Connect is still in its pilot phase, such preferential tax policy is good for attracting individuals to invest in the Hong Kong market and promotes the establishment of Shanghai–Hong Kong Stock Connect. Second, as of November 17, 2014, Hong Kong investors are exempted from income tax and business tax on gains obtained through

Shanghai Stock Connect, which meets current domestic and Hong Kong tax systems and is convenient for taxation management. Third, in cases of buying and selling, inheritance, and gifts of shares, securities/stocks transaction/ stamp tax is imposed in accordance with the tax system in place where the trading object is situated, which reflects the principle of reciprocity and makes it convenient for taxation. Transaction tax for Shanghai Stock Connect is collected by HKSCC and handed over to CSDC, while stamp tax for Hong Kong Stock Connect is collected by CSDC and handed over to HKSCC or HKEx; each party then pays tax to the appropriate tax authority. Fourth, from November 17, 2014, QFII and RQFII are exempted from corporate income tax on income gained by transferring shares and other equity investment assets from within the Chinese territory.

g. Market supervision. While making it convenience for investors to make investment both on the mainland and in Hong Kong, Shanghai–Hong Kong Stock Connect increases cross-market transaction exposure. Supervision and penalties should be clarified in respect of domestic investor and overseas investor breaches of laws and regulations in Hong Kong and Shanghai respectively, such as market manipulation, so as to maintain stable market operations and safeguard the legal rights of investors. Regulatory authorities in both markets will improve their current cooperation on regulation and strengthen law enforcement cooperation in the following ways: improve information-sharing mechanisms for breaches of laws and regulations; jointly mount effective investigations into cross-border breaches of laws and regulations, such as false statements, insider trading, and market manipulation; carry out reciprocal exchanges and training in law enforcement; and improve levels of cross-border law enforcement and cooperation.

4.2.1.3 Effects of Shanghai–Hong Kong Stock Connect
Shanghai–Hong Kong Stock Connect has given rise to favorable market expectations. On April 10, 2014, as the Shanghai–Hong Kong Stock Connect pilot program was announced, the market began to heat up in response. The market generally holds that Shanghai–Hong Kong Stock Connect is hopeful of attracting external incremental funds and bringing "flowing water" to the domestic stock market; at the same time, overseas investors attach importance to long-term value investment and will hopefully boost the vitality of the domestic blue-chip stock market which is of lower stock index. In other words, the market believes Shanghai–Hong

Kong Stock Connect is great news for the domestic stock market; in seizing market opportunities, investors actively chase stocks within the scope of Shanghai–Hong Kong Stock Connect. From April 10 to November 16, the SSE 180 and SSE 380 indexes increased by 15.9% and 24.9% respectively, while in the same time period, the SSE Composite Index increased by 17.8%, and the SME index and GEM index increased by 9.9% and 5.2% respectively.[20]

The opening of Shanghai–Hong Kong Stock Connect was full of setbacks. Following the April 10, 2014 joint announcement by the CSRC and the HKEx of the official establishment as of that date of Shanghai–Hong Kong Stock Connect, requiring six months of preparation, the market generally believed Shanghai–Hong Kong Stock Connect would be launched on November 27, 2014. Some held that the complexity of Shanghai–Hong Kong Stock Connect meant it would only be launched when preparations were complete in every respect, ; there was also a belief that Hong Kong's "Occupy Central" movement might delay the program until 2015. The CSRC and the HK regulatory department made several explanatory statements. While the market was in turmoil, on November 10, the CSRC and the Securities & Futures Commission of Hong Kong made a further joint announcement that Shanghai–Hong Kong Stock Connect would be officially opened on November 17.

The first day of opening went smoothly. On November 17, the eye-catching Shanghai–Hong Kong Stock Connect was officially opened. The Shanghai Stock Connect did not hit the raising limit within one second as was anticipated by the market, and the 13 billion yuan quota limit was used up before 1400. Compared with Shanghai Stock Connect, the transactions of Hong Kong Stock Connect were much lower than the market expectation, with transaction volume of the whole day amounting to only 1.7 billion yuan,[21] only 16% of the daily quota of 10.5 billion yuan, showing a prudent attitude by domestic investors towards Hong Kong stock investment. On November 17, the SSE Composite Index and SZSE Component Index fell by 0.19% and 0.52% respectively; of the 568 individual shares covered by Shanghai Stock Connect, nearly 60% went up. The Hong Kong stock market was even worse as the Hang Seng index fell by 1.21% and the HKEx shares declined as much as 4.5%,[22] creating a record for the largest daily decline in four months. If the previous steady rise of shares was closely related to the market's expectations of Shanghai–Hong Kong Stock Connect, the opening realized the expectations, and the day's market decline was just a normal reaction by the market. Though the market went down, various links such as transaction settlement, quota control, and exchange swap operated normally on that day, and the first day's operation was steady.

The trading volume of Shanghai–Hong Kong Stock Connect is relatively low. Apart from November 17 when the daily quota was used up, quota surplus has been significant on Shanghai Stock Connect since November 18: the average use of the daily quota in the first week was 4.7 billion yuan, average use rate being 37%; in the first month it was 3.1 billion yuan, with an average use rate of 24%. On the Hong Kong Stock Connect side, average daily quota use was 0.46 billion, and the average use rate was 4.4% in the first month.[23] What is noteworthy is that the basis for calculating and controlling quotas in Shanghai–Hong Kong Stock Connect is the offset balance between the buying price and selling price, so the actual trading activity is higher than what is reflected in the use of quota. Even so, Shanghai–Hong Kong Stock Connect's trading is, on the whole, still relatively low. However, its success cannot be measured by trading activity, as its real significance lies not in the throughput of the highway connecting domestic and overseas capital markets but in its restoration. As the market develops and investors become more prepared, the trading activity of Shanghai–Hong Kong Stock Connect will of course increase greatly in the future.

Shanghai–Hong Kong Stock Connect is "cold in the south and hot in the north." Ever since its opening, overseas investors' enthusiasm for buying A shares is obviously higher than that of domestic investors for buying Hong Kong stocks, and the daily quota use on Shanghai Stock Connect is significantly larger than on Hong Kong Stock Connect, presenting distinct difference between the south and the north. In the month from November 17 to December 16, the average daily quota use on Shanghai Stock Connect was 3.1 billion yuan, while that of Hong Kong Stock Connect was only 0.46 billion yuan, the former being nearly seven times the latter.[24] The following reasons may account for these differences. On the one hand, Hong Kong Stock Connect sets a relatively high investment threshold for domestic investors (not less than 500,000 yuan in securities account and capital account). High-net-worth investors who reach this standard have mostly already invested in Hong Kong stocks through official or unofficial channels such as QDII, personal banking business in foreign-funded banks, etc. To individual investors, the Hong Kong stock market is on the whole unfamiliar, and the trading mechanisms on HKEx are also different from those on the mainland; higher charges on the Hong Kong market also affect investor enthusiasm.

To institutional investors, the balance of securities investment funds, insurance, and others annotbe adjusted in time in investment portfolios due to the limitations of asset consignors, so the capital stock cannot reach Shanghai–Hong Kong Stock Connect quickly, and incremental funds also need more time to get there. On the other hand, overseas investors participating in Shanghai Stock Connect are mostly institutional investors who are quite familiar with the A share market, while some of them have already invested in A shares through QFII and RQFII and have wide investment experience with A shares; in addition, domestic blue-chip stocks are of relatively low value, which makes them very attractive to overseas institutional investors since Chinese macro-economic growth still has great potential so that overseas investors make a greater effort to buy through Shanghai Stock Connect.

The "cold in the south and hot in the north" situation of Shanghai–Hong Kong Stock Connect leads to net inflow of overseas funds to the A share market. According to statistics, in the first week of its opening, the net fund inflow was 20.7 billion yuan, and the numbers in the second, third, and forth week were respectively 16.2 billion, 11.4 billion, and 4.8 billion yuan.[25] As with the decrease of total trading volume, the net inflow has also weakened. The net inflow of overseas funds to the A share market meets the expectations of the Chinese regulatory department and helps boost the domestic stock market.

4.2.2 Reform of the GEM System

On March 21, 2014, the CSRC invited public opinion on the revised "Interim Measures on Administration of Initial Public Offering and Listing on Growth Enterprise Board" (hereinafter referred to as the IPO Measures) and the newly drafted "Interim Measures on the Administration of Securities Issue of Companies Listed on GEM" (hereinafter referred to as Refinancing Measures). On May 14, the two measures were officially published following revision and improvement. The notable reform of the GEM system was thus officially launched.

4.2.2.1 Reform of the GEM IPO System

Background

The GEM (growth enterprise market) was set up to support national scientific and technological innovations. In March 2009, the CSRC issued the "Interim Measures on Administration of Initial Public Offering and

Listing on Growth Enterprise Board" and later a succession of supplementary systems and rules; in October of that year, GEM was officially launched and welcomed the first batch of 28 listed companies. Since its establishment, GEM has been developing rapidly; by the end of 2013, the number of listed companies on GEM reached 355, accounting for 23% of all listed companies on SZSE.[26] In the past five years, GEM has made an outstanding contribution to supporting the development of the real economy and promoting scientific and technological innovation, ushered in a large group of leading enterprises in the area of scientific and technological innovation: in short, GEM has become an important platform for new points of economic growth.

However, when GEM was set up, the entire stock-issue system centered on the verification system and thresholds for companies to issue shares and be listed on the market were relatively high. To coordinate with issue systems pertaining to main boards and SME boards, and with a view to clear market position, successful launch, and steady operation, two sets of financial standards for access to GEM IPO were set up, both of which stress the requirement for continuous growth of performance, i.e., the continuous growth of net profit or operation revenue in the last two years to be no lower than 30%. In fact, most innovative enterprises are at the initial stages of establishment, which involves large-scale investment, unstable operations, great fluctuations in performance, and difficulty turning a profit even for many years. However, performance growth that is not continuous does not mean the company has zero growth, as some enterprises show great potential in respect of new products and market expansion, which is even more important than current performance. Especially under the "new normal" state with macro-economic growth geared down from high speed to medium and high speed, the requirement of continuous growth will keep many innovative SMEs outside the capital market and go against the need to adapt to and lead the new normal state of economy. Besides, several rounds of reform of new share-issue system have already occurred since 2009, which have increasingly improved the marketization of new share issues; in addition, the reform of the new share-issue registration system is ready to launch, its keynote being relaxing access to the market and strengthening supervision. Therefore, the revision of the GEM IPO measures is an inevitable part of the adaptation to market development and a must in the interests of the real economy.

Content

First, relaxations on financial indicator restrictions for GEM access. Compared with the 2009 version, the revised GEM IPO measures continue the two sets of financial standards for market access but abandon the requirement for continuous growth. The former provision was "continuous profits in the last two years and profit accumulation in the last two years of no less than 10 million yuan": "continuous growth" has been deleted. In "profits in the last year and operational revenue in the last year of no less than 50 million yuan," the requirement "growth rate of operational revenue in the last two years of no lower than 30%" has been deleted. In addition, the old Article 14 stipulating that the issuer has no conditions that affect its continuous profitability, Article 15 stipulating that the issuer's results do not rely heavily on tax preference, and Article 16 stipulating that the issuer has no major issues pending such as guarantees, lawsuits, or arbitration that affect its continuous operation, have all been deleted. Overall financial standards for GEM IPO access are relaxed to accord with the characteristics of innovative SMEs, which will facilitate the expansion of GEM coverage.

Second, broaden the range of industries on GEM boards. At the same time of issuing the new GEM IPO Measures, the "Guidelines on Further Doing a Good Job of GEM Sponsoring" were abolished. The guidelines required sponsor institutions to accurately assess the position of the GEM, emphasized sponsorship of those enterprises that accord with the national strategic development direction of emerging industries such as energy, materials, information, pharmaceuticals, energy conservation and environmental protection, aeronautics and aerospace, maritime, advanced manufacture, high-tech services, etc., and of enterprises showing independent innovation ability and growth potential in other areas. In practice, 90% of enterprises applying to be listed on the GEM are from the above-mentioned nine strategic emerging industries. Along with the development of new types of business and new industries, the nine industries can no longer cover innovative growth enterprises. The abolition of the guidelines removes restrictions on GEM enterprises within the nine industrial sectors and further improves the range of service industries acceptable on the GEM. It should be noted that enterprises in industries with excess production capacity, high pollution, and high energy consumption which are clearly restricted by national industrial policy still cannot be listed on the GEM.

Third, improve the efficiency of issuance examination. The old IPO measures did not have clear time limits for the approval of GEM issue applications, while the new measures clearly stipulate that the CSRC should make decisions on approvals, suspension of verification, termination of verification, and rejection in three months from the date the CSRC receives the application file. This will greatly improve the efficiency of issue examination, changing the current indefinite time for issue examination, and effectively alleviate queuing problems with GEM listing applications. For enterprises and securities intermediaries, this is undoubtedly good news and boosts their confidence to march towards GEM. In addition to clear time limit for approval, issuers are given a longer time to issue shares; the previous six months to complete issuing from the date of approval have been increased to 12 months, giving issuers more flexibility to pick their time for issuing.

Fourth, strengthen in-process and follow-up supervision. The revision of the GEM IPO system followed the principle of in-process and follow-up supervision centering round information disclosure that applied to the new round of new share-issue systems at the end of 2013 and has stressed the supervisory responsibilities concerning information disclosure. For example, it clarifies that the issuer bears the primary responsibility for information disclosure and should provide accurate and complete financial accounting information and other materials to sponsors and securities service institutions and cooperate securities service institutions in every way in due diligence investigations. It specifies that from the date the application file is received, various relevant responsible bodies will bear corresponding legal responsibilities for the accuracy, completeness, and timeliness of issue application files; issuers and sponsors should take responsibility for the pre-disclosed prospectus (application draft), which cannot be changed at will after filing and pre-disclosing. This should ensure no major mistakes such as intentional concealment.

Comment

The reform of the GEM IPO system responds to the demands of the market and constitutes a major aspect of improving China's multi-tier market system. The reform follows the same lines as the new round of reform in respect of new share-issue systems which started at the end of 2013. The two are highly consistent as regards basic guidelines relaxing market access, strengthening information disclosure, etc. The reform will bring new incentives for the development of the GEM and will, hopefully, facilitate new jumps in the market. In the whole of 2014, a total of 125 new shares were issued, 51 of which are listed on the GEM, accounting for almost half of the total.[27] At present, as economic development enters the new normal state, the GEM has a larger role to play, not only in supporting SMEs and stimulating the vitality of the private economy but also in boosting innovative enterprises and promoting economic transition and upgrade. This reform is of great significance in promoting the position of the GEM in economic society.

Needless to say, the reform of the GEM IPO system is not yet adequate and is still transitional in nature. Though it has relaxed the financial indicators for GEM access, it does not mean GEM standards have been lowered. Standards of "continuous profits in the last two years and profit accumulation in the last two years of no less than 10 million yuan; or profit gaining in the last year and operational revenue in the last year of no less than 50 million yuan" are still not easily attainable for most enterprises. The decision of the Third Plenary Session of the 18th CPC Central Committee clearly determined that the core content of promoting the reform of share-issue registration system is cancellation of the profit requirement for enterprises issuing shares, and the regulatory department no longer makes substantive judgment regarding the profitability of enterprises. The reform of the share-issue registration system is currently advancing actively and steadily; as an important link in the reform process, the GEM IPO system's ultimate target should be to abolish conditions regarding the profits of applying enterprises.

4.2.2.2 GEM Refinancing System Established

Background
The GEM board was set up in 2009 and only has a short history. As it aims to serve high-tech enterprises, the market has high expectation for the growth of GEM companies and gives a warm reception to their stocks, which causes the "three highs" phenomenon in GEM companies' IPO—high turnover rate, high fluctuations, and high valuation. Taking the first 28 listed companies, for example, their average PE ratio is 56.7 times, while that of BODE Energy Equipment reaches 81.67 times, far higher than the PE ratio of the whole A share market and the SME market. Listed companies on the GEM over-fulfill their funding objective one after another; by the end of 2013, the average over-fulfilled fund-raising rate of 335 listed companies on GEM reached 115%.[28] Some listed com-

panies deposit the extra funds in the bank or use them to buy wealth management products. From 2009 to 2013, the financial expenses of GEM companies were all negative values, indicating that they had more interest income. In other words, GEM companies at early stage of development have adequate funds for development and basically have no demand for refinancing, which was also one of the main reasons that no refinancing system had been set up for the GEM board.

However, as macro-economic development in China on the whole took a downturn after 2010 and the profitability of listed companies continued to decline, some GEM companies also met with operational difficulties, enormous consumption of capital, and increasing demands for refinancing. In 2013, the financial expenses of 355 GEM companies totaled −268 million yuan, showing a large increase compared with −187.3 million yuan in 2012; 131 of these companies have financial expenses in positive values, adding up to 235.3 million yuan, showing a large increase compared with a total of 119.5 million yuan of financial expenses for 99 companies; in the first three quarters of 2014,[29] the financial expense of GEM companies had already turned to positive values. This indicates that quite a few GEM companies have begun raising funds through bank credit. In addition, since the new round of new share-issue system reform at the end of 2013, over-fulfilled fundraising has almost disappeared among newly listed companies; in future real demands for continuous financing will be inevitable. The refinancing system is a major component of the capital market system and has been established for years in the main board market. In recent years, the refinancing scale on the main board far exceeds the scale of IPOs. Under such circumstances, setting up a refinancing system for the GEM board is not only necessary but also urgent.

Content
Regarding the means of refinancing, the GEM Refinancing Measures specify that companies listed on the GEM board can refinance by issuing shares, convertible bonds, and other varieties approved by the CSRC. Security varieties issued by GEM can be offered publicly to no particular entities, or privately to specified entities, a combination which allows listed companies on GEM to refinance in basically the same way as listed companies on the main board by multiple means, including public additional issue, rationed shares, directional additional issue, convertible bonds, and so on to meet their various demands for investment and financing.

Regarding the conditions for refinancing, the GEM Refinancing Measures stipulate that, to issue securities, GEM companies should meet conditions provided by the Securities Law and satisfy the following requirements: (1) net profit in the last two years, from which non-recurring gains should be deducted; (2) cash dividends paid in the last two years according to the articles of association of listed companies; (3) cash dividends paid according to the articles of association of the company; (4) over 45% asset-to-liability ratio at the end of the last period, except for private placement of listed companies; and (5) normality of other basic accounting work, completed corporate governance, etc. In addition, companies with lower asset-to-liability ratios whose capital requirements can be met through bank loans and corporate bonds are not expected to refinance with publicly offered shares which will dilute the rights and benefits of medium and small investors.

Regarding the use of refinanced funds, the Refinancing Measures stipulate that listed companies whose previously raised funds have not been used up, or where the progress and effects of fund usage are very different from its disclosure, should not refinance. Refinancing funds should be used in accordance with the provisions of national industrial policies and laws and administrative laws and regulations; except for financial enterprises, refinanced funds cannot be used for financial investments in the way of holding tradable financial assets and available-for-sale financial assets, lending to others, commissioning wealth management, etc., or for direct or indirect investment in companies whose main business is buying and selling negotiable securities; in addition, investments with raised funds should not involve controlling shareholders and actual controllers in horizontal competition or affect the independence of the company's production and operation, and in such cases refinancing will not be granted.

Regarding directional additional issues, the reform has established a directional additional issue mechanism specifying "small amount, speediness, and flexibility." The specific institutional arrangement is as follows: first, the upper limit of the financed amount of directional additional issue is set at 10% of the company's net assets for a 12-month accumulated amount, not exceeding 50 million yuan and 10% of the company's net assets per issue; second, simple verification and approval procedures are applied so that the regulatory department can approve or reject the application within fifteen working days of its receipt; third, a system of one-off decisions by annual shareholders' meeting but multiple implementation by the board of directors is set up to improve decision-making efficiency;

fourth, the issuer is allowed to sell shares on their own without hiring sponsors and underwriters so as to reduce financing costs; fifth, the interval between share offering and listing is shortened to lower market risks.

Regarding the issue of convertible bonds, companies listed on GEM can issue convertible corporate bonds with a minimum term of one year, convertible bonds can be converted to shares 6 months after the completion of offering, and the share conversion period can be decided by the company according to the duration of the convertible bonds and the financial condition of the company. The converted share price should not be lower than the average share prices of twenty trading days and one trading day before the notification day of the prospectus.

Comment

As with the rapid development of GEM, the lack of refinancing systems had been an increasingly prominent factor holding it back. The establishment of refinancing systems for GEM is the main component that completes the GEM system and rules, helping to solve the refinancing requirements of GEM companies and promoting the further development of GEM. The directional additional issue mechanism of "small amount, speediness, and flexibility" completely matches the characteristics of a growth enterprise market, and may become the main refinancing method for GEM companies. Under the circumstances of the share-issue system's gradual transition to a registration system, the refinancing system of the main board market also requires revision and improvement, whereas the GEM refinancing system provides a good reference for the main board.

4.2.3 Reform of Delisting System

The CSRC invited public comments on "Several Opinions on Reforming and Strictly Implementing the Delisting System (Exposure Draft)" on July 4, 2014, and officially issued "Several Opinions on Reforming and Strictly Implementing the Delisting System" (hereinafter referred to as Delisting Opinions), which took effect on November 16. This was a new round of reform of the delisting system, two years after the reform of 2012.

4.2.3.1 Background

The delisting system is of fundamental importance in the capital market. Mature overseas capital markets have all set up fairly complete delisting systems as a major way of ensuring resource allocation of the market, achieving survival of the fittest, and cleaning up the operating environment of the market. Therefore, delisting is a universal phenomenon in main securities markets overseas and is generally recognized by markets and investors. Taking the USA as an example, from 1995 to 2012, the NYSE had 3,052 delisted companies while NASDAQ had 7,975 delisted companies.[30] Under the share-issue registration system, the listing threshold for the American stock market is low, so every year large numbers of new enterprises are listed; the US mature delisting system ensures unblocked entrance to and exit from the capital market, enables "survival of the fittest" in dynamic development, and maintains the strong vitality of the American stock market.

Since the establishment of the capital market in China, a corresponding delisting system has been set up based on company law and securities law. The delisting system has been revised on many occasions, the last time being the reform of 2012. This reform added delisting indicators such as net assets, operational revenue, and audit reports for companies to delist from Shanghai and Shenzhen main boards; it imposed stricter requirements for resumption of listing, such as positive values of net profits both before and after deducting non-recurring profit and loss, operational revenue not lower than 10 million yuan, positive value of net assets at end of periods, etc.; it simplified delisting and resumption of listing procedures, and specified a time limit for verification; it set up a risk warning board for the trading shares of companies warned of delisting and other major risks; it adopted the necessary restrictive measures on trading, on market monitoring, and on eligibility management of investors. Shenzhen's SME board and GEM board have similar delisting arrangements. The reform has been implemented more on the technical level and leaves some substantial matters unchanged.

Overall, the delisting system in China has the following outstanding problems. First, there is no active delisting system. Listed companies are public companies, with socialized and dispersed stock rights and highly transparent operating information. For the company, this is a two-edged sword. If the company believes listing in the market does not accord with its interests, delisting becomes a natural choice. Taking the US market as an example, companies mostly delist by choice. From 2003 to 2007, the annual delisting rate on NYSE was 6%, about half of which was active delisting; the annual delisting rate of NASDAQ was 8%, of which active delisting accounted for nearly two-thirds.[31] In China, listed status has always been rare, so companies have seldom had an incentive to actively delist from the market. However, advances in the share issue registration system will greatly change this situation, and some companies will have a significantly stronger incentive to delist.

Second, compulsory delisting is difficult to achieve. The previous delisting system was mainly compulsory delisting, that is, when the financial or trading indicators of the company reach the delisting standard, their transactions on the exchange would be terminated. The rarity of listed status means, on the one hand, that listed companies will manipulate financial or trading indicators, and on the other hand, that other entities including local government and investors will also thwart the delisting process; indefinite and non-specific law-enforcement standards for delisting made it extremely difficult for listed companies to delist. By the end of 2014, there had been less than 80 delisted companies in total in China, with a delisting rate far lower than mature markets like the USA. It has led to the phenomenon that some badly performing companies even become the object of market speculation . More importantly, the difficulty of delisting strongly impacted the normal function of the "survival of the fittest" market mechanism.

Since the new round of new share-issue system reform started at the end of 2013, the issue of new shareshas been further marketized. Under the new share-issue system, the supervisory department and Issuance Examination Committee do not make a judgment about the continuous profitability and investment value of the issuer but focus on the compliance of new share-issue application documents. Since new share issues were re-launched in 2014, their efficiency have obviously been promoted, the tempo has greatly accelerated, and there have been 125 new share issues over the whole year. At the same time, in accordance with the decision of the Third Plenary Meeting of the 18th CPC Central Committee, the supervisory department has been driving forward the reform of the share-issue registration system, the implementation of which will bring radical changes to the stock market, altering the rarity of listed status and allowing more enterprises to enter the capital market. In other words, the supervisory department no longer guarantees the profitability and growth of listed companies, some enterprises that have not yet made a profit can also be in the capital market, and share issuing and listing of more and more enterprises will decrease the general quality of listed companies. Under such circumstance, if companies badly performing companies and serious breaches of the law cannot be eliminated from the market, the overall quality of the capital market will be seriously affected Therefore, completion and strict implementation of the delisting system is a must.

4.2.3.2 Main Content

The active delisting system has been finalized. The Delisting Opinions point out that if, for reasons of development strategy, maintaining rational valuation, stabilizing control, and cost effectiveness, a listed company believes listing on the market is no longer a need or is detrimental to its development, it can actively apply to the stock exchange to terminate trading in its shares. The Delisting Opinions list seven situations for active delisting, including listed companies no longer qualifying for listing because of acquisition, repurchase, consolidation by merger, and other market activities, and active withdrawal of share transaction by listed companies after necessary decision procedures. Active delisting is not arbitrary delisting, which requires listed companies to carry out relevant internal decision procedures including getting two-thirds of the votes of both general shareholders and medium and small shareholders who attend the shareholders' meeting, examination by independent financial advisors, opinions of an independent board of directors, etc. Besides, to lead marketized active delisting, the Delisting Opinions require a series of relevant supporting policies and measures to address repo operation of listed companies, share repurchase program, merger and acquistion, and bankruptcy liquidation.

Compulsory delisting of companies occurs for major violations of laws. The Delisting Opinions specify that major violations refers to companies that have received administrative penalties from the CSRC for fraudulent conduct in issue and listing, and false or misleading statements or major omissions in important information disclosure documents, or companies that have been referred to public security authorities by the CSRC on suspicion of criminal behavior. For companies committing major breaches of the law, the Delisting Opinions require the CSRC to suspend their stock trading and terminate their listing status within one year of the the CSRC decision to impose a penalty or refer to public security. The conditions under which listed companies on suspension can resume listing are provided, with different arrangements for those responsible for fraudulent conduct and major information disclosure breaches: the shares of these companies can be re-listed on the market as long as they correct the breaches, dismiss staff responsible, and make proper arrangements for civil compensation within the specified time limit. Companies found to have acted fraudulently during issue have the listed status of their stocks terminated within the specified time limit.

Indicators for compulsory delisting for failure to satisfy trading standards are strictly observed. Exchanges have already set up compulsory delisting indicators for listed companies who do not satisfy trading standards and requirements, while the Delisting Opinions require these delisting indicators to continue being implemented together with appropriate supplementary and adjustment indicators such as total capital stock, share distribution, trading volume, market value of shares, etc. For total capital stock, share distribution, and trading volume, the Delisting Opinions allow securities exchanges to have differentiated arrangements according to the characteristics of different boards and to make suitable adjustments. It also means standards of total capital stock, share distribution, and trading volume are probably lower than others and can rarely become the main drivers of compulsory delisting. For shares' market value delisting indicators, the Delisting Opinions specify that companies whose shares have closing prices lower than par value for 20 consecutive trading days (excluding suspended days) will be obliged to delist.

Compulsory delisting indicators that reflect the company's financial situation are strictly adhered to. Like compulsory delisting indicators for failure to satisfy trading standards, systems and rules regarding financial situation delisting indicators have also been established in exchanges, while the Delisting Opinions require that these delisting indicators continue to be implemented, together with appropriate supplementary and adjustment indicators such as net profits, net assets, operational revenue, audit reports, and accuracy of information disclosure within a specified time limit according to the law. The Delisting Opinions provide that listed companies whose listing and trading are suspended because they meet financial situation delisting indicators will be obliged to delist if any one of the relevant indicators in the most recent annual financial accounting report still fails to meet the requirements. Among financial situation delisting indicators, it is net profit that has received the most attention, since the market has varied opinions about it. Some hold it should be retained to ensure the quality of listed companies, while others believe that because it is out of keeping with the spirit of reforms which allow enterprises that have not yet shown a profit to issue and be listed on the market, it should be weakened or abolished. The Delisting Opinions retain the "losses in three consecutive years" as a delisting indicator, mainly because of the provision in the current securities law which is still under revision.

Supporting institutional arrangements for delisting have been completed. First, exchanges are required strictly to implement procedures for resumption of listing and for termination of the listing status of companies suspended from listing that do not apply for resumed listing or fail to meet requirements of resumed listing within the specified time limit. Second, to protect the legal rights and interests of investors, the Delisting Opinions ask listed companies to act in accordance with their public commitment to restrict their reduction of share holdings. Third, it requires securities exchanges to set a "delisting preparation period" of 30 trading days for stock trading of compulsorily delisted companies before they are delisted. It also requires exchanges to set up investor eligibility systems in the "delisting preparation period" to prevent some investors, especially small and medium retail investors, trading shares of the delisted company for the purposes of speculation. Fourth, it specifies the disposition and trading arrangement of delisted companies. Actively delisted companies can make their own arrangements, while shares of compulsorily delisted companies will all be listed and traded on a special level of the National Equity Exchange and Quotations. Fifth, it stipulates that delisted companies can apply to be re-listed when they meet listing requirements, and securities exchanges can have a range of arrangements for resumption of the listing of delisted companies in varied situations.

Protection of investors in delisted companies is strengthened. As company delisting involves the interests of general medium and small investors, the protection of investors, especially the legal rights and benefits of medium and small investors, is the priority in all delisting arrangements. The Delisting Opinions requires the general requirements of the "Opinions of the State Council on Further Enhancing Protection of Legal Rights and Benefits of Medium and Small Investors in the Capital Market" to be implemented at each stage of the delisting arrangements. It also requires that listed companies' obligations to disclose information before delisting is strengthened, illegal conduct such as false statements, insider trading, market manipulation, and so on are strictly punished, protection for dissenting shareholders in active delisting companies is improved, and civil compensation liabilities are clarified in respect of companies committing major violations of the law and the staff responsible.

4.2.3.3   Comment
Compared with previous reforms of the delisting system, the delisting system set up this time is more significant, has further improved

in terms of top-level design and embodies both flexibility and strictness. Its flexibility is reflected in full respect for the intentions of listed companies in the process of active delisting. In developed countries' stock markets, active delisting has become the main way of delisting. Considering the special national conditions of China, active delisting cannot become the mainstay in a short time, but it will be an inevitable trend in the medium and long term. Strictness means that delisting standards become more specific and their implementation stricter. On November 16, 2014, after the official release of the Delisting Opinions, the market viewed it as "the strictest delisting system in history." The strictness compensates for the weak link in the previous delisting system and builds up a "great wall" for delisting. Once listed companies hit the wall, they will be evicted from the capital market. In practice, some listed companies that cannot meet trading and financial requirements are faced with the risk of delisting, while those involved in major violations such as fraudulent issue and illegal information disclosure will be directly delisted from the market.

The strict implementation of the Delisting Opinions will have a great impact on the Chinese stock market where previously companies had only entered but never left. First, it provides a favorable market environment for the reform of the share-issue registration system, which will significantly increase the supply of shares, so a strict delisting system will help achieve the survival of the fittest and ensure the overall quality of listed companies on the stock market. Second, it introduces reassessment of the overall market value system. The delisting system will become a red line for all listed companies, and every listed company is able to delist. More and more delisting of listed companies will bring about a re-measurement of share values, leaving some badly performing companies with no investors. Third, it will improve the investment atmosphere of the stock market. For a long time, badly performing companies were regarded as "phoenixes" that never died, giving wide scope to the imagination of investors and inviting them to indulge in speculative trading. However, with the implementation of a stricter delisting system, investors will risk losing everything if they take part in speculation in underperforming shares; this will lead to a decrease in speculative behavior and a great improvement in the investment culture and atmosphere of the capital market.

4.2.4 Establishment of Central Supervisory Information Platform for the Capital Market

Xiao Gang, President of the CSRC, made a speech "vigorously promoting regulatory mode transition" at the 2014 national securities and futures regulation work conference, making "advancing the establishment of central supervisory information platform for the capital market" one of the nine tasks of regulatory transition. At the 2015 conference, Xiao Gang once again emphasized the establishment of a central supervisory information platform (hereinafter referred to as regulatory platform) and put forward the requirement of "continuously promoting the establishment of a central supervisory information platform." It can be seen that the construction of the regulatory platform is important in the CSRC system and will have a profound influence on CSRC regulation.

4.2.4.1 Background

In recent years, as the Chinese economy has continued to develop rapidly, and information science and technology are advancing and changing every day, it has become fashionable to improve information technology and electronic development in business. E-commerce companies, Internet companies and financial institutions are all setting up their data centers. For the regulatory department, the increasingly expanding market volume and the explosive growth of data information mean that traditional "manual" regulatory methods can no longer meet demands for regulation, while the efficiency of regulation is in urgent need of improvement with the use of information technology. Therefore, in recent years, several national commissions/ministries and regulatory departments have been actively attempting to build highly efficient supervisory information systems that feature logic centralization.

For example, to improve the efficiency of banking regulation, the CSRC started building an off-site supervisory information system in 2003 which took over 5 years to complete. An off-site supervisory information system gathers basic data from around 4,000 subjects of regulation and has three aims: micro regulation of individual banks, macro regulation of the overall operation of the banking industry, and macroprudential regulation. The regulatory departments of various businesses, analysis and research departments, and the risk monitoring departments of the CSRC all use the same off-site supervisory information system, with one platform for both collecting and downloading data.

After more than two decades of development, the volume of China's securities market is now growing rapidly. Currently, there are more than 2,600 listed companies with a total market value of over 35 trillion yuan and 140 million investor accounts in the securities market; the bond market has a total scale of 35 trillion yuan and includes a complete range of bond varieties such as national debt, financial bond, enterprise bond, etc.;[32] varieties of commodity futures and financial futures keep increasing; the private placement market is growing rapidly. Trading methods have also multiplied including securities margin trading, stock option, repurchase, and so on. The securities market has the most centralized information and generates enormous data every day, in which trading, settlement and other market activities can all be reflected. Under these circumstances, effective market regulation must rely on a strong supervisory information system. Especially when cross-market, cross-variety, and cross-border trading become more frequent, regulation is beyond the scope of a single department and must use more powerful regulatory methods.

The CSRC has set up multiple supervisory information systems, but their independent construction and usage make them into islands with problems such as different data standards, data redundancy, and data inconsistency, which greatly reduces their effectiveness and means there is no straightforward connection and information-sharing mechanism covering various regulatory matters. Moreover, the individual systems cannot adapt to information classification, integration, and mining requirements in the era of big data, and do not make full use of information technology for smart regulation functions such as risk warning and evidence identification. Therefore, the establishment of a central supervisory information platform for the capital market is a fundamental task with long-term benefits and an is the inevitable choice to promote regulatory transition.

4.2.4.2 An Overview of the Central Supervisory Information Platform of the Capital Market

The establishment of a supervisory information platform is an internal CSRC task and there is little published material about it. However, from Xiao Gang's speech at the national securities and futures regulation work conference, we can have a rough idea of its orientation, architecture, concept, construction planning, difficulties, etc.

Orientation

The central supervisory information platform is an application platform based on the requirements of various agencies and departments in the CSRC and is its highest supervisory information platform. The platform gathers and integrates data and resources from the whole system, promotes the logical centralization of the regulatory system, and achieves unification, comprehensiveness, and sharing of regulatory data information. It has three core tasks: first, to solve the problem of the repeated construction of individual information systems and realize their organic unification; second, to resolve multi-thread data collection, different standards, and data conflicts and achieve standardization and unification of data; third, to solve the problem of underdeveloped information-processing methods and low efficiency, and to comprehensively promote the informationization of regulation.

Architecture

The central supervisory information platform consists of two parts: core installation and business functions. The core installation module includes a central data-submission system, a central database, an external data-exchange system, public information distribution and a feedback system; the central database is at the heart of the whole platform, holding complete data information from the CSRC system which various business sectors all rely on for their regulation. The business function module is a business regulation system developed on the base installation according to the demands of various business sectors for regulation and is mainly used to support the CSRC's administrative licensing, case investigation, daily supervision, macro regulation, and internal management. The main design concept of the platform can be seen from its structure, which builds a unified data collection and exchange system and a central database by setting up a data governance and control system, achieves unified collection and management of whole-market regulatory data, avoids repeated, multi-thread data submission, and meets various regulatory requirements.

Construction Planning

Construction of the central supervisory information platform began in 2014 and was regarded as the lead project for various organizations, requiring each department head to personally manage the demands of the information system and to appoint key staff to the construction of the platform. There will be no other new independent regulatory systems and all planned business supervisory information systems will be included in the central supervisory information platform. Business regulatory systems will be implemented gradually in priority order, and the whole platform is scheduled for completion in three years. In 2014, investigation of the whole-system business demand was conducted, the overall plan, implementation plan, management rules, and standard norms of the platform were established, and the core installation and business regulation modules of the supervisory information system were partially completed; in 2015, the development of new business regulatory system is to be completed and the system will run online; in 2016, upgrading and reconstruction of old systems will be completed, and the whole system will be fully operational.

Difficult Points
The regulatory platform is a complicated and enormous project that involves a wide range of regulatory matters and thus is very difficult to implement. At the 2015 national securities and futures regulation work conference, Xiao Gang pointed out that the construction of the platform had made progress in the last year but had also faced many difficulties and outstanding problems which affected the progress and quality of construction. Some agencies and departments did not attach due importance to the project and had not invested much effort, sticking instead to the old practice of individual systems and not complying with the concept of regulatory mode transition. These problems have led to low quality in some business requirements, difficulties with data centralization and integration, and difficulty in overall planning and coordination. To counter these difficulties, Xiao Gang re-emphasized that regulatory platform construction is a major tool in regulatory mode transition, an important base and method for future regulatory work, and also a measure of the regulatory mode transition of different agencies and departments; he also required each department head to give high priority to, support, and cooperate in the construction of the regulatory platform and make an effort to achieve a major breakthrough in 2015.

4.2.4.3 The Significance of the Supervisory Information Platform for Improving Regulatory Efficiency
The CSRC's effort to promote the construction of a central supervisory information platform appears to be its own internal affair. But, as the saying goes, "the artisan must sharpen his tools first to do good work." The construction of the regulatory platform is an important way of achieving

regulatory mode transition and improving regulatory effectiveness and is bound to exert a great influence on the whole market.

A major task of the CSRC in 2014 and the following several years is to promote regulatory mode transition. There are six transitions: the transition from shattered, segmented regulatory mode to sharing, functional regulation; from opaque, unstable regulation to fair, transparent, rigorous, highly efficient operation, and so on. The construction of the regulatory platform will promote transition in the following ways. First, it will promote the transition from institutional regulation to functional regulation. The central supervisory information platform will establish unified information standards, strengthen information centralization and sharing, facilitate the breakdown of segmentation between departments and business sectors, conquer departmental selfishness, and lay the foundations of information technology for functional regulation. Second, it will improve the transparency of regulatory work. The central supervisory information platform supports whole-course supervision and achieves regulatory data information sharing, which not only helps to reduce manual operations, but also favors the construction of anti-corruption system combining prevention and disciplinary action. Third, it reduces the cost of regulatory work. All off-site data is collected through the off-site data collection platform, reducing the effort of independent data collection by each department and effectively avoiding inconsistent data standards and repeated data submission. The smart collection of data information through the off-site data collection platform will reduce on-site investigation and manual operations and improve efficiency in inspection and law enforcement, investigation of institutions, and other forms of on-site investigation.

It will increase the amount of smart technology in regulation. The current capital market businesses are highly reliant on electronic information technology systems, and generate enormous amounts of information that can scarcely be processed and mined manually. After the establishment of the central supervisory information platform, all supervisory business data information will be stored in the central database, through which data information, especially cross-market, cross-variety information can be automatically related, mined, and integrated by constructing data models, applying big-data technologies, etc. so as to serve business supervision and risk monitoring and improve the level of smart technology in regulation. According to published data from the CSRC, since the launch of the big-data analysis system in the second half of 2013, 375 items of evidence of insider trading have been investigated, 142 of which have been recorded officially, an annual increase of 21% and 33% respectively, showing an obvious improvement of efficiency in inspection and law enforcement; during the surge of the stock market at the end of 2014, the CSRC relied on a big-data system for in-depth analysis and mining of evidence of market manipulation, registered and investigated institutions and individuals involved in cases of eighteen stocks including ST Cloud Network and Baiyuan Trousers.[33] These cases of market manipulation were of short duration and highly disguised, could hardly have been found by traditional means but were easily detected by the big-data system.

It enhances the ability to prevent systemic risks. The current securities market is becoming more complicated with cross-market transactions becoming universal, posing severe challenges to the prevention of systemic financial risks. International financial regulatory institutions such as the International Monetary Fund and the Financial Stability Board hold that in the 2008 global financial risk, data omission, opacity, improper conduct, and difficulties with information sharing at key moments were major obstacle to regulators being able to accurately anticipate and respond to systemic risks. Hence appropriate collection and sharing of information by reinforcing modern IT infrastructures and optimizing their legal structures needs to be strengthened. The construction of the central supervisory information platform meets the latest regulation requirements of international financial regulatory institutions to prevent systemic financial risks; by integrating the required supervisory data information on a single platform, it is possible to use relevant systemic risk monitoring and precautionary models to warn the market and prevent or resolve systemic financial risks in time.

Column: Unified ID for Securities Accounts

For a long time, backstage technical service platforms for registration and settlement of the capital market were established separately according to markets and varieties, so there were instances of repeated platform construction, conflicting standards, low market efficiency, etc.; meanwhile, since there was no connection between different securities accounts, it was hard to count the number of investors, which affected investor service and market regulation. In accordance with the requirement of "improving centralized and unified registration and settlement system" in the new State 9 Articles, the CSDC launched securities account integration from 2012. The general objective is to establish a unified account platform, which provides a unified ID number for each investor in order to associate different securities accounts of a particular investor with a single ID and thus achieve unified recognition of the investor's identification, unified collection of investor information, and unified registration of investor securities assets. The main content can be summarized as: a single set of accounts, a single set of rules, and a single set of systems. "A single set of accounts" means assigning a unified ID to each investor so that various securities accounts can be brought together as sub-accounts under the general account with a unified ID; "a single set of rules" means comprehensively unifying rules and process flows concerning account services, eliminating 49 differences between the account services of the Shanghai and Shenzhen stock markets, and improving customer experience and efficiency in account transactions; "a single set of systems" means establishing a unified account platform for the unified operation of account services so as to eliminate the problem of securities companies needing to deal with multiple account systems, and realizing the reception of account services of various markets at a single counter. On October 8, 2014, the unified ID account platform was officially launched.

Unified ID account is the general securities account set up by the CSDC on the basis of an investor's existing securities accounts to record the investor's identification information and securities assets. Existing investor securities accounts include Shanghai and Shenzhen A share accounts, B share accounts, closed-ended fund accounts, credit trading accounts, derivative contract accounts, national share transfer system for SMEs accounts, and open-ended fund accounts registered in the CSDC's TA system, all of which are sub-accounts that record the investor's activity in each trading venue and investments in certain varieties. The CSDC adds a unified ID account to each investor; securities sub-accounts deal with specific service transactions, while the Unified ID gathers all the sub-account information. The legal position of existing securities accounts acts as proof of the investor's right to hold and change the holding status of securities.

A unified ID system for securities accounts is significant in several ways. On the macro level, firstly, it helps to unify and standardize account systems between various levels of markets, facilitates the organic connections between different market levels, and greatly improves market efficiency; secondly, it combines flexibility and expansiveness and thus can provide strong support for multiple services of the securities market such as asset management, cross-market product innovation, etc.; third, securities companies can strengthen their risk identification of customers by using the new account system and conduct eligibility management of investors, which favors the prevention and control of systemic and major risks in the capital market; fourth, it facilitates the transition from the management of accounts to that of investors and centralizes investor information, which can provide centralized data for market supervisors in a more efficient way and supports supervisory work.

For investors, first, it provides great convenience for investor account information management, in that investors can check and change account data at any securities company which they have commissioned for business without needing to show account cards for any transactions, making service easier; second, newly opened accounts in the Shanghai and Shenzhen markets are identically set as usable in T+1 day (the next trading day after opening account), while cancellation of accounts will take effect in T+0 day (the day of the cancellation), making it more convenient for investors to cancel accounts; third, the "one person one account" restriction in the Administrative Rules of Securities Accounts has been abolished so that investors with actual needs are allowed to open multiple securities accounts; fourth, seven charges have been reduced to one, an standard account opening fee, which has been greatly reduced; fifth, investors are not required to go through repeated risk evaluations for different services and can apply for direct asset transfer transactions such as transfers from B to A, company delisting, new third-board listing, cross-market acquisitions and mergers, etc.

4.3 Outlook for Securities Regulation

4.3.1 Macro-Economic Environment for Development of the Securities Industry in 2015

The recovery of the global economy was weaker than expected in 2014, and difference between the main economies were quite apparent; it is anticipated that in 2015 the global economy will continue the developing pattern that the US economy carries on the powerful recovery, the European and Japanese economies lack momentum for growth, and emerging economies are slowing down their speed of development. As economic fundamentals decide the direction of monetary policy, in early 2015 the USA will probably start raising interest rates, while the Eurozone and Japan will continue with quantitative easing monetary policies and ultra-low interest rates to stimulate economic growth. Rising US interest rates and continuing USD appreciation will influence the global economy in multiple ways. Some emerging economies may face challenges of capital outflow and currency depreciation. International financial markets and bulk commodity markets may experience great fluctuations, which will introduce uncertainty in economic operations. Generally speaking, the Chinese securities market still faces a complex international environment in 2015. Especially since the opening of the channel between domestic and overseas capital markets through Shanghai–Hong Kong Stock Connect, overseas factors will have a significantly increasing impact on the domestic capital market, and the internationalization of capital markets will present severe challenges to securities regulation.

As for the domestic economy, the pressure of economic downturn was relatively large in 2014, and annual GDP increased by 7.4% on a year-on-year basis, the lowest growth rate since 1990. What is noteworthy is that the year-on-year growth rate in the fourth quarter was 7.3%, basically the same as that of the third quarter, indicating that the economic downturn had been mitigated. The Central Economic Work Conference at the end of 2014, analyzing China's current and future economic situation, suggested that the Chinese economy is now evolving towards a more advanced form, a more complicated division of work, and a more reasonable structure, and economic development is entering a "new normal" state. Under the new normal state, economic growth will be go down a gear from high speed to medium-high speed, but the change of speed does not mean reduction of momentum: economic development remains the first priority, but the quality of economic growth will be significantly improved. Taking a look at the three driving forces of the Chinese economy, it is hard to see great improvement but it is possible to sustain steady growth. Especially since 2014, comprehensive reform has advanced progressively while dividends brought by key area reforms such as state-owned asset reform, free trade zone, and "One Belt, One Road" have been released gradually, boosting steady economic growth. On the whole, though, the Chinese economy still faces downturn pressure in 2015, and GDP growth is estimated at around 7%.

The securities and futures market is currently in a key period that combines opportunities and challenges. On the one hand, entering the new normal state will inevitably improve the foundations of and environment for the development of the capital market, greatly expand its scope, and provide a rare historic opportunity for the innovative development of the capital market. As the market-oriented financial reform has been carried forward continuously, financial resources have been reallocated, market liquidity has generally been sufficient, and the risk-free rate of return has gradually declined, all of which have created favorable conditions for development of the capital market. On the other hand, the development of the capital market has also entered a brand-new phase where market operating conditions have gone through substantial changes, presenting severe challenges to securities regulation. First, the multi-tier market system is becoming increasingly complete, while market volume and degree of complexity is significantly increasing, challenging the ability of the regulatory department to control complicated situations. Second, Shanghai–Hong Kong Stock Connect links domestic and overseas capital markets, and the Chinese capital market has gone from a relatively closed state to bilateral opening up, which tests the regulatory department's ability from global perspective. Third, securities market reform has entered deep water, key reforms such as the stock-issue registration system involve profound adjustments of the pattern of benefits and faces significant resistance. Of course, since the second half of 2014, the Chinese stock market has steadily risen to become the best bull market in the world, a favorable time for the regulatory department to drive forward reforms and innovation. The regulatory department should proceed with confidence, take advantage of the opportunity, and have the courage to take responsibility and overcome difficulties, so as to promote broader development of the securities market.

4.3.2 Policy Direction of Securities Regulation in 2015

In 2013, the Third Plenary Session of the 18th CPC Central Committee systemically initiated the deepening of overall reform; the core of economic system reform is to let the market play a decisive role in resource allocation. As a naturally highly marketized place of resource allocation, the capital market is an important element in the overall deepening of reform and also an important platform supporting economic system reform. Therefore, the Third Plenary Session's decision has clearly outlined tasks for reform and development of the capital market, which is to "complete the multi-tier capital market system, promote the reform of the stock-issue registration system, drive forward equity financing through multiple channels, develop and standardize the bond market, improve the proportion of direct financing," "optimize investor return mechanisms," and "protect legal rights and benefits of investors, especially medium and small investors." It illustrates the future development direction of the capital market. In May 2014, the State Council issued the "new State 9

Articles", further clarifying general requirements and policy measures to accelerate the development of the multi-tier capital market. Implementing these policies and measures is the long-term task of the securities regulatory department. The main work of the regulatory department in the next few years is closely related to the "new State 9 Articles."

Considering the current development of China's economic society and capital market, there will probably be two main aspects of securities regulation in 2015. First, the function of the capital market should be fully brought out to serve the new normal state of economic development. In its comprehensive summary at the end of 2014, the central economic conference set out the objective of "speed adjustment but no reduction of momentum, volume increase with better quality." The new normal state requires the economic structure to be transformed, models to be developed, and growth to become a driving force, all of which are inseparable from support of the capital market and thus provide a historic opportunity for the innovative development of the capital market. The regulatory department will certainly accelerate the construction of the multi-tier market system in 2015, expand the breadth and depth of the market, establish improved market mechanisms, and effectively bring out its resource allocation, investment and financing functions, together with wealth management and risk management, aiming to let the capital market become the invisible hand that serves and leads the new normal state of the Chinese economy and the important catalyst in the realization of the Chinese dream.

Second, the CSRC is exploring the establishment of new mechanism of in-process and follow-up supervision. The year 2014 saw a good beginning for the CSRC's vigorous efforts to promote regulatory mode transition; a great deal of effective work was done on the transition of regulation focus and methods. At the 2015 national securities and futures regulation work conference, Mr Xiao Gang's speech centered round "focusing on regulatory mode transition and improving regulatory efficiency", indicating that regulatory mode transition will be carried forward thoroughly in 2015. The main objective of the 2015 regulatory mode transition is real-problem-oriented gradual exploration of the establishment of in-process and follow-up supervision mechanisms, which means the focus on examination and approval in advance will be shifted to in-process and follow-up supervision; the emphasis of regulation is geared towards regulatory rule enactment, inspection and law enforcement, while there are four main methods: on-site examination, off-site supervision, education and training, and inspection and law enforcement. According to Mr Xiao Gang, regulation under the new mechanism of in-process and follow-upafterwards supervision will be stimulating, information driven, knowledge intensive, and cost effective.

4.3.3 Outlook for Securities Regulation in 2015

At the moment, all sectors of society have high expectations for the capital market, which is facing both opportunities and challenges. In 2014, the securities regulatory department launched quite a few reform initiatives and innovations which will be implemented in 2015. Many tasks are yet to be started in accordance with the Third Plenary's decision and the new State 9 Articles. In general, the following achievements and breakthroughs may arise in securities regulation in 2015.

4.3.3.1 Promoting the Reform of the Stock-Issue Registration System

Promoting the reform of stock-issue registration system is an important task set by the decision of the Third Plenary Session of the 18th CPC Central Committee. In 2014, the CSRC took the lead in establishing a stock-issue registration system reform team to deliberate and report to the State Council. Reform of the stock-issue registration system began as soon as it was approved by the State Council. At the 2015 national securities and futures regulation work conference, Mr Xiao Gang pointed out that registration system reform is the top priority in the capital market reforms of 2015, an essential project that involves market participants, and an important starting point for the CSRC to promote regulatory mode transition. The general objective of the reform is to establish a stock issue and listing system dominated by the market, based on information disclosure, with clear divisions of responsibility, precise expectations, and effective regulation. Once the registration system reform plan is approved, the CSRC will devise a specific implementation plan, revise the related businesses rules, , and issue related supporting measures. This will be a highly complicated systemic project involving a wide range of interested parties, difficult to plan and coordinate, requiring a progressive, steady, and continuous process that cannot be completed all at once. In particular, it requires revision of the Securities Law to specify the legal force of the stock-issue registration system. It is unlikely that the stock-issue registration system will be comprehensively implemented in 2015 but regional pilot projects are anticipated.

4.3.3.2 The Launch of Shenzhen–Hong Kong Stock Connect

Since the opening of Shanghai–Hong Kong Stock Connect on November 17, 2014, the overall market operation has been steady while the depth and breadth of both markets have expanded, winning acclaim from various sectors of society. The comprehensive opening up of the capital market is an irresistible trend, and the launch of the Shenzhen–Hong Kong Stock Connect following on from the Shanghai–Hong Kong Stock Connect favors expansion of the range of bilateral investment objectives for Hong Kong and domestic markets, strengthens the connection between the A share market and the H share market, and accelerates the internationalization of A shares. On January 5, 2015, during his inspection in Shenzhen, Premier Li Keqiang stated that a Shenzhen–Hong Kong Stock Connect should follow on from the Shanghai–Hong Kong Stock Connect, which immediately made theShenzhen–Hong Kong Stock Connect both a hot topic for the market and a political task. It is reported that the Shenzhen Stock Exchange has lost no time in studying and deliberating on the Shenzhen–Hong Kong Stock Connect initiative and regards its implementation as the principal task for 2015. With the successful experience of Shanghai–Hong Kong Stock Connect, aspects such as trading rules, coordination and communication between two markets will be much easier. Of course, owing to the characteristics of the Shenzhen market, the Shenzhen–Hong Kong Stock Connect will not simply be a copy of Shanghai–Hong Kong Stock Connect—it will be an upgraded version. There is no definite timescale for the launch of the Shenzhen–Hong Kong Stock Connect, but the experience of the Shanghai–Hong Kong Stock Connect suggests it will need a period of preparation and may be launched in the second half of the year.

4.3.3.3 Release of Crude Oil Futures

China is the world's fourth-largest oil-producing country and the second-largest oil-consuming and importing country. The building of a China-dominated international crude oil market will provide the necessary risk evasion tools for oil production, consumption, and transportation enterprises, promote the influence of China on pricing in the international crude oil market, and maintain China's energy and economic security. In 2013, the CSRC approved the building by Shanghai Futures Exchange of the Shanghai International Energy Trading Center Co., Ltd. in China (Shanghai) Free Trade Pilot Zone, which will take charge of the construction of an international crude oil futures platform. In December 2014, the CSRC approved the organization of crude oil futures trading by Shanghai International Energy Trading Center. Crude oil futures trade is quite different from trading in other varieties of commodity futures and will bring in overseas investors, making the market organization, rules, technical system, etc. more complex and requiring more supporting policies. Since the second half of 2014, the international crude oil market has seen a sharp price decline, bringing both opportunities and challenges for the listing of China's crude oil futures. The time of its listing is not fixed yet and will be decided by the regulatory department depending on preparation and market status, most likely in the first half of 2015.

4.3.3.4 Establishment of Board Transfer Mechanisms

Mature capital markets are mostly pyramid types of structure: the higher levels have fewer companies while the lower levels have more. There are smooth transfer mechanisms for a company to go up or down between the different levels of the market. China's equity market has had an inverted pyramid type of structure for a long time; the main board market within the exchange is fully developed, but the third and fourth board markets are still lagging behind. Although this market structure has changed for the better since 2013, transfer mechanisms between different market levels have not yet been established, which is a significant defect of the system. By the end of 2014, the number of listed companies in the new third board had reached 1,572 and a faster increase is still expected; listed companies in regional equity markets also exceeded 2,000. Under these circumstances, building transfer mechanisms between multi-level markets seems relatively urgent and significant for the development of direct financing and to resolve financing problems in the real economy. In October 2014, the CSRC approved the reform of Shenzhen's capital market, where one innovation is the establishment of a special level for the GEM board in the Shenzhen Stock Exchange to allow Internet and technology innovation enterprises that have not yet shown a profit to issue and be listed on the GEM board a year after being listed on the national share transfer system for SMEs so as to support the healthy development of the GEM board. Judging from this, the mechanism for transferring from the new third board to the GEM board is expected to be established first.

4.3.3.5 Inclusion of a Share in the International Index

In recent years, as China's capital market has continue to grow and open up to the outside world, both the regulatory department and general investors have hoped that global main index companies can include their A share in their global index series so as to improve the global influence of the Chinese market and bring large-scale long-term investment capital into the domestic market. International investors are optimistic about the prospects of A share market investment and also wish to include A shares in global index series. It is reported that MSCI and the UK's FTSE have had discussions with the CSRC about including A shares in their index series.

In June 2014, MSCI announced the result of their 2014 global market classification review and rejected the inclusion of China's A share in emerging market indexes, to the great disappointment of domestic investors. According to MSCI, issues such as quota allocation, capital flow restriction, and uncertainty of capital gains tax are the main reasons for the decision not to incorporate A shares for the time being. However, MSCI is keeping China's A share on the list of possible emerging markets as part of its 2015 review. With the opening of Shanghai–Hong Kong Stock Connect and the launch of Shenzhen–Hong Kong Stock Connect, problems such as excessive quota restrictions and uncertainty of capital gains tax will be resolved effectively so that the A share is more suitable for inclusion in global indexes. In addition, the total value of China's stock market now ranks second in the world, and the market still has plenty of scope for development. Therefore, it is very possible that in 2015 the A share can be included in the global index series of global main index providers. Though its weight in the early stages might be small and its incremental capital flow limited, its influence on the domestic stock market will be continuous and profound.

4.3.4 Outlook for Securities Regulation in the Next Few Years

Since 2013, the CSRC has vigorously promoted regulatory mode transition and has achieved much, but there are also many problems, difficulties, and conflicts that mean regulatory mode transition has a long way to go. Xiao Gang, President of the CSRC, has also clearly stated that "at present and in a period of time, we will still be in the grinding-in phase of regulatory mode transition, the stage of regulatory mechanism reform, the period of regulatory capacity construction, and the time of regulation quality improvement." There is no going back, and regulatory mode transition will still be the main emphasis of securities regulation in next few years. Its main tasks are to continuing cancelling and delegating advance examination and approval items on one hand, and to explore establishment of in-process and follow-up regulation mechanisms to improve regulation efficiency on the other.

To be more specific, securities regulation in next few years will emphasize the following aspects. First, it will continue to deepen the reform of administrative approval systems for the capital market. Administrative approval and registration matters will be greatly simplified and market access will be further relaxed to reduce intervention in micro activities of market participants. The CSRC's authority list and duty list will be considered and formulated in such a way as to clarify the boundary between government and market.

Second, it will strengthen the construction of a multi-tier capital market. The core content is to expand market breadth and depth and strengthen the capacity of the capital market to serve the development of the real economy. The stock-issue registration system will be progressively advanced and steadily implemented. Internal levels of exchange places will be optimized, board transfer mechanisms for the multi-tier market will be established, and financial products and trading tools enriched to expand the proportion of direct financing and improve service coverage of the capital market in every way.

Third, it will extend the bilateral opening up of the capital market. Compared with the degree of bilateral opening in China's real economy, the opening up of China's capital market is obviously lagging behind. To adapt to and lead the going out of economic entities, the capital market is required to accelerate bilateral opening up to facilitate reform and development. The regulatory department will provide further convenience for domestic and overseas economic entities to engage in cross-border investment and financing, support the internationalized operation of securities and futures operating agencies, and provide new kinds of risk management instruments and financial services.

Fourth, it will strengthen the protection of investors. Individual investors are the largest group of market participants in China's capital market, and they are in a weak position. Protecting legal rights and benefits of investors, especially medium and small investors, is at the heart of the development of the capital market. The regulatory department will set up and improve investor protection mechanisms and adopt multiple means to genuinely safeguard rights and benefits of investors.

Fifth, it will strengthen inspection and law enforcement. With the relaxation of market access, more participants will enter the market and may introduce disorder. Market order must rely on strong and powerful inspection and law enforcement. The regulatory department will enlarge the inspection and law enforcement team, improve inspection and law enforcement tools, and severely penalize breaches of laws and regulations such as fraudulent issues, breaches of information disclosure requirements, and market manipulation.

Notes

1. Data from CSRC, http://www.csrc.gov.cn/pub/newsite/zjhxwfb/xwdd/201307/t20130712_230675.html.
2. Data from http://finance.people.com.cn/stock/n/2015/0318/c67815-26714125.html.
3. Data from Wind.
4. Data from http://www.ccstock.cn/stock/gupiaoyaowen/2015-01-19/A1421604872812.html.
5. Data from http://www.ccstock.cn/stock/gupiaoyaowen/2015-01-19/A1421604872812.html.
6. http://fund.stockstar.com/SS2014122300002889.shtml.
7. Research group for China financial stability report: *China Financial Stability Report (2015)*, Beijing: China Financial Publishing House, Mai 2015.
8. Data from Wind.
9. Mao, Qizheng. 2015. "Report on Financial Markt (2014)." *China Finance*, Vol. 3, 2015, pp 57.
10. Data from Wind.
11. Data from http://www.chinabond.com.cn/Info/19762422.
12. Data from Wind.
13. Research group for China financial stability report: *China Financial Stability Report (2015)*, Beijing: China Financial Publishing House, Mai 2015.
14. Data from China Futures Association, http://www.cfachina.org.
15. Data from China Securities Regulatory Commission.
16. http://www.chinairn.com/news/20141113/100917140.shtml.
17. http://finance.ifeng.com/a/20140804/12855072_0.shtml.
18. http://www.chinadaily.com.cn/hqcj/zgjj/2014-11-18/content_12731607.html.
19. CSRC, http://www.csrc.gov.cn/pub/newsite/zjhxwfb/xwdd/201404/t20140410_246762.html.

20. Data from Wind.
21. http://sc.stock.cnfol.com/gppdgdzx/20141118/19483799.shtml.
22. Data from Wind.
23. Data from Wind.
24. Data from Wind.
25. Data from Wind.
26. Data from Wind.
27. http://stock.cngold.org/c/2014-12-26/c2961854.html.
28. Data from Wind.
29. Data from Wind.
30. http://www.csrc.gov.cn/pub/newsite/zjhxwfb/xwdd/201407/t20140704_257271.html.
31. http://www.csrc.gov.cn/pub/newsite/zjhxwfb/xwdd/201407/t20140704_257271.html.
32. Data from Wind.
33. http://www.csrc.gov.cn/pub/newsite/zjhxwfb/xwdd/201501/t20150109_266364.html.

References

CC Stock. http://www.ccstock.cn
China Daily. http://www.chinadaily.com.cn
China Futures Association. http://www.cfachina.org
China Securities Regulatory Commission, CSRC. http://www.csrc.gov.cn
Chinairn. http://www.chinairn.com
CNFL. http://sc.stock.cnfol.com
Finance. http://finance.ifeng.com.
http://stock.cngold.org/c/2014-12-26/c2961854.html
Mao, Qizheng. 2015. Report on financial market (2014). *China Finance* 3.
Research group for China financial stability report: *China Financial Stability Report (2015)*. Beijing: China Financial Publishing House, Mai 2015.
Stockstar. http://fund.stockstar.com
Wind data bank. http://www.wind.com.cn/

CHAPTER 5

Annual Report on Foreign Exchange Administration

Liu Tang

5.1 Review of Reforms of Foreign Exchange Administration and International Balance of Payments in 2014

5.1.1 *Review of Reforms of Foreign Exchange Administration*

In the aftermath of the financial crisis, as the main administrator of foreign exchange and its risks, the foreign exchange administration authorities face great changes in the international economic and financial environment and their profound effect on foreign trade and investment and the international balance of payments. The State Administration for Foreign Exchange (SAFE), as the principal executor of the country's external strategy, are at the forefront of reform and the establishment of new adminis-

---

Liu Tang, a PhD in Economics, is an Associate Researcher, and visiting scholar at Harvard University, and is now working at the International Finance and International Economics Laboratory of the CASS Institute of Finance and Banking. Her areas of interest include international financial regulation and international economics.

L. Tang
Institute of Finance and Banking, Chinese Academy of Social Science, Beijing, China

© The Editor(s) (if applicable) and The Author(s) 2016
B. Hu et al. (eds.), *Development of China's Financial Supervision and Regulation*, DOI 10.1057/978-1-137-52225-2_5

trative systems to promote economic rebalancing and internationalization of the RMB.

Since 2010, strengthening the administration of capital inflow has become an important aspect of foreign exchange administration. Investigation and penalization of breaches by enterprises and banks have been strengthened and quantitative management tools to restrain surging capital inflow have been introduced, such as the lower limit of foreign exchange position balance in settlement and sale, foreign exchange loan-to-deposit ratio limits, etc.

The administration of the foreign exchange reserve has become more active and more positive. SAFE has progressively released rules supporting enterprises and individuals to hold and use foreign currencies to promote the transition from "storing foreign currencies in the national treasury" to "storing foreign currencies among the people." SAFE has also promoted new changes in foreign exchange reserve administration to actively cooperate the general national strategy and innovate operation modes of foreign exchange reserves to bring the role of foreign exchange reserve in supporting the development of the national economic society into better play,: these are strategic operations such as entrusted loans and foreign exchange reserve cooperation with BRICS countries.

Capital account management systems are provided to support RMB internationalization, which requires an increase in the degree of marketization in the domestic financial market, and requires the regulator to possess instruments and capacities to manage cross-border capital flow and respond to all kinds of sudden financial risks. Therefore, SAFE has put forward administrative proposals including streamlining administration and delegating power, gradually simplifying formalities and procedures for receipt and payment of foreign exchange in trades and services, strengthening monitoring and analysis, stressing follow-up management and subject management, etc., in preparation for the further opening up of the capital account.

5.1.2 The International Balance of Payments in 2014

According to SAFE's statistics, China's international balance of payments in 2014 once again showed a current account surplus and financial capital account deficit, and the growth of foreign exchange reserves slowed down.

Since the financial crisis, the world has entered a period of economic rebalancing. Due to an ever-enlarging service trade deficit, the growth trend in our current account surplus is gradually slowing down. In 2014, China's current account surplus was 213.8 billion USD, 2% of GDP, sustaining the steady trend as of 2011.[1]

Since 2011, the primary change in China's international balance of payments is that the long-term surplus of capital and financial accounts has changed to alternate surplus and deficit, showing obvious fluctuations in cross-border capital flow. In 2014, China's capital and financial account deficit was 96 billion USD, a repeat of the 2012 capital net outflow situation. The main factor affecting the balance of capital and financial accounts remains the constant change in the balance of other investments. According to the data from the first three quarters of 2014, on the asset side, the balance of China's overseas deposits greatly increased compared with the same period of the previous year; on the side of liabilities, the balance of overseas trade credit or loans decreased compared with the same period of the previous year. The microeconomic expression of this phenomenon the reverse adjustment by the private sector and financial institutions of the previous term's asset and liability currency allocation, and increasing foreign currency asset operations and decreasing foreign currency debts.

The growth of the foreign exchange reserve in 2014 clearly slowed down. The foreign exchange reserve in 2014 increased by 118.8 billion USD, which was a 73% reduction on the previous year, a slight current account surplus and a capital and financial accounts deficit.

5.1.3 RMB Exchange Rate

According to average monthly RMB exchange-rate data from 2014, the RMB to USD exchange rate experienced a rollercoaster of depreciation and appreciation. Since July 2013, the RMB exchange rate has been in a constant state of bidirectional fluctuation. Influenced by the USA's announcement of their plan to gradually cease quantitative easing policies and the market pullback after a continuous increase in the RMB exchange rate in the previous period, the RMB exchange rate began a gradual decline in early 2014, reaching rock bottom in terms of annual average level in May 2014, when 1 USD could be exchanged for 6.1636 RMB, a depreciation of 1 %compared with January. This was followed by a slight rise to 1USD for 6.1238 RMB in December 2014, the accumulated range of appreciation in the later period being 0.6%, but it had only increased by 0.1% compared with the end of the previous year. After May 2014, the nominal effective exchange rate and the real effective exchange rate of RMB increased significantly to reach 121.53 and 126.16 respectively by the end of the year (Fig. 5.1).[2]

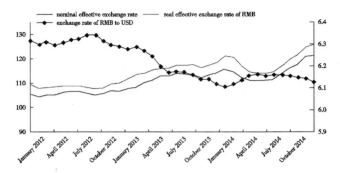

Fig. 5.1 RMB exchange-rate trend in 2014.
Data source: CEIC, BIS (BIS, http://www.bis.org)

5.2 The Reform of Foreign Exchange Administration in 2014

Since 2010, SAFE has proposed "five transitions" in the concept and methods of foreign exchange administration. RMB internationalization is one of the major driving forces in foreign exchange administration. As with the growth of cross-border RMB business and the deepening of administration reform, China's foreign exchange administration has shown new characteristics:: the transition from major risk prevention to "convenience orientation and risk prevention;" from micro behavior supervision to macroprudential supervision; from monitoring that lays partial emphasis on foreign currency as a statistical standard to due importance attached to both home and foreign currencies; and from differentiated management of Chinese capital and foreign capital to unified national treatment. In 2014, the reform of foreign exchange administration mainly included the following five aspects.

5.2.1 The Opening of the Capital Account to the Outside World

5.2.1.1 Present Trend of Reform
In recent years, the central bank has been giving policy signals such as "promoting bilateral opening of the capital market," "progressively improving the exchangeability of personal capital account," and so on. As far as the specific administration of foreign exchange is concerned, the authorities

have continuously increased the quota limit of QFII and QDII; expanded the range of eligible investors; launched the RQFII service and expanded the range of overseas investors; further relaxed restrictions on capital operation under direct investment; started the process of relaxing private individuals' participation in foreign securities investment and trading; and allowed individuals' domestic legal capital to participate in overseas stock ownership incentive schemes.

Compared with the past, the 2014 foreign exchange administration reform of the capital account showed noticeable vigor. The main administrative rules on foreign exchange issued in 2014 include: "SAFE Circular on Further Improving and Adjusting Foreign Exchange Administration Policies under the Capital Account," "Provisions on Foreign Exchange Administration for Cross-border Guarantees," "Provisions on Foreign Exchange Administration for Conversion of Foreign Debt to Loan," "Administrative Provisions on Centralized Operation of Foreign Exchange Funds of Transnational Corporation (trial)," "Relevant Issues concerning Foreign Exchange Administration for Overseas Listing," and "SAFE Circular on Foreign Exchange Administration of Overseas Investments and Financing and Round-Trip Investments by Domestic Residents via Special Purpose Vehicles." In addition, in the process of sorting out and integrating rules and regulations, the number of administrative licensing items under the capital account has been reduced from 59 sub-accounts to 20 sub-accounts, a decrease of 66 %; in the first half of 2014, eighteen relative normative documents were abolished, twelve of which concerned cross-border guarantees.[3]

5.2.1.2 Streamlining Administration and Delegating Power to the Lower Levels So As to Set Up a Clearer Administrative Policy Framework

This round of reforms has the following features:

Transition from Examination and Approval System to Registration System

The "Provisions on Foreign Exchange Administration for Cross-border Guarantees" propose to "cancel or greatly simplify administrative examination and approval procedures as related to cross-border guarantee, and only include 'some newly added cross-border guarantees provided by residents for liabilities or creditor's rights of non-residents after performance of guarantee' in the scope of one-by-one registration." Another example is the "SAFE Circular on Further Improving and Adjusting Foreign Exchange Administration Policies under the Capital Account" issued in February 2014, which includes such content as "carry out follow-up registration for foreign financial leasing service"and "cancel the SAFE's examination and approval procedure for foreign exchange receipts and payments and exchanges incurred in financial assets management companies' foreign business of disposing non-performing assets."

Emphasis on Simplification and Improvement Such as "Optimizing Procedure" and "Streamlining Administration"
The "SAFE Circular on Foreign Exchange Administration of Overseas Investments and Financing and Round-Trip Investments by Domestic Residents via Special Purpose Vehicles" issued in July 2014 proposes to "simplify business documents," "cancel procedures of registration of foundation, financing, and financing changes for overseas special purpose vehicles, and meanwhile simplify contents of change of registration." "On Deepening Reform of Foreign Exchange Administration under Capital Account and Promoting Trade and Investment Facilitation" proposes to "simplify verification of profit remittance of domestic institutions," "improve management of securities companies' foreign exchange business license," and so on.

Emphasis on Follow-up Risk Prevention, and Differentiated Administration of Entities
The "Provisions on Foreign Exchange Administration for Cross-border Guarantees" "weakens the one-by-one compliance management of secured transactions but more emphasizes the management of domestic subjects in secured transactions, and at the same time as simplifying subject classification standard, carries out differentiated, classified management of different types of entities, for example, looser management for banks compared with non-banking institutions, and looser management for large institutions compared with medium and small institutions."[4]

5.2.1.3 New Progresses in Securities Investment
In the area of securities investment, foreign exchange trading and exchange management are strictly restricted in China. The opening up of the capital

account in this area always follows the principles of prudence, gradualness, controllability, and order, but its advances in 2014 were prominent and included the following measures.

Continuous Capacity Expansion of QFII, QDII and RQFII

According to the newly published SAFE "Sheet of QFII Investment Quota Approval," by December 30, 2014, the total QFII quota approved by the SAFE had increased to 66.923 billion USD, while the number of approved institutions reached 270. By the same date, the total QDII quota approved by the SAFE was 83.323 billion USD, while the number of approved institutions reached 127. For RQFII, by the end of November 2014, the number of approved institutional investors reached 108; by the end of December 2014, the approved RQFII quota had been 299.7 billion yuan, mainly concentrated in Hong Kong.

Experimental Opeing up of the Capital Market
On April 10, the CSRC and Securities and Futures Commission of Hong Kong made a joint announcement to approve the pilot mechanism of the interconnection between Shanghai and Hong Kong stock markets (known as Shanghai–Hong Kong Stock Connect). In Shanghai–Hong Kong Stock Connect, the CSRC and Securities and Futures Commission of Hong Kong allow investors of both markets to buy listed stocks on each other's exchange within a prescribed range via local securities companies (or broker's agency). To prevent abnormal capital flow, Shanghai–Hong Kong Stock Connect has set a rather controversial limit on the total and daily quota of cross-border investment. Both daily quota and total investment quota are limited compared with the sum of transactions and market value of Shanghai and Hong Kong markets.

Trial Promotion of Free Trade Zone
On December 12, 2013, the central bank issued "Opinions concerning Financial Support for the Construction of China (Shanghai) Pilot Free Trade Zone." At the heart of the reform is an experiment in the areas of capital account convertibility, cross-border use of RMB, interest-rate liberalization, etc., and the establishment of a foreign exchange administration system appropriate to the free trade zone. This pilot program involves multiple major capital account opening up projects such as cross-border direct investment in enterprises, bilateral opening up of the capital mar-

ket, cross-border use of RMB, and so on. Currently, the main measures that support capital account liberalization in the free trade zone are: establishing free trade account and separate accounting systems, allowing participation in derivative trading in international financial markets according to provisions, and implementing voluntary settlement of capital fund exchanges. As yet the plan to comprehensively open up the capital account has not been implemented.

Recently, the State Council has decided to promote the experience of the Shanghai Pilot Free Trade Zone by setting up another three free trade zones in Guangdong, Tianjin, and Fujian and expanding the scope of the Shanghai free trade zone.

In January 2015, Shanghai the free trade zone's experience of foreign exchange administration of capital account was implemented nationally. The main contents were voluntary settlement of capital fund exchange for foreign-invested enterprises, foreign exchange settlement and sale related to banks' OTC trading of bulk commodity derivatives, delegation of foreign exchange registration and extension of direct investment account registration to banks.

Policy Interpretation
According to the IMF's Annual Report on Exchange Arrangements and Exchange Restrictions in 2011, the degree of capital control is still relatively high. Among 40 sub-accounts under the capital account, about 35% (fourteen sub-accounts) realized basic convertibility, mainly including credit instruments, direct investment, direct investment liquidation, etc.; 55% (22 sub-accounts) realized partial convertibility, mainly including bond market transactions, stock market transactions, real estate transactions, and personal capital transactions; four inconvertible accounts made up about 10% of the total, mainly non-residents' participation in the international money market, fund and trust markets, and derivative trading. The latter two mainly concern securities investment accounts (Table 5.1).[5]

Looking back at the history of reform, whether in the period when capital liberalization became the mainstream or during the present stage of re-evaluating capital account administration, the Chinese government has not changed its fundamental view of capital account convertibility reform, which emphasizes "gradual realization of RMB capital account convertibility." From the essential content of capital account opening up, the administrative authorities still follow the prin-

Table 5.1 China capital account convertibility restriction list

	Inconvertible	Partially convertible	Basically convertible	Totally convertible	Total
Capital and money market instrument transactions	2	10	4	0	16
Derivatives and other instrument transactions	2	2		0	4
Credit instrument transactions		1	5	0	6
Direct investment		1	1		2
Direct investment liquidation			1		1
Real estate transactions		2	1		3
Personal capital transactions		6	2		8
Total	4	22	14	0	40

Data source: Research group of Statistics and Analysis Department, People's Bank of China (2012)

ciples of gradualness, prudence, order, and controllability, combining the advance of capital account convertibility with overall risk prevention arrangements.

Though the administrative level relaxed external restrictions on the capital account in 2014, the relaxation was mostly about simplifying procedures but not cancelling quota management, and it only removed restrictions on investment and financing with a smaller range of influence. In contrast, in the reform of foreign exchange administration for cross-border guarantees, especially in the area of domestic guarantees of foreign debts, the management methods has changed from advance examination and approval to registration and self-regulation, and the free convertibility has obviously been improved.

As to the pace of opening up, because RMB internationalization requires a freer capital account and capital market, and the international financial crisis also reveals the importance of capital account administration, setting the tone for reform of the capital account opening up has become a hot topic in the industry. Since the international financial crisis, mainstream opinion about capital account liberalization has suffered a shock, international society and the international academic circle of economists, including the IMF, have changed their attitudes capital control, and thus methods and effectiveness of capital control have become issues that various governments and academic economics circles want to reconsider. In China, in view of the promotion of RMB internationalization, some scholars believe the opening up of the capital account should be accelerated. For example, Li Xiangyang (2014) established an index of the degree of opening of the capital account, included it in decisive factors of international reserve currency constitution, and by testing it with a fixed-effect model, affirmed the decisive effect of capital account opening upon RMB internationalization.[6] Li Chao (2013) held that promoting capital account convertibility has more benefits than harm because the rise of the comprehensive national strength of China greatly enhances its ability to resist risks.[7] Ma Jun (2012) believed that RMB internationalization should occur in concert with capital account opening up which should be accelerated year by year, and the opening of the domestic capital market should be improved 1% each year on average.[8] Yu Yongding (2014) took a different view and thought China's capital control has supported financial stability since the financial crisis, while the current domestic and foreign economic situation and financial situation do not support accelerated opening up of the capital account in China;[9] Lin Yifu (2013) held the same opinion.[10]

5.2.2 The "New Normal" State of Foreign Exchange Market Reform and Exchange Rate Fluctuation

5.2.2.1 Present Reform Trend

In recent years, reform has been vigorous in the areas of expanding the breadth and depth of the foreign exchange market, and marketizing foreign exchange prices and supply and demand. For the domestic market, the main administrative regulations related to foreign exchange market reform in 2014 include: "SAFE Circular on Adjusting the Relevant Management Policies Regarding Entry into the Interbank Foreign Exchange Market by Financial Institutions," "Provisions on the Administration of Bank RMB and Foreign Exchange Derivative Products Services," PBC's "Administration of Exchange Rate in Interbank Foreign Exchange Market and Listed Exchange Rate in Banks," and "Measures for Administration of Bank Foreign Exchange Settlement and Sale

Services", which further promote marketization reform of the RMB exchange-rate formation mechanism under the principle of streamlining administration and delegating power to lower levels. For offshore markets, China took the opportunity of RMB cross-border liquidation to reach liquidation agreements with Hong Kong, Singapore, London, and Switzerland in order to promote RMB internationalization by relying on developed offshore financial centers. Offshore RMB foreign exchange markets have been developing rapidly as a result, and their scale has already exceeded that of the domestic foreign exchange market.

The "Trinity" Framework and Reform of the RMB Exchange Rate Formation Mechanism

First, methods of exchange-rate adjustment have been improving. In recent years, the government has continued to stress "progressively expansion of the bidirectional fluctuation range of the RMB exchange rate" and "the fundamental role of market supply and demand in exchange rate formation." Following the PBC's April 2013 decision to expand the RMB/USD fluctuation range on the foreign exchange market, on March 15, 2014, the PBC made another announcement expanding the RMB/USD exchange-rate fluctuation range on the interbank spot foreign exchange market from 1% above and below the median price to 2% as of March 17; the interbank market fluctuation range only imposes restrictions on daily fluctuation but not overnight fluctuation. The regulatory department has repeatedly stated that "since this year, the PBC has greatly reduced intervention in foreign exchange," or "the PBC is gradually quitting routine intervention in the foreign exchange market."

Second, the foreign exchange market has been fostered and developed. The main trading results are: simplified market access; increased foreign exchange products; relaxation of restrictions on clients' selling option or option combination types; "enriching exchange rate hedging instruments with emphasis on foreign exchange option, supporting banks' diversified option services including buying, selling, combination, etc. on the premise of normal European-style options and real-need transactions." In respect of trading currency, on December 26, the foreign exchange transaction center subordinate to China's central bank announced the launch of forward and swaps RMB/ruble exchange transactions. As to trading entities, as of January 1, 2015, the procedure of advance permission for financial institutions to enter the interbank foreign exchange market was abolished so that domestic financial institutions, even including money brokerage agencies, can participate in spot and derivative transactions on the foreign exchange market with SAFE's approval.

Third, the foreign exchange supply and demand relationship has been straightened out. Administrative restrictions on foreign exchange receipts and disbursements are gradually being relaxed; exchange rates are decided in the interbank market, while the price is implemented during the transaction between bank and market. Through this year's reform, the foreign exchange supply and demand mechanism between banks and customers has been gradually marketized. On July 2, 2014, the PBC "cancelled banks' bid-ask spread management of USD listed trading by clients, allowing independent pricing of banks according to market supply and demand;" at this point, banks' restrictions on the exchange rate range for clients' listed foreign currency trading have been completely abolished, and the adjustment role of market mechanisms can thus be fully brought out.

In the process of "trinity" marketization reform, the administrative department has been emphasizing the establishment of a "new framework of foreign exchange market administration that combines government supervision and market self-regulation" so as to transfer the requirements of business supervision to the banks' internal management and ask financial institutions to strengthen their awareness of foreign exchange risk and management efficiency. Meanwhile SAFE will focus on the responsibility of follow-up supervision.

The Rapidly Increasing Scale of the Offshore RMB Foreign Exchange Market
As with the advances in RMB internationalization and the establishment of offshore RMB financial centers, the scale and structure of the RMB foreign exchange market have undergone great changes. According to BIS statistics, the scale of transactions on the RMB foreign exchange market has grown very fast, and the RMB offshore growth rate is much higher than that of the onshore market. The daily foreign exchange transaction volume of RMB was 119.6 billion USD;[1] this was an increase as a proportion of global foreign exchange market transactions from 0.1% in 2004 to 2.2% in 2013, ranking 9th in the world and next to Mexico's peso in 2013. According to region-based calculations, the foreign exchange transactions

Table 5.2 Offshore foreign exchange transactions of the BRIC countries in 2013 (daily transaction volume)

	Offshore transactions (billion USD)	Offshore proportion (%)						
		World	Home country	Region[a]	UK	USA	Eurozone	Others
China RMB	861	72.0	45.5	43.7	18.0	5.8	1.5	1.2
Mexico peso	1096	81.0	0.4	0.3	27.5	45.7	4.3	3.2
Russia ruble	440	51.6	0.6	0.0	35.9	7.4	4.5	3.1
Brazil real	471	79.6	0.2	0.1	29.3	39.8	7.9	2.5

[a]The proportion of daily transaction in regional financial centers including Asia's Hong Kong and Singapore, Latin America's Brazil and Mexico, Turkey and Russia.

Data source: BIS et al. (2013)

in China amount to 22 billion USD, 0.7% of the global foreign exchange market; the UK and the USA which rank highly had 2,726 billion USD and 1,263 billion USD of daily foreign exchange transaction volumes respectively in 2013. Among foreign exchange transaction volumes of the BRIC countries, the RMB's offshore foreign exchange transactions rank alongside only Mexico's peso, which are 86.1 billion USD. As to regional influence, however, the daily RMB offshore foreign exchange transaction volume accounts for 43.7% of its daily foreign exchange transaction volume, being the only currency with regional influence among the BRICs (Table 5.2).

5.2.2.2 Influence of Repeated Calculation Has Been Deducted from These Data

Policy Interpretation

Exchange-rate marketization reform has received widespread recognition from the market, and the marketization reform of both exchange rate and interest rate is the future trend. The marketization of the RMB exchange-rate formation mechanism is favorable to the establishment of a unified, integrative RMB foreign exchange market and helps to change the previous passive situation of the central bank's monetary policies. Wu

Jinglian states that "financial reform and marketization reform centering round exchange-rate and interest-rate marketization are proceeding progressively;"[11] Li Yang holds that the present exchange-rate reform has achieved great progress, and exchange rate has already approached a balanced level through China's monetary authorities' adjustment in recent years;[12] Chen Yulu believes "RMB exchange rate marketization reform hasn't taken decisive steps yet," its fluctuation range still being subject to the implementation of monetary policies, and "as to time arrangement, the time when the exchange rate is truly decided by the market will come later than interest rate marketization."[13]

The positive influence of the bidirectional fluctuation of the RMB exchange rate is gradually becoming apparent. First, it favors autonomous market clearing of the RMB exchange rate. According to official statistics, this year, the daily price difference between CNH, the overseas RMB exchange rate, and CNY, the domestic RMB exchange rate, is continuously converging from 169 basic points in the first quarter to 42 basic points in the third quarter, and the relative values of the two keep alternating.[14] Second, it facilitates bidirectional cross-border capital flow and changes the continuously expanding trend of foreign exchange reserve assets. This year, according to the balance of banks' foreign exchange settlements, and sales and balance of net foreign exchange settlement of forward before maturity, the market motivation of foreign exchange settlements is weak but the willingness to purchase foreign currency is growing. The marketized fluctuation of the exchange rate is helping to change unilateral speculative behavior in the market and can buffer the continuous growth of the foreign exchange reserve.

On the basis of "trinity" marketization reform, the positive influences of foreign exchange market reform are mainly reflected in the following aspects. First, in the current international balance of payments conditions, along with the marketization reform of China's exchange-rate formation mechanism, decisive factors for the RMB exchange rate are no longer merely trade surplus and interest margin of home and foreign currencies but have become more and more extensive, and market expectation also emerges as a factor, making "the asset price property of the RMB exchange rate more and more obvious."[15] Second, the scale of the domestic foreign exchange market continues to expand, with the market becoming more energetic. In the first half of 2014, total deals of 6.05 trillion USD were concluded in the RMB foreign exchange market (daily transactions being 50.8 billion USD), showing an increase of 15.0% year on year; among these, various derivatives like forward, swap and option, took up 2.5 trillion USD, increasing by 0.62 trillion USD and 5.6% year on year. Third, entities in China's foreign exchange market have become more abundant, and the marketized exchange rate will generate more supplt and demand in products and services. In the international foreign exchange market, non-banking institutions are the main market player, motivated by actively taking trading positions based on prediction of the exchange-rate trend. This reform has introduced these active trading entities to promote foreign exchange transactions to reflect the expectations of an increasing number of market entities and better realize the price discovery function of foreign exchange transactions. Industry circles believes it will "enable foreign exchange trading prices to better reflect expectations of more market institutions."[16] Fourth, the derivative options foreign exchange market has been developed to further enrich exchange-rate hedging instruments, which can better satisfy customerdemand for risk management having regard to exchange-rate fluctuations and can enlarge the transaction scale and activity of the foreign exchange market.

At the same time, the development and reform of the foreign exchange market still face various challenges. These include the following. Product structure and risk management need to be perfected. Though this year restrictions on client selling options and the operation of option combinations are relaxed, RMB option products are still of limited varieties and a simple product structure. Varieties of foreign exchange derivatives are also not complete. Enterprises' internal control systems for derivatives and corresponding accounting systems also need improvement. According to official statistics, in the first half of 2014, the increment in interbank foreign exchange derivative trading was mainly driven by the interbank foreign exchange market, while bank forward and swap trading volumes for clients decreased. According to SAFE statistics, in the first half of 2014, the option market concluded a total of 36.5 billion USD of deals, and daily trading volume decreased by 1.6% year on year. Among these, the option market between banks and clients stands at 23.3 billion USD, and the daily trading volume has decreased by 29.2% year on year.[17] Such phenomena show that during the marketization transition, trade companies' and non-banking institutions' ways of participating in derivatives trading and realizing optimization of risk management are major tasks in the future.

Supervision of foreign exchange derivatives needs to be specified. For example, the supervision of foreign exchange derivatives involves multiple regulatory departments, frequently causing obscure or overlapping regulatory authority in practice. Uncertainty over subjects of regulation and trading methods hinders the construction of China's foreign exchange futures market; as yet no contract varieties of this kind have been issued.

The offshore RMB foreign exchange market will test China's monetary and financial stability. International experience shows that offshore financial activities create difficulties for the central bank in determining the money supply and controlling bank credit. The central bank can hardly tell how much money has become offshore deposits and how many offshore deposits return to the domestic credit system. By influencing the money supply of one country, offshore financial activities influence the interest rate yield curve and the exchange rate. The influence of offshore financial activities on financial stability is also two-edged. On the one hand, for given risk exposure, offshore finance means more complicated and extensive investment activities, which can effectively spread risks so as to reduce over-reliance on one big bank and decrease systemic risk; on the other hand, offshore finance involves multiple countries and currencies in such a way that national risk, credit risk, interest-rate risk, exchange-rate risk, and liquidity risk all affect the robustness of the home country's or host country's banking system, and then, because of the close interconnectedness of transnational finance, aggravate the accumulation of risk and the infection of the global financial market. With regard to the continuing opening up of the capital account, the question of how to respond to offshore RMB foreign exchange market risks in order to ensure domestic financial stability is gradually increasing in importance.

5.2.3 Foreign Exchange Administration Reform that Supports the "One Belt, One Road" Strategy

5.2.3.1 Present Reform Trend

Since 2000, supporting enterprises "going out", that is, investing overseas, has been an important constituent of our foreign policy. Since the financial crisis, establishing a new order of international finance and realizing economic rebalance became the focus of China's foreign relations. The Third Plenary Session of the 18th CPC Central Committee further proposed to "enlarge external investments of enterprises and individuals, establish enterprises and individuals' position as subjects of external investments, and allow them to bring out their advantages in overseas investment and cooperation;" "accelerate the implementation of free trade zone strategy based on peripheral areas;" and "push forward the construction of the silk road economic belt and the maritime silk road." This last is known as the "One Belt, One Road" foreign investment strategy.

The "One Belt, One Road" strategy will form a new pattern of comprehensive opening up in trade, investment, energy, industry, services, etc. and provide an important boost to the transition and upgrade of China's opening economy in the new era. Accordingly, various financial management systems, including foreign exchange administration, require the implementation of supporting reforms. SAFE's reform focus has changed from "trade facilitation" to "trade and investment and financing facilitation," which is more open. After the strict implementation of goods trading and service facilitation reforms, foreign exchange administration of foreign direct investment in China has been further streamlined and delegated to lower levels. As with the steady advance of RMB internationalization, more and more foreign exchange administration and investment management policies and reforms are aiming to relax and support exchange and the use of overseas investment.

5.2.3.2 Promoting the Facilitation of Trade and Foreign Investment
As regards promoting trade facilitation, the reform of foreign exchange administration systems for goods trading has been carried out nationwide since 2012. The reform has simplified transaction procedures for foreign exchange receipts and payments in import and export trade and has spread to the area of service trade. To promote free trade at the border, in March 2014, having regard to the demand for market transactions, SAFE took measures to simplify procedures, including abolishing administrative approval for border trading enterprises and clarifying foreign exchange cash settlement to promote the turnover and operational efficiency of capital in border trade enterprises. In the area of foreign exchange concerning foreign direct investment, since 2012, foreign exchange registration procedures and foreign exchange account management for foreign investments have been simplified; from 2014, pilot reform of the voluntary settlement of exchange of capital funds for foreign-invested enterprises has been carried out in some areas, and the previous expense management system for overseas direct investment has been relaxed.

Strategic Combination of National Investment and Enterprise Investment

The investment fields for the foreign exchange reserve have been enlarged, and the foreign investment strategy of enterprises has been included in the national investment strategy. In January 2013, the central bank and SAFE founded the SAFE Co-Financing Office within the foreign exchange reserve operation and management agency to take charge of progressing applications for foreign exchange reserve. After that, the General Office of the State Council published "Guiding Opinions on Financial Support for Economic Structural Adjustment, Transition and Upgrade," involving "innovate in foreign exchange reserve applications, expand entrusted loan platforms and commercial bank sub-loan channels for foreign exchange reserve, and integrate and apply multiple methods to provide financing support for foreign exchange users" so as to support the "going out" of enterprises. External investment takes the form of "entrusted loans", in which the SAFE provides funds and entrusts China Development Bank to issue loans to a specified borrower; the China Development Bank determines the interest rate, term, and amount of the loan, while the SAFE, the capital provider, bears the risk; the main prospective borrowers are "going-out" Chinese enterprises. In December 2014, it was reported that the Silk Road Fund had already been founded. Foreign exchange reserves will contribute a large amount of capital for investment in infrastructure construction and interconnection between countries along the Silk Road.[18]

Supporting Enterprises to "Go Out" and Accelerate the Export of Capital

First, domestic enterprises opening up to the outside world are being supported, and policies are being introduced to facilitate investment and financing. For example, domestic enterprises are allowed to extend loans to affiliated overseas enterprises in which they directly or indirectly hold shares, and the two-year limit on the effective term for overseas loans has been abolished; finance leasing companies' overseas finance leasing business is not subject to the current restriction on overseas loans for domestic enterprises; foreign exchange administration has been reformed to facilitate overseas listing of enterprises; foreign exchange settlement approval procedures have been abolished for the return of funds raised overseas under overseas-listed foreign share accounts; company and shareholder accounts have been integrated; fund remittance between domestic companies and shareholders is facilitated; individual residents are allowed to purchase overseas special purpose vehicles and overseas working capital with foreign currency; restrictions on domestic enterprises' extension of overseas loans to special purpose vehicles have been abolished; the mandatory fund-return provision that "foreign exchange receipts such as profits, dividends, and capital changes obtained from special purpose vehicles should return home in 180 days upon receipt" has been abolished, allowing overseas-financed funds and other related funds to be kept and used overseas; within prescribed foreign debt and foreign loan limits, domestic and international accounts are interconnected to help businesses to regulate fund surpluses and deficiencies internally.

Second, in the interests of RMB cross-border guarantee services, administrative provisions have been introduced for foreign exchange guarantees. In addition to the above-mentioned relaxation of the examination and approval of foreign exchange investment and financing for individual areas, the "Provisions on Foreign Exchange Administration for Cross-border Guarantees" represents a major reform of cross-border investment and financing facilitation, and has differentiated the institutional arrangements for cross-border guarantees of various types. Since the progressive development of RMB cross-border guarantee services in China, the PBC and SAFE have stipulated a division of responsibilities and business management in cross-border RMB business; advance verification and registration are not required for banks transacting foreign guarantees of RMB financing, while there is provision for banks to report and submit letters of guarantee and performance information to the RMB Cross-Border Payment Management Information System (RCPMIS). To achieve equality in the treatment of Chinese and foreign enterprises regarding cross-border guarantees, free exchange between foreign currency and RMB ensures the facilitation of investment and financing. Accordingly, SAFE issued "Provisions on Foreign Exchange Administration for Cross-border Guarantees," which provides that "all advance examination and approval procedures related to cross-border guarantees, together with advance verification of guarantee performance and most restrictions on business qualifications and conditions, are abolished and replaced by proportionate self-regulation and registration management;" for "domestic guarantees of foreign loans (which become external creditor's rights after performance of guarantee), multifarious management procedures are abolished; for foreign guarantees of domestic loans (which become foreign debts after performance of guarantees) that may cause capital inflows, appropriate regulation and restrictions continue." At the same time, regulations have been sorted out and integrated, twelve normative documents concerning foreign exchange administration for cross-border guarantees abolished, and the transparency of foreign exchange administration policies improved.

Third, the steady development of direct transactions between RMB and foreign currencies is being promoted to facilitate exchange. Since the 2009 cross-border RMB business pilot program, China has realized direct transactions between RMB and eight currencies in the interbank foreign exchange markets of both parties. The daily volume of RMB direct transactions has hit 10.222 billion RMB, 8.4 times larger than that of the year before the promotion of direct transactions.[19] Direct transaction of foreign currencies not only enriches the products of the foreign exchange market and promotes marketization of foreign exchange supply and demand, but also contributes to decreasing exchange costs, drives forward the facilitation of trade and investment and financing, and supports the export of RMB.

5.2.3.3 Policy Interpretation

Before the year 2000, China's direct investment foreign exchange administration followed the principle of "relaxed inflow but restricted outflow." Along with the emergence of "double surpluses", i.e., deposit surplus and foreign exchange surplus,[20] China began the "going out" strategy after 2000. The National Development and Reform Commission, the Ministry of Commerce, and SAFE jointly coordinate responsibility for the approval and administration of overseas investments and cooperate on their management. Since the launch of the "going out" strategy, foreign exchange administration policies have gradually been transformed from the restriction of overseas investment in the past to the encouragement of overseas investment and relaxation of strict restrictions on foreign exchange and the entry and exit of overseas investments. Since 2002, SAFE has gradually abolished profit remittance guarantee deposits for overseas investments, simplified and gradually abolished the examination of foreign exchange fund sources so that domestic enterprises' freedom to use foreign exchange in direct investment is greatly improved. However, by 2009, the freedom of Chinese enterprises to use foreign exchange was limited to their own foreign exchange funds and profits earned through overseas investments, while SAFE's verification was still required for foreign exchange loans and direct purchase of foreign exchange with RMB. In the last two years, SAFE has been actively exploring ways to further facilitate cross-border investment and financing using pilot program before comprehensive popularizing them under the principle of progressiveness and controllability.

The significance of promoting trade and investment and financing facilitation reform and then driving forward the construction of "One Belt, One Road" is as follows. It answers to China's demand for strategic transformation and upgrading. For a large trading country like China, according equal importance to both import and export, promoting balanced trade development, transforming from commodity export to capital export and from a large trading country to a large investment country have become the routes to transformation and upgrading in the opening economy.[21] Foreign exchange administration reform that supports enterprises' overseas investments will facilitate the acceleration of China's transition to capital export, realize basic exchange between home and foreign currencies on the basis of trade transactions, help enhance the economic integration of China with Europe and Asia, and further promote RMB internationalization.

It helps to solve the difficult and expensive financing problem facing "going-out" enterprises. Cross-border guarantee activities such as domestic guarantees of foreign loans and foreign guarantees of domestic loans can improve the efficiency of capital application at home and abroad and make the most of domestic and overseas interest-rate spread and exchange-rate spread. New regulations have abolished restrictions on entities or transactions, have allowed overseas assets to provide guarantees for overseas or domestic creditors, and presented enterprises with further options for cross-border investment and financing not limited to specific relationships and enterprises' own funds.

It accords with the current trend towards opening up. Before reform, the main regulations on foreign exchange administration for cross-border guarantees dated back to the 1990s. However, as with the rapid growth of foreign-related business in China, cross-border guarantees are becoming increasingly complicated and diversified, and cross-border use of RMB in particular involves cross-over use of foreign currencies and home currency. The reform includes all kinds of cross-border guarantees with payment as guarantee performance, which may exert an important influence on the international balance of payments, and greatly eases foreign exchange administration for cross-border guarantees.

5.2.4 Construction of Foreign Debt Management System Under the Macroprudential Framework

5.2.4.1 Evolution of China's Foreign Debt Management

For a long time, China had neither domestic debts nor foreign debts. Since the reform and opening up, China has changed its attitude to foreign debt management, has attached importance to the exploitation of both international and domestic markets and two kinds of resources, has promoted the active role of foreign debts in serving the real economy, and has gradually established a foreign debt management system that accords with the socialist market economy. In the 1980s, China published relevant regulations such as "Interim Regulations of the PRC on Foreign Exchange Administration" and "Interim Provisions on Foreign Debt Statistics and Monitoring," conducted two different management systems of foreign loans by Chinese and foreign-funded institutions, and excluded foreign-funded investment corporations loans from foreign debts statistics. In the 1990s, foreign direct investment exceeded foreign debt and became the main way to use foreign capital; since the use efficiency of foreign debts was low, China began to adjust its foreign debt policy and took temporary measures such as restricting enterprises from purchasing foreign exchange and repaying loans ahead of time to restrict capital flight. In 2003, China published "Interim Measures for Foreign Debt Management" to gradually promote national treatment of Chinese and foreign-funded institutions in foreign debt management, to improve foreign debt statistical reporting to international standards, and to consider both facilitation and risk prevention in management.

Joint supervision is China's method of foreign debt management. Since the 1980s, the cross-department cooperative supervision model has been adopted under the leadership of the State Council. In this, the National Development and Reform Commission is responsible for verifying medium- and long-term foreign debt targets, SAFE is responsible for verifying short-term debts, foreign debt exchange and statistics from financial institutions and Chinese-funded enterprises, the Ministry of Finance for sovereign debt, and the Ministry of Commerce for determining the upper limit of foreign debts (Table 5.3).[22]

5.2.4.2 Present Reform Trend

Foreign debt management is closely related to the opening up of the capital account. According to the general direction of reform, the Chinese

Table 5.3 Current foreign debt management model in China

Department	National Development and Reform Commission	SAFE	Ministry of Commerce	Ministry of Finance
Management function	Determines the total scale of the country's foreign debt, medium- and long-term foreign debt targets of financial institutions and Chinese-funded enterprises, approves establishment of foreign-invested enterprises, compiles feasibility research reports	Short-term foreign debts of financial institutions and Chinese-funded enterprises, exchange and statistics of all foreign debts	Approves contracts and regulations of foreign-invested enterprises	Signs contracts; use of sovereign debts
Type of debtor	Chinese and foreign-funded financial institutions and enterprises	All kinds of domestic debtors	Foreign-invested enterprises	On-lending institutions and final fund users of sovereign debts

Data source: Li Chao (2012) (Li Chao, "China's Foreign Debt Management Issues." *Journal of Financial Research*, Issue 4, 2014.)

government's requirement for reform is gradually deepening. The 12th Five-year Plan for Development and Reform of the Financial Industry proposed to "improve management of foreign credit and debt," "focus on facilitation of cross-border financing, accelerate foreign exchange administration reform of credit business, deepen reform of foreign debt management systems, and regulate the management and monitoring of external credit's rights." The Third Plenary Session of the 18th CPC Central Committee further proposed to "establish and improve foreign debt and capital flow management systems under a macroprudential management framework and accelerate the realization of RMB capital account convertibility."

The implementation of supervision currently mainly relies on "Regulations of the PRC on Foreign Exchange Control," "Interim Measures for Foreign Debt Management," formulated in 2003, and "Measures for Foreign Debt Management of Foreign-funded Banks" in 2004, which still impose strict controls on the overseas debts of enterprises and financial institutions. Although SAFE has relaxed restrictions on short-term foreign debts of Chinese-funded enterprises in 2010, there remain strict provisions about borrower institutions, limit, term, and use of short-term foreign debts. Although China carried out reform of cross-border financing guarantees in 2014, foreign debt management of capital inflow still exists, as SAFE stated that they "only cancelled restrictions on foreign exchange administration in the link of signing guarantee contracts", and "there are still necessary restrictive provisions concerning foreign debt management, cross-border investment, property right guarantees, and so on."

Policy Interpretation
According to official statistics, since 2001 when the external debts of foreign-funded institutions started being included in statistics, the scale of China's short-term foreign debts has continuously increased, and its proportion to debt also keeps rising. By 2013, the total balance of China's foreign debts was 863.17 billion USD, with the balance of short-term foreign debts at 676.64 billion USD, accounting for 78.39 % of the total (Fig. 5.2); unlike other developing countries, China's short-term debts are mainly trade credit closely related to import and export. According to official statistics, trade credit among enterprises was 49.73 % of short-

Fig. 5.2 Scale and proportions of short-term debt in China (*left axis*: Billion USD; *right axis*: %).
Data source: State Administration of Foreign Exchange (State Administration of Foreign Exchange, http://www.safe.gov.cn).
Note: As of 2001, China has adjusted the original range of foreign debts according to international standards

term debt, while bank trade financing was 21.08%. Foreign debts, especially short-term foreign debts, have grown rapidly in recent years, but, according to preliminary calculations, China's foreign debt-to-GDP ratio was only 9.40% by the end of 2013; debt-to-export-earnings ratio was 35.59%; debt servicing ratio was 1.57%; the proportion of short-term debts to foreign exchange reserve was 17.71%, all within the world-recognized safe limit. That being the case, why has China recently started considering "establishing foreign debt management system under the macroprudential framework"? The author believes there are two reasons.

For one, short-term debts may cause a large fluctuation in cross-border capital. As for the growth trend of short-term debts, since 2010, China's short-term debts have grown rapidly from 375.7 billion USD to 676.6 billion USD, increasing by 80%. At this time, China was experiencing high economic growth and RMB unilateral appreciation expectations, and the country faced an aggravated risk of "hot money inflow". It was at this time that China's "debt balance" of other investment accounts, with trade credit as a major part, appeared as obvious fluctuations closely related to the foreign exchange expectation of banks, enterprises and other private-sector players. Enterprises and banks can strive for "debt dollarization and asset localization" by legal means and may also carry out speculative currency arbitrage activities and interest arbitrage through fake trades. Besides, economic entities seeking alternative financing channels at times of tightening home currency credit will also accelerate changes in short-term debt. Relevant empirical research shows that the relation between China's foreign debt and money supply (M2) is already higher that that between foreign debt and import and export, etc. In November 2012, Hu Xiaolian, Vice President of the central bank, clearly stated that "having realized convertibility, a country can still conduct monitoring and necessary management of cross-border capital flow in areas concerning short-term capital flow such as macroprudential foreign debt management, anti-money-laundering and anti-terrorist financing management, take temporary special measures at times of sharp fluctuations of capital flow to maintain the economic and financial stability of the nation".

For another, RMB export causes an increase in RMB liabilities. Along with the advance of RMB internationalization, more and more overseas non-residents will hold RMB assets. Taking Hong Kong RMB offshore center as an example, the HKMA's data reveal that by the end of the first half of 2014, the RMB deposits of Hong Kong had reached 1,125 billion yuan, 12 times larger than the 90 billion yuan in the same period of 2010;

trade settlements handled by Hong Kong's banks reached 2,926 billion yuan, 107 times those of the same period in 2010; balance of bond issues reached 384 billion yuan, while that in the same period of 2010 was only 30 billion; the daily transaction amount of Hong Kong's RMB real-time settlement system reached 700 billion yuan, nearly 1,000 times larger than that of the same period in 2010.[23]

Looking back, China has accumulated a certain amount of experience in foreign debt management and has alleviated the impact of cross-border capital flow on economic development. For example, before the explosion of the Asian financial crisis, China took the initiative of adjusting foreign debt policy and reducing the scale of foreign debt; after the crisis, the regulatory department launched temporary measures such as restricting enterprises purchasing foreign exchange and repaying loans ahead of time, and restricted capital flight. Before the onset of the global financial crisis, SAFE issued the "Notice on Relevant Issues concerning 2007 Short-term Foreign Debt Management of Financial Institutions" and reduced the limit on foreign debts for various types of banking institution; after the explosion of the crisis, China also felt the impact of capital inflow coming from foreign debt channels caused by exchange-rate expectation. Response plans were launched twice in November 2010 and March 2011 to strengthen foreign exchange administration concerning banks' foreign exchange settlement position and sale, foreign exchange receipts and settlement in exports, short-term foreign debts, etc. and to further lower the total 2011 short-term foreign debt target for domestic financial institutions. The specific examination of foreign exchange capital fund settlement and short-term foreign debts were carried out mainly in financial institutions and large enterprises so that investigators could concentrate oncases of major breach and combat illegal capital inflows like "hot money." In May 2013, "Administrative Measures for Foreign Debt Registration" was issued, according to which, SAFE will rely on capital account information systems to strengthen foreign debt statistics monitoring and analysis and off-site verification, while at the same time simplifying foreign debt registration management so as to actively prevent foreign debt risks.

In the future, the regulatory department should take the following actions on policy design. First, improve the data collection and foreign debt statistics monitoring systems. Besides foreign debt statistics denominated in foreign currencies, SAFE will gradually establish foreign debt statistics denominated in home currency to improve the completeness of foreign debt statistics. Second, continue to improve policy and data transparency; enhance information sharing and use among administrative departments. Third, in combination with cross-border capital flow management, actively explore macroprudential supervisory tools that fit in with China's system of foreign debt management.

5.2.5 Construction of Cross-Border Capital Flow Management System Under the Macroprudential Framework

5.2.5.1 The Gradually Intensifying Trend of Bidirectional Cross-Border Capital Flows

For a rather long time, the condition of China's international balance of payments was mostly "double surpluses" of both current account and capital account, but obvious bidirectional flows appeared after the financial crisis. According to international balance-of-payment capital fund statistics, the balance of the capital account has been growing since 2010, and the trend towards bidirectional fluctuation has intensified (Fig. 5.3).

5.2.5.2 Present Reform Trend

Though there is controversy about the actual effect of capital flow management among different countries, China's regulatory department believes "it is necessary carry out necessary monitoring of cross-border financial transactions" and "proper management of short-term speculative cross-border capital flows."[24] In recent years, SAFE's main reform has been to explore relevant risk emergency management methods and mac-

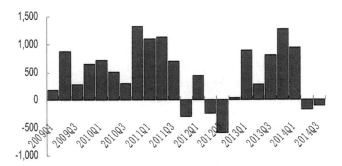

Fig. 5.3 2009–2014 balances of capital and financial accounts (unit: one hundred million USD).
Data source: State Administration of Foreign Exchange (State Administration of Foreign Exchange, http://www.safe.gov.cn)

roprudential policy tools and improve bidirectional monitoring and warning mechanisms of cross-border capital flow risks on the basis of enhanced data and statistics.

Data and system resources have been integrated. Cross-border capital flow monitoring of economic entities has been enhanced and gradually changed to the supervision of entities. In December 2012, a domestic bank was required to report and submit foreign exchange settlement and sale and account information on the foreign exchange account and the bank's capital account data (including the bank's entrusted businesses such as QFII, RQFII, QDII, stock incentive plan, etc. and banks' monthly assets and liabilities), and the three original independent systems were integrated into a single capital account information system. In May 2013, the capital account information system was promoted nationwide, requiring SAFE and its branches and domestic banks to transact capital account business for domestic entities through the capital account information system. On January 1, 2014, the "Measures for Statistical Reporting of International Balance of Payments" took effect.

The nature of capital flow statistics has been improved. In view of the new cross-border capital flow in 2012, the 2012 "China Cross-border Capital Flow Monitoring Report" proposed using the "residual method," which deducts foreign exchange reserve increments; in 2013, in accordance with international practice and relying on the balance of international payments, cross-border capital flows were classified into several categories, including cross-border capital flow of high stability and greater relevance to the real economy (total balance of current account and direct investment) and cross-border capital flow with larger fluctuations (indirect investment capital flow).

Emergency management tools and policy tools for risk management have been explored. In the Shanghai Pilot Free Trade Zone, in addition to unified supervisory standards such as capital adequacy ratio and liquidity regulation, the regulatory department is also considering the introduction of new relevant measures such as setting up dynamic monitoring and warning mechanisms for high-frequency, large-sum trading accounts. When short-term abnormal capital flow appears in a free trade account, temporary capital control measures can be applied, such as extending the deposit term of the account, imposing special deposit reserves or interest-free deposit reserves on the account, setting up account inflow/outflow limit management, etc.[25] In the Shanghai Pilot Free Trade Zone, the regulatory department plans in-depth research into price regulating measures such as

Tobin Tax, interest-free deposit reserves, and foreign exchange transaction fees to restrict short-term speculative capital flow and interest arbitrage.[26]

5.2.5.3 Policy Interpretation

The current international situation is complex and changeable: monetary policy trends in the USA, Europe and Japan also differ, interest rates and the exchange rate levels of different countries are unpredictable, which aggravates frequent cross-border capital flow and poses new challenges to our cross-border capital flow management. The authorities believe the USA's cessation of quantitative easing has so far had limited effect on China,[27] mainly because of the expectation of USD appreciation and the slowing down of the domestic economy, which urges Chinese enterprises to make financial adjustments to their external assets and liabilities, enables the autonomous regional balance of foreign exchange supply and demand, favors "storing foreign exchange among the people" as a policy direction, and reduces intervention by the central bank (Guan Tao et al. 2014).[28] The future influence of the US action on China's cross-border capital flow, however, will continue to receive attention from the authorities and academic circles.

China's current management of short-term capital inflow mainly concentrates on quantitative control. For example, foreign debt limits and balance management, measures to manage banks' foreign exchange settlement and sale position, and the interim foreign exchange loan-to-deposit ratios of banks are SAFE's main measures for controlling capital inflow over recent years. However, quantitative control is defective in that it works in short term, but its effects wear off in the long term and affect normal trade and investment activities. Price management tools such as Tobin Tax will enhance cross-border capital management, reduce the fluctuations of the foreign exchange market, maintain the stability of the capital market, and achieve balanced management of capital flow. Since the introduction of Tobin Tax, its implementation has aroused great controversy worldwide, but the discussion over its implementation is of particular importance. The explosion of the financial crisis and the European debt crisis have shown Europe the cost of capital impact; such unfairness has caused differentiation of the American and European alignment, which together with the rise of developing countries may make Tobin Tax a future trend (Fan Limeng et al. 2012).[29]

The construction of macroprudential cross-border capital flow systems is first of all about how to construct cross-border capital flow management system. The IMF has proposed a policy framework for capital flow management and has ranked administrative policy tools. The IMF believes the first thing is to carry out structural reforms, increase the depth and liquidity of the domestic financial market, and improve the financial system's ability to resist shocks; the second thing to consider is macro-economic measures like currency appreciation, reserve increases, financial and monetary policies, while the last resort is capital control measures (Li Chao 2012).[30] Therefore, such a policy framework emphasizes the unilateral application of multiple macro-economic policies concerning exchange rates, money, finance, reserves, and so on.

Second, while deliberating on relevant management tools, due attention should also be given to the compatibility of the domestic economic and financial conditions of the country that is opening. The IMF's recent research on the buffering effect of a country's economic and financial features on capital inflow is noteworthy.[31] According to the result of the IMF's recent analysis of Chile, Malaysia, and the Czech Republic's capital flows, emerging markets and economies with stronger resistance have the following characteristics: (1) financial policy is more counter-cyclical, monetary policy more complete; (2) the system is more complete; (3) exchange-rate mechanisms are more flexible; and (4) financial regulation is more vigorous. These economies provide more private, not official, buffers for capital inflow so that net capital flows are more stable. Boucekkine et al. (2013) believed capital control policy is conditional and can only be carried out when certain domestic debt and economic scale conditions are met; sub-optimal capital control measures should be counter-cyclical.[32]

At last, international cooperation and domestic coordination should be enhanced. Cross-border capital flow is the result of the combined actions of various factors, including domestic and foreign politics, economics and finance, prices, etc., so the monitoring of cross-border flow requires coordination and cooperation by international and national regulatory departments. On the international level, China should take an active part in international supervision, expand the scope of supervision cooperation, set up information-sharing systems with foreign supervisory agencies and exchanges, sign supervision cooperation agreements, and take part in international supervisory organizations that are formulating rules for the foreign exchange derivatives market according to their standards so as to increase channels of information exchange. On the domestic level, Li Yang stressed that the deficiency of the financial system was reflected in the regulatory system; the current agency regulation was only an initial condition and more emphasis should be put on function regulation and regulation coordination.[33] With respect to foreign exchange administration, the regulatory plan of the Shanghai Free Trade Zone has already mentioned coordination and cooperation between various departments and the need to further enhance supervision cooperation nationwide. For example, as the scale of cross-border RMB business keeps expanding, the supervision of RMB cross-border flows and foreign exchange fund cross-border flows are equally important, but at present the supervision coordination mechanism for cross-border capital flows of home and foreign currency has not been clearly established.

5.3 Future Outlook

5.3.1 "New Normal" State of Basic Equilibrium of International Balance of Payments

After the crisis, following the new trend towards economic rebalancing, active adjustments and reforms have been carried out in China's foreign economic strategy, the range of its current account surplus has been narrowed, and cross-border capital takes on a bidirectional flow. Furthermore, the 2014 central economic work conference proposed to "more actively promote the balance of domestic and overseas market demands, of import and export, of foreign capital introduction and overseas investment, gradually realize basic equilibrium of international balance of payment, and build new systems for opening the economy." The conference also stressed "China still has its competitive edge in export." Currently, the US economy is recovering, and the expectation of USD appreciation is intensifying; China's economic growth trend is still as before, and its exchange-rate and interest-rate marketization reforms are deepening. In the future, under the guidance of a new foreign investment strategy, along with the rapid development of cross-border RMB business, the trend towards autonomous equilibrium of the international balance of payment will intensify, and "current account surplus and capital account deficit" may become the "new normal" state of basic equilibrium of the international balance of payments.

5.3.2 Outlook of Foreign Exchange Administration

In January 2015, the comprehensive foreign exchange administration work conference was held, which "followed and carried out the spirit of the Eighteenth National Congress of the Communist Party of China, the Third and Fourth Plenaries of the 18th CPC Central Committee, and the central economic work conference", and "made in-depth analysis of the current economic and financial situations and international balance of payments trends, deliberated on the arrangement of 2015 foreign exchange administration". Based on this, the next few years may see SAFE focusing on the following aspects.

a. Legal Exercise of administrative power. As rule by law is "to insist on the integrated construction of national government, and society under the rule of law" and "to realize legalization of various works of the country",[34] SAFE as an important administrative department for the country's foreign economic activities must speed up the compilation and formulation of the foreign exchange regulation system administration, strengthen legislation and sort out laws and regulations in key areas, including "establish and improve long-term mechanism of regulation sort-out, regularly update the 'Catalog', improve policy transparency, provide convenience for banks, enterprises, and individuals to understand and use regulations of foreign exchange administration, and promote administration by law in the foreign exchange area."[35]

b. Insistence on "the decisive role of the market in resource allocation." There are two main aspects to this principle as it concerns the system of foreign exchange administration. First it means maintaining good relations between the government and the market and reforming attitudes to foreign exchange administration methods. SAFE will continue to streamline administration and delegate power to lower levels, introduce negative list management, promote trade facilitation, and reduce unnecessary intervention in the market. Second, it means maintaining a good relationship between the real economy and the virtual economy, insisting on the fundamentals of serving the real economy, combating illegal capital inflow, making good policy plans to respond to bidirectional cross-border capital flow risks, and improving ability to prevent risks with foreign exchange and international balance of payments.

c. Support for the strategic deployment of the "One Belt, One Road" steady advance of RMB internationalization. Under the guidance of the new central leadership, Chinese economic development will continue "going out" and achieve increasingly open upgrades and economic transformation.

d. Achieving basic equilibrium in the international balance of payments, promoting the export of overseas direct investment, and supporting the steady advance of RMB internationalization, carrying out pilot programs to open up capital accounts, supporting interactions with neighboring countries, and promoting equal treatment of both domestic and foreign capitals. During the process of opening up, implement a "combination of control and relaxation," establish cross-border capital flow monitoring and management systems for home and foreign currencies, and improve foreign debt and cross-border capital flow management systems under the macroprudential framework so as to enhance the effectiveness of follow-up regulation.

NOTES

1. State Administration of Foreign Exchange, http://www.safe.gov.cn.
2. Data from CEIC.
3. Quoted from the SAFE's news release on September 25, State Administration of Foreign Exchange, http://www.safe.gov.cn.
4. State Administration of Foreign Exchange, http://www.safe.gov.cn.
5. Research Group of PBC Statistics and Analysis Department: Conditions to Quicken Capital Account Opening up in China are Basically Mature, *China Finance*, 2012 (5).
6. Li, Xiangyang. "RMB Internationalization: from the Perspective of Capital Account Opening up." *Studies of International Finance*, 2014 (5): 10–15.
7. Li, Chao. "Transition of IMF Capital Flow Management Framework and its Revelation." *International Economic Review*, 2013 (5): 9–20.
8. Ma, Jun. "RMB Offshore Market and Capital Account Opening up. " *International Economic Review*, 2012 (4): 1–10.
9. Yu, Yongding. "Seeking for Consensus on Capital Account Opening Up." *Studies of International Finance*, 2014 (7): 3–6.
10. Lin, Yifu. "Why Don't I Support Capital Account Opening Up?" Keynote speech on CF 40 Forum Biweekly Round Table Seminar.
11. See Wu Jinglian's speech on the "Fifth Caixin Summit." *Nanfang Daily*, December 23, 2014.
12. See Li Yang's speech of "China under the New Normal State of Economic Development" on the 2014 Annual Meeting of Economic Strategy of the CASS National Academy of Economic Strategy, quoted from Chinanews.com.
13. See Chen Yulu's interview with media concerning 2014 Report on RMB Internationalization, July 20, 2014, quoted from China Finance Information Network.
14. State Administration of Foreign Exchange, http://www.safe.gov.cn.
15. See China's Balance of Payments Report for the first half of 2014.
16. Zhang, Chenqu. "Foreign Exchange Market Ushers in Non-Banking Retail Investors." *Innovative Finance Observation*, December 22, 2014.
17. State Administration of Foreign Exchange, http://www.safe.gov.cn.
18. Zhao, Jing. "2015: Essential Progress of "One Belt and One Road." *Economic Information Daily*, January 5, 2015.
19. Quoted from the PBC's 2014 fourth-quarter money policy report.

20. Yao, Zhihong et al. "Developing Trend and Policy Outlook of China's Overseas Direct Investment." *International Economic Review*, Issue 2, 2011.
21. Wang, Yang. 2013. *Building New System for Opening Economy, printed in Counseling Book for the CPC Central Committee's Decision of Several Issues concerning Comprehensively Deepening Reform*. Beijing: People's Publishing House.
22. Li, Chao. "China's Foreign Debt Management Issues." *Journal of Financial Research*, Issue 4, 2014.
23. See the website of HKMA.
24. Zhou, Xiaochuan. "Outlook and Route of RMB Capital Account Convertibility." *Journal of Financial Studies*, Issue 1, 2012.
25. Zhang, Xin. "Exploring Classified, Progressive and Manageable Capital Account Convertibility." *China Finance*, Issue 11, 2014.
26. Yi, Gang. "Reform Foreign Exchange Administration: An Important and Urgent Task." *Qiu Shi*, Issue 1, 2014.
27. Quoted from the SAFE's 2013 Report of International Balance of Payment.
28. Guan, Tao et al. "Federal Reserve's Quit of Quantitative Easing Monetary Policy and Financial Stability." *International Economic Review*, Issue 6, 2014.
29. Fan, Limeng et al. Tobin Tax, "Focus of Controversy and Comment." *Economic Perspectives*, 2012 (8).
30. Li, Chao. "Transition of IMF Capital Flow Management Framework and Its Revelation." *International Economic Review*, Issue 5, 2013.
31. Benes et al. "The Ying and Yang of Capital Flow Management: Balancing Capital Inflows with Capital Outflows [R]." *World Economic Outlook*, 2013 (10).
32. Boucekkine et al. "On the Timing and Optimality of Capital Controls: Public Expenditures, Debt Dynamics and Welfare." *International Journal of Economic Theory*, 2013 (9).
33. See Li Yang's speech of "China under the New Normal State of Economic Development" on the 2014 Annual Meeting of Economic Strategy of the CASS National Academy of Economic Strategy.
34. Quoted from the Decision of the CPC Central Committee on Several Important Issues concerning Comprehensively Promoting Rule by Law.
35. Quoted from State Administration of Foreign Exchange, http://www.safe.gov.cn.

References

Benes, Jaromir, Jaime Guajardo, Damiano Sandri, and John Simon 2013. The Ying and Yang of capital flow management: balancing capital inflows with capital outflows [R]. *World Economic Outlook* 10, pp 113–132.
BIS. 2013. *BIS Quarterly Review*, December. http://www.bis.org

CEIC. 2015. http://www.ceicdata.com

China's Balance of Payments Report for the first half of 2014.

Decision of the CPC Central Committee on Several Important Issues concerning Comprehensively Promoting Rule by Law.

Fan, Limeng and Zhang Xiaowen. 2012. Tobin tax, "Focus of Controversy and Comment." *Economic Perspectives*, 8, pp 12–19.

Guan, Tao and Chen Zhi Ping. 2014. Federal reserve's quit of quantitative easing monetary policy and financial stability. *International Economic Review*, Issue 6, pp 21–32.

HKMA. 2015. http://www.hkma.gov.hk/

Li Yang's speech of "China under the New Normal State of Economic Development" on the 2014 Annual Meeting of Economic Strategy of the CASS National Academy of Economic Strategy.

Li, Chao. 2013. Transition of IMF capital flow management framework and its revelation. *International Economic Review* 5, pp 43–56.

Li, Chao. 2014. China's foreign debt management issues. *Journal of Financial Research* 4, pp 84–97.

Li, Xiangyang. 2014. RMB internationalization: from the perspective of capital account opening up. *Studies of International Finance*, 5, pp 10–15.

Lin, Yifu. 2013. Why don't I support capital account opening up? Keynote speech on CF 40 Forum Biweekly Round Table Seminar.

Ma, Jun. 2012. RMB offshore market and capital account opening up. *International Economic Review*, 4, pp 21–32.

PBC Statistics and Analysis Department: Conditions to Quicken Capital Account Opening up in China are Basically Mature. *China Finance*, 2012 (5), pp 06–12.

PBC 2015. PBC's 2014 fourth-quarter money policy report.

Raouf, Boucekkine, Pommeret Aude, and Prieur Fabien. 2013. On the timing and optimality of capital controls: public expenditures, debt dynamics and welfare. *International Journal of Economic Theory*, 9, pp 252–260.

SAFE. 2015. http://www.safe.gov.cn

Wang, Yang. 2013. Building new system for opening economy. Edited by the CPC Central Committee. In *Counseling book for the CPC Central Committee's Decision of Several Issues concerning Comprehensively Deepening Reform*. People's Publishing House, Beijing.

Yao, Zhizhong and Li Zhongmin. 2011. Developing trend and policy outlook of China's overseas direct investment. *International Economic Review*, Issue 2, pp 127–140.

Yi, Gang. 2014. Reform foreign exchange administration: an important and urgent task. *Qiu Shi*, Issue 1, pp 13–17.

Yu, Yongding. 2014. Seeking for consensus on capital account opening up. *Studies of International Finance*, 7, pp 1–12.

Zhang, Chenqu. 2014. Foreign exchange market ushers in non-banking retail investors. *Innovative Finance Observation*, December 22.

Zhang, Xin. 2014. Exploring classified, progressive, and manageable capital account convertibility. *China Finance*, Issue 11, pp 12–14.

Zhao, Jing. 2015. 2015: essential progress of 'One Belt and One Road'. *Economic Information Daily*, January 5.

Zhou, Xiaochuan. 2012. Outlook and route of RMB capital account convertibility. *Journal of Financial Studies*, 1, pp 1–19.

CHAPTER 6

Research on the Financial Reform and Innovation and Corresponding Regulation in China (Shanghai) Pilot Free Trade Zone

Qian Xie

6.1 SHANGHAI FREE TRADE ZONE: GENERAL ANALYSIS OF OPERATING CONDITIONS

6.1.1 Preliminary Establishment of an Institutional Framework for the Shanghai Free Trade Zone

The core task of the China (Shanghai) Free Trade Zone pilot project is to build an innovative, sophisticated institutional system rather than to discard policy. Established on September 29, 2013, the free trade zone has been operating formally for more than a year. Generally speaking, the free trade zone has established the fundamental institutional framework, including various trade facilitation and investment management systems, and financial and government administration frameworks.

Qian Xie, a Ph.D. in Economics, is a Research Fellow at the Institute of Economics, CASS.

Q. Xie
Institute of Economics, Chinese Academy of Social Science, Beijing, China

© The Editor(s) (if applicable) and The Author(s) 2016
B. Hu et al. (eds.), *Development of China's Financial Supervision and Regulation*, DOI 10.1057/978-1-137-52225-2_6

6.1.1.1 Institutional Innovation for the Facilitation of Trade

The establishment of the Shanghai Free Trade Zone has improved the level of trade facilitation. The free trade zone adheres to the regulatory framework of "the first line (national frontier) of openness, the second line (the line between the pilot zone and non-pilot zone) of safety and high level of control, free trade within the zone" in the following ways: (1) measures facilitating trade, import and export through innovation in customs supervision; (2) measures to facilitate trade through reform of the inspection and quarantine systems. Comprehensive new customs supervision measures have introduced a "one declaration, one check, and one clearance" system. Businesses are allowed to "enter before declaration" and "declare batches of import and export through exploration". The inspection and quarantine department has established an "all-in-one window" and a paperless clearance system. These measures have greatly improved the efficiency of clearance.

6.1.1.2 New Measures in Investment Management Systems

New investment management measures within the Shanghai Free Trade Zone are mainly reflected in the trial run of a "negative list". This is part of a fundamental change in foreign investment management and marks an important first step in the transformation of government functions. It will also further encourage deepening reforms in the area of foreign investment and will expand the opening-up process in the pilot free trade zone and even throughout the country. On the basis of the 2013 negative list, Shanghai made substantial deletions and revisions of special management measures for the 2014 list, reducing the number of items from 190 down to 139. In accordance with the requirements for building a new more open China, there is still room for deletions and revisions on the 2015 negative list, where special management measures expected to be below 100. This will be applied, depending on the circumstances, to the recently established free trade zones in Tianjin, Guangdong, and Fujian. In the area of commercial registration systems reform, a registered capital subscription system has been implemented for enterprises. This is accompanied by two systems for businesses: the "all-in-one window" and the "business license before administrative license" systems. A filing system is being trialled as part of overseas investment management reform.

6.1.1.3 Financial System Innovation

Since the establishment of the Shanghai Free Trade Zone in 2013, the "one bank and three commissions" (People's Bank of China, China Securities Regulatory Commission, China Banking Regulatory Commission, and China Insurance Regulatory Commission) have issued a series of measures, opinions, and detailed rules concerning financial support for the construction of the free trade zone, providing policy and legal support for financial reforms and innovations. At the heart of the reforms is the implementation of a separate accounting system: this provides the foundations for deepening financial reform in the free trade zone. Against this backdrop there has been great progress in the areas of interest rate marketization reform, cross-border RMB use, and the reform of foreign exchange management systems and cross-border financing systems. By the end of August 2014, the total number of financial institutions, quasi-financial institutions, financial information services, asset management companies, and so on totaled 3,015; financial enterprises accounted for 25% of newly established enterprises. At the same time, a total of 4,110 FTE (Free Trade Enterprise) accounts were opened in the free trade zone.

6.1.1.4 Innovation from Government Management

New management systems in the Shanghai Free Trade Zone are mainly reflected in the formation of an "in-process and follow-up" regulation system, which is gradually transforming government functions. As the "in-process and afterwards" regulation system matures, the reform can be replicated across the country. This framework comprises six main systems: social credit, safety review, information sharing, comprehensive law enforcement, Tax management, and trading facilities. The free trade zone has also established the publication of corporate annual reports, a system for reporting operational abnormalities, and adjustments to the relevant laws and regulations.

6.1.2 Challenges Facing the Development of the Shanghai Free Trade Zone

Despite its achievements, the Shanghai Free Trade Zone still faces various challenges on the road ahead. There is still room for improvement in its industries, business, and policies and systems.

6.1.2.1 Weakness in the Industrial Function

The industrial function of the Shanghai Free Trade Zone lays particular emphasis on service industries. However, Shanghai has a highly developed manufacturing industry, and the neighboring provinces of Jiangsu and Zhejiang also have a solid manufacturing base. Shanghai also has a port with the largest cargo handling capacity in the world. If an Asia-Pacific distribution center can be built within the free trade zone, it is also possible to develop an international production line that covers the Asia-Pacific area. This production line could take advantage of the opportunities in global raw material pricing to process raw materials and transport finished and half-finished products, guaranteeing a strong role in the manufacturing industry chain. The current predicament is that the Shanghai Free Trade Zone has limited land reserves to develop manufacturing industry. The zones's expansion is an inevitable step towards the development of foreign trade.

6.1.2.2 Offshore Service Functions Are Still Weak

Shanghai Free Trade Zone provides certain conditions for developing offshore trade, and still lags behind other offshore trade centers around the world. Its current management foundation is still weak and the free trade zone has so far not set up management rules for offshore trading operations or set limits on the establishment offshore accounts. Offshore trade service providers are highly sensitive to tax issues, but measures concerning tax preferences for offshore goods and enterprises are non-existent, which does not help the further development of offshore trading.

6.1.2.3 Tax Reform Should Be Accelerated

First, a preferential tax policy attracts multinational corporations and is the key factor in the competition in the offshore business. Shanghai still lags behind Hong Kong, Singapore, etc. in aspects of the treatment of offshore trade corporate income tax and individual income tax. Second, its preferential tax policy for international ship registration is not favorable to multinationals. "The Pilot Project of International Ship Registration Systems in China's (Shanghai) Pilot Free Trade Zone" has been officially approved, marking a breakthrough in aspects of ship registration conditions, vessel age limits, crew allocation, ship registration types, etc. However there is no benefit for ship hull import duties and value-added tax. The influence of offshore trade development and the national registration of Chinese ships is affecting the Shanghai international trade center and the construction of the shipping center.

6.1.2.4 Enterprises Lack Vitality in the Zone

By the end of August 2014, over 10,000 new enterprises had been set up in the pilot free trade zone, less than a third of them reported tax revenues. A large number of enterprises entered the free trade zone through virtual registration, making the free trade zone the "registration zone". The reason is that space in the free trade zone is limited, and rent is continuously rising. Some office buildings saw their rents soar from 1.5 yuan to 11 yuan per square meter per day in two weeks. Some businesses have to remain outside the free trade zone due to its limitations in terms of both size and rent.

6.2 Position, Principles and Analysis of Financial Services in the Shanghai Free Trade Zone

6.2.1 Financial Reform and Innovation in the Free Trade Zone

The Third Plenary Session of the 18th CPC Central Committee proposed the establishment of a new, open economy. At the heart of the new system is innovation and the opening up of systems and mechanisms of international trade, both in the mainland area and in the expanding service industry. The China (Shanghai) Pilot Free Trade Zone not only involves trading in goods but also aims to open services in trade (Pei Changhong 2014).

The general plan of the Shanghai Free Trade Zone released by the State Council makes specific mention of the opening of the service industry, of which six major fields and 18 sub-fields are mentioned. The openness of the financial services industry is rather low in comparison with the entire service industry in China. Reform and innovation in the financial industry is certainly the main constituent in the development of Shanghai Free Trade Zone and this is embodied in the general plan, which cites financial reform and innovation in the zone as a pioneering mission, to be followed by replication of the experience and practice nationwide (Table 6.1). Financial reform and innovation in the free trade zone will also support transformation and upgrade to serve a new type of trade business.

6.2.2 Principles of Financial Reform and Innovation in the Free Trade Zone

First, the ultimate goal of financial reform is to serve the real economy; as far as the free trade zone is concerned, it is to improve investment levels

Table 6.1 Degree of openness in various sectors of China's service industry, percentage

	Promised opening	Completely opening	Partly opening	Non-opening
Commerce	60.9	22.8	38.1	39.1
Communications	62.5	19.8	42.7	37.5
Architecture	100	25	75	0
Sales and distribution	100	35	65	0
Education	100	25	75	0
Environment	100	25	75	0
Finance	76.5	16.2	60.3	23.5
Tourism	50	25	25	50
Transportation	20	11.3	8.7	80
Entertainment	0	0	0	100
Health care	0	0	0	100
Other	0	0	0	100
Average	67	21	46	33

Source: Pei Changhong, The Openness Scale in the New Round from the Perspective of Global Governance based on Observation of Shanghai Free Trade Zone, *Reform*, Issue 12, 2014.

and trade facilitation. Second, as part of the national mission to build a new type of open economy, financial reform and innovation in the free trade zone should lead to national financial reform. Third, financial institutions and financial markets should always be subject to reform and innovation, which includes not only the implementation of reform but also the practicalities of constructing a system. Finally, the importance of financial risk prevention should be borne in mind, while financial reform and openness proceed in a reasonable and orderly manner.

6.2.3 Path Selection of Financial Reform in the Free Trade Zone

Since September 2013, The Shanghai Free Trade Zone has experienced and essential development. Compared with other China's economic zone, Shanghai selected a different way to conduct the new reform and openness policy. First, the Free Trade Zone is a comprehensive reform approach including current account and captial account. Second, the Free Trade Zone conducts a negative list management framework. Third, it uses the principle of Pre-establishment National Treatment. See Table 6.2.

Table 6.2 Documents issued after the establishment of Shanghai Free Trade Zone and their core contents

Order	Date	Department	Title	Core content
1	September 27, 2013	State Council	Notice of Printing and Distributing the General Plan of China Shanghai Pilot Free Trade Zone	1. General requirements 2. Main tasks and measures 3. Environment of regulation and taxation systems 4. Solid work of organization and implementation.
2	September 29, 2013	Shanghai Municipal People's Government	China (Shanghai) Pilot Free Trade Zone Special Management Measures on Foreign Investment Access (Negative List)	CBRC, CSRC, and CIRC respectively issued related policies to support Shanghai Free Trade Zone.
3	December 2, 2013	People's Bank of China	Opinions concerning Financial Support for the Construction of China (Shanghai) Pilot Free Trade Zone	1. General principles 2. New accounting system that favors risk management 3. Explore exchange facilitation for investment and financing 4. Expand cross-border use of RMB 5. Steadily promote interest rate marketization 6. Deepen foreign exchange management reform 7. Monitor and regulate.
4	February 18, 2014	People's Bank of China, Shanghai Headquarters	Notice on the Support of Expansion of Cross-border RMB Use in China (Shanghai) Pilot Free Trade Zone	1. Detailed rules on the expansion of cross-border RMB use and exploration of exchange facilitation for investment in "30 Clauses on Finance" 2. Overseas RMB loans 3. Cross-border RMB settlement under current and investment accounts 4. Start cross-border RMB electronic settlement in e-commerce 5. Cross-border RMB transaction service.

(*continued*)

Table 6.2 (continued)

Order	Date	Department	Title	Core content
5	February 26, 2014	Headquar-ters of People's Bank of China	Notice on the Interest Rate Upper Limit of Small-amount Foreign Currency Deposit in China (Shanghai) Pilot Free Trade Zone	Strengthen the construction of pricing mechanism for foreign currency interest rate, improve relevant management systems, and set up prevention mechanism.
6	February 28, 2014	SAFE Shanghai Branch	Notice on Printing and Distributing the Implementation Rules of Supporting the Construction of Foreign Exchange Management in China (Shanghai) Free Trade Zone	1. Simplify the verification of documents for receipt, settlement, purchase, and payment of foreign exchange under current account 2. Simplify foreign exchange registration procedure for direct investment 3. Improve pilot policies concerning centralized operation and management of foreign exchange capitals of multinational headquarters, foreign currency capital pool, and foreign exchange management of international trade settlement center 4. Relax restrictions on the conditions of pilot enterprises, and simplify approval and account management procedures 5. Strengthen requirements to submit foreign exchange settlement and sale management data; 6. Strengthen off-site supervision and on-site verification and examination.

Table 6.2 (continued)

Order	Date	Department	Title	Core content
7	May 12, 2014		Notice on Trial Implementation of Related Institutional Arrangement of Banking Regulation in China (Shanghai) Pilot Free Trade Zone	1. General regulation requirements of pilot zone business 2. Banking industry special monitoring financial statement system in the pilot zone 3. Regulation requirements of internal institutions in the pilot zone 4. Functional layout and resource support for the banking industry in the pilot zone.
8	May 15, 2014	CIRC	Notice on Further Simplifying Administrative Approval to Support the Development of China (Shanghai) Pilot Free Trade Zone	1. Allow Shanghai Institute of Marine Insurance to launch the pilot project developing shipping insurance clauses of association 2. Cancel the advance approval requirement for the establishment of branches of Shanghai shipping insurance operation centers and reinsurance companies in the free trade zone, and carry out filing management by CIRC Shanghai Bureau 3. Cancel the advance approval requirement for qualification of top managers in insurance branch companies in the free trade zone 4. CIRC Shanghai Bureau to carry out filing management.

(*continued*)

Table 6.2 (continued)

Order	Date	Department	Title	Core content
9	May 21, 2014	People's Bank of China, Shanghai Headquarters	Notice on Printing and Distributing *Implementation Rules of Separate Accounting Business in China (Shanghai) Pilot Free Trade Zone (Trial)* and *Detailed Rules of Prudential Risk Management for Separate Accounting Business in China (Shanghai) Pilot Free Trade Zone (Trial)*	1. Separate accounting management 2. Free trade account management 3. Supervision and management.

Source: Summary of Xie Qian from relevant documents concerning China (Shanghai) Pilot Free Trade Zone

6.3 Key Areas of Financial Reform in Shanghai Free Trade Zone

6.3.1 Establishment of Separate Accounting System in the Free Trade Zone

On May 21, the Shanghai Headquarters of the People's Bank of China issued detailed accounting rules for implementation and for prudent risk management, which was regarded as the largest breakthrough in financial innovation since the foundation of Shanghai Free Trade Zone. The rules not only cover institutional innovations but also function as supporting regulatory measures.

The basic principle of a separate accounting system in the free trade zone is "a macro-prudent management of caution along the first line" and "limited permeation through the second line"; the establishment of such a system basically forms an "electronic encircling gear" in the financial landscape. Businesses in the free trade zone and overseas companies can transact businesses with cross-border settlement, financing, guarantee, etc. via free trade account, enabling the free exchange of foreign currency in the accounts. Meanwhile, capital can be transferred freely in both directions between a free trade account and an overseas enterprise's overseas account, domestic non-resident account, offshore account, and other free trade accounts under the same account name or different names. Enterprises in the free trade zone can also maintain or open non-free trade accounts for domestic settlements with foreign enterprises in China (capital can be transferred freely in both directions) or for international settlements with enterprises overseas or foreign enterprises in China.

The second line of a macro-prudential management is about the free trade accounts and limited permeation out of FTZ. In view of the requirements of legitimate cross-border transactions, including current account business, credit repayment, real-economy investment, etc., capital transfers between accounts bearing the same name can be transacted under limited permeation between free trade accounts and non-free trade accounts in the free trade zone. Not only does the significance of the establishment of a separate accounting system mean two sets of detailed rules, but more importantly in the future it will serve the real economy, improve investment and facilitate financial services. In accordance with the risk management framework, the system is the key to financial reform in the free trade zone.

As the free trade zone's separate accounting systems currently operate, what has so far permeated through the second line are mainly services in the real economy (with current account business, credit repayment

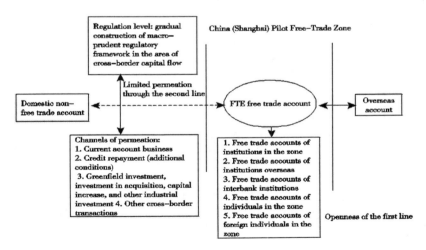

Fig.1 Operation of the separate accounting systems in Shanghai Free Trade Zone

(additional conditions), new investment, mergers and acquisitions, industrial investment, and other cross-border transactions). However exchange business for cross-border investment and financing is of greater significance for the opening up of the economy, and this has not yet been officially incorporated into the system. The core of investment and financing facilitation is complete capital account convertibility. In light of the current global financial conditions, capital account convertibility in China will proceed in a managed, differentiated and gradual way (Table 6.1).

6.3.2 Interest Rate Marketization in the Financial Markets

The essence of interest rate marketization in the financial markets is that interest rates should be determined based on supply and demand factors for the money market, in other words, the market decides the price of capital, ensuring a reasonable capital flow and improved efficiency in the capital utilization ratio. On February 26, 2014, the Shanghai Headquarters of the People's Bank of China issued "Notice on the Interest Rate Upper Limit of Small-amount Foreign Currency Deposit in China (Shanghai) Pilot Free Trade Zone", marking the full liberalization of interest rates by financial institutions in the Shanghai Free Trade Zone, and officiating market deposit rates in the Shanghai FTZ pilot, which will also be gradually extended to the whole city of Shanghai.

These arrangements comply fully with the central bank's strategic deployment of interest rate marketization, that is, "loan before deposit, foreign currency before home currency." The interest rate marketization of small amounts of foreign currency deposits actually accounts for only a very small fraction of the entire interest rate marketization business in the free trade zone, but it plays a leading and exemplary role. The central bank's financial support for the construction of the Shanghai Free Trade Zone shows that the national government's strategy for interest rate marketization is to promote its systematic establishment in the pilot zone according to the degree of maturity of basic related conditions.

Three short-term goals for interest rate marketization in the free trade zone have been suggested: to continuously improve the market-oriented interest rate pricing monitoring mechanism for home and foreign currencies in the free trade accounts of residents and non-residents in the free trade zone; to select excellent financial institutions to issue large amounts of negotiable deposit receipts; and gradually to extend the upper limit of the interest rate for deposits of foreign currencies in small amounts within the free trade zone. China can now be said to be adopting a dual pricing structure for interest rates. This means mechanisms for determining the interest rate within and outside the free trade zone coexist and influence each other (Luo Sumei and Guangyou 2014). The future goal of interest rate marketization in the Chinese financial market is to achieve coordination and consistency between interest rate mechanisms in each free trade zone and the domestic financial market (Table 6.2).

6.3.3 Institutional Innovation of Cross-Border Financing

In its General Plan for Innovation within the Financial System, the State Council aimed to "encourage enterprises to make full use of resources and markets both at home and abroad, to realize liberalization of cross-border financing; to deepen the reform of foreign debt management to facilitate cross-border financing." Compared with the domestic environment, cross-border financing system innovation in the pilot free trade zone has in general terms promoted the liberalization and facilitation of overseas financing for businesses (especially domestic businesses).

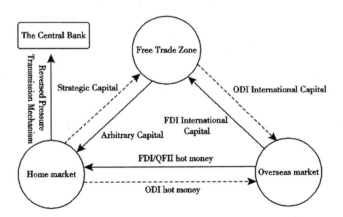

Chart 6.2 Interest rate determination mechanism under dual pricing system. *Source*: Luo Sumei & Zhou Guangyou, The Periodic Characteristics of Interest Rate Marketization: based on the Demand of Shanghai Free Trade Zone, Reform, Issue 10, 2014

At the same time, the design of the cross-border financing system in the free trade zone is closer to marketization than several other regional initiatives in China. This is mainly reflected in the following aspects. First, in the pilot free trade zone, the overseas financing limit is related to contributing capital, and the same standard applies to both domestic and foreign enterprises, which complies with international conventions of fair competition. Second, the leverage ratio of contributing capital and the parameters of macroprudential policy are reflected in the overseas financing quota, which makes it convenient for the central bank to make flexible adjustments according to specific countries' credit ratings and supports the prevention and control of financial risks. Third, institutional initiatives in the pilot free trade zone can be copied throughout the country when the timing is right, so the experiment is of even more significance for the innovation of China's financial system (Table 6.3).

6.3.4 Foreign Exchange Management System Innovation

The establishment of the Shanghai Free Trade Zone provides new opportunities for China to deepen and improve its foreign exchange management system. On February 28, 2014, the Shanghai headquarters of the People's Bank of China issued "Notice on Printing and Distributing the Implementation Rules Supporting the Construction of Foreign Exchange Management in China (Shanghai) Free Trade Zone." Four aspects were to be examined to an unprecedented degree: improving exchange facilitation; streamlining transmission mechanisms for foreign exchange management policy; exploring negative list management; and setting up and improving the macroprudential regulatory system for foreign debt and capital flow. First, on the level of foreign exchange management, enterprises in the free trade zone are encouraged to make effective use of domestic and foreign markets, while cross-border trade and investment is facilitated in the interests of the real economy. Second, reducing administrative checks and approvals in the foreign exchange business integrates and supports trade and economic development. Off-site supervision and on-site verification and examination are strengthened, while inter-departmental joint regulation mechanisms are improved, reducing systemic and regional financial risks (Ma Cuilian 2014). Needless to say, on the whole, the reform of foreign exchange management systems in Shanghai Free Trade Zone has not fully met the requirement of "overall realization of trade and investment

Table 6.3 Comparison of cross-border financing systems in four places around China and evaluation of the cross-border financing system in the pilot free trade zone

Region content	Pilot free trade zone	Suzhou	Shenzhen	Khorgas port
Background	To explore financial system innovation in China	China-Singapore pilot cooperation program	Development and construction of Shenzhen-Hong Kong modern service industry cooperation zone	To promote China-Kazakhstan cooperation and RMB internationalization in Central Asia
Time of start	March 2014	June 2014	December 2012	September 2013
Source of overseas financing	No limitation	Limited to Singapore banking institutions	Limited to Hong Kong banks with RMB business	No limitation
Quota limit of overseas financing	Related to contributed capital and macroprudential policy parameters	Balance management	Balance management	No limitation, not limited by the domestic quota for foreign debt
Direction of financing	Within the zone and overseas	Within Suzhou Industrial Park	Used for the construction and development of Qianhai	Used for project construction in the border cooperation center, overseas project construction, and non-resident trade
Model of popularization	Yes	No	No	No
Overall evaluation of the pilot free trade zone	In respect of overseas financing, a management system that conforms to fair competition principles, international conventions, and the principle of controllable risk has been established; cautionary policy parameters are established by the financing quota limit, which seeks to prevent financial risk; clarifies that replication would be possible with mature timing, making it more meaningful as an experimental initiative in China's financial system			

Note: See Notice of Shanghai Headquarters of People's Bank of China on Supporting China (Shanghai) Pilot Free Trade Zone to Expand Cross-border Use of RMB (Bank Headquarters Issue [2014] No. 22), Interim Measures for the Management of the Pilot Cross-border RMB Innovative Business in Suzhou Industrial Bank, Notice on Printing and Issuing the Interim Measures for the Management of Cross-border RMB Loans in Qianhai (Shenzhen PBC Issue [2012] No. 173), and Management Measures for China Kazakhstan Khorgas International Border Cooperation Center Pilot Cross-border RMB Innovative Business (Urumqi Bank Issue [2013] No. 119) facilitation". The foreign exchange management system innovation pilot should be extended into the areas of foreign exchange for non-trade payments and other capital purposes (Table 6.4).

Table 6.4 Overall evaluation and comparison: The foreign exchange management system within and outside the free trade zone

Core innovation	Non-free trade zone in China	Free trade zone	General Plan's requirement for innovative foreign exchange management system	Breakthrough point and core of further reform
Foreign exchange capital pool	Separate management of membership company accounts	Centralizing operation of capital from domestic member organizations; centralized exchange receipt and payment settlements under current account	Explore international-oriented foreign exchange management reform pilot project, establish foreign exchange management system that fits the condition of free trade zone, realizing trade and investment facilitation	*Breakthrough*: innovative foreign exchange management pilot project centers around requirements for enterprises, especially foreign exchange receipt and payment business under current account. *Aspects of further reform*: there are still gaps between "overall realization of trade and investment facilitation". The foreign exchange management system pilot project initiative should be extended to areas of foreign exchange payment for non-trade purposes and capital account.
Relaxation of debt management	Strict administrative review and approval required for debt management	Debt examination and approval canceled for external guarantee, overseas guarantee payment and overseas financing and lease		

Source: Based on the Notice of SAFE Shanghai Branch on Printing and Distributing the Implementation Rules of Supporting the Construction of Foreign Exchange Management (Shanghai SAFE Issue [2014] No. 26)

6.4 Shanghai Free Trade Zone Financial Regulatory Framework Establishment and Policy Analysis

6.4.1 Building a Macroprudential Regulatory System with Both Macro and Micro Views of Caution Towards Regulation

For a long time, the emphasis in financial regulation in China rested on microprudential regulation focused on quota management. However, with globalization and the expansion of the Chinese economy, especially after the onslaught of the financial crisis which began in the USA in 2008, microprudential regulation became less effective in the prevention of systemic risks. Since the financial crisis, financial reforms in various countries have been directed towards the strengthening of a macroprudential regulatory system. Financial markets are closely intertwined, a crisis in a single financial institution can easily spiral into shocks in the entire financial system, even starting a financial crisis. Financial reforms in Shanghai Free Trade Zone are extremely extensive and include: RMB capital account exchangeability; RMB cross-border use; interest rate marketization; and new foreign exchange management systems Meanwhile the continuing process of financial openness brings a series of challenges for financial market regulation in China.

To ensure the smooth and steady progress of financial reform in the Shanghai Free Trade Zone, the central bank stated its intention of implementing a macroprudential regulatory system in the free trade zone, though specific operational details have yet to be issued. The choice of regulation model has not yet been determined, but fundamental principles of financial regulation are two pillars: the first is the accounts and deals are open and free in FTZ' and the second is the acounts and deals are regulated and controlled out of the FTZ'. The ultimate goal of macroprudential regulation is operability. Macroprudential regulation should be based on microprudential regulation, which relies on a highly effective early warning system to detect risk. As for regulatory bodies, aside from the leading role of "one bank and three commissions", a special macroprudential regulatory agency should be set up in the Shanghai Free Trade Zone to monitor overall risk in the financial market, as well as collecting and analyzing data required by macroprudential regulation. Such an agency would also establish effective targets for macroprudential regulation through a process of model design, pressure tests, etc. (Su Ying 2014).

6.4.2 Improving the Regulation System for Separate Accounting

The establishment of free-trade accounts is the highlight of the Shanghai Free Trade Zone's financial reforms. The official implementation and smooth operation of free trade accounts benefits investment and financing for both enterprises and individuals in the free trade zone. Undeniably, financial risk rises in tandem with financial reform and innovation.

For this reason, when it laid down detailed implementation of the separate accounting system, the central bank also published detailed rules concerning macroprudential risk management for separate accounting. The issue and implementation of the detailed regulation of separate accounting systems for businesses within and outside the free trade zone produced a relatively scientific mechanism for risk assessment, monitoring, and regulation. Although risk monitoring and analysis conforms to international financial regulation standards, various aspects of the separate accounting system will require continuous improvement, including risk assessment, pressure tests, monitoring index system design, and regulation mechanisms.

6.4.3 Regulation of Interest Rate Marketization

The pioneering experiment with interest rate marketization in the free trade zone is in line with China's new steps towards opening up the economy. At the same time, it has had a relatively strong impact on the stability of China's financial markets. It increases risks from exchange rate fluctuations and "hot money" inflow, as well as the risk of bankruptcy of some financial institutions. According to the history of interest rate marketization reform, radical reform coupled with weakening regulation has led to failure when countries had incomplete supporting regulatory policies. Countries that have been relatively successful at interest rate marketization, however, strengthened regulation at an early stage of the reform, combining it with other corresponding regulatory measures later (typical examplesinclude Indonesia and Japan).

In view of this, interest rate marketization reform in our free trade zone should go hand in hand with completion of the regulatory framework. First, large-scale short-term capital arbitrage should be prevented to maintain the safety and stability of the financial market in the free trade zone (large-scale deposit removals and large-scale cross-border capital flow for arbitrage purposes).

Second, the focus of regulation should be the establishment and improvement of the deposit insurance system. A deposit insurance system strengthens against systemic risks that can stem from the bankruptcy of financial institutions or problems arising from their mismanagement (Wang Qian and Ji 2014). Therefore, on November 30, 2014, the Office of Legislative Affairs of the State Council published the Deposit Insurance Regulations (draft for public consultation), marking China's first crucial step towards establishing and improving a deposit insurance system. Finally, supervision should be improved to strengthen process regulation, conduct real-time monitoring of interest rate fluctuations in the banking industry in the free trade zone, and gradually improve liquidity and raise the standard of interest regulations in the monitoring index system.

References

Luo, Sumei, and Guangyou Zhou. 2014. The periodic characteristics of interest rate marketization: Based on the demand of Shanghai Free Trade Zone. *Reform*, Issue 10 pp 28-36.

Pei, Changhong. 2014. The openness scale in the new round from the perspective of global governance based on observation of Shanghai Free Trade Zone. *Reform*, Issue 12 pp 30-40.

Su, Ying. 2014. On the macro-prudenl financial regulatory policies in Shanghai Free Trade Zone. *Political Science and Law Review*, Issue 8 pp 73-81.

Wang, Qian, and Ji Zhang. 2014. A research on the opening of China's financial service industry and issues concerning law and regulation—Based on the analysis of Shanghai Free Trade Zone. *Journal of Shanghai University of International Business and Economics*, Issue 3 pp 27–38.

CHAPTER 7

Shanghai–Hong Kong Stock Connect: Main Characteristics, Strategic Significance, and Regulatory Response

Jianjun Li

7.1 SHANGHAI–HONG KONG STOCK CONNECT: CONCEPT AND MAIN ARRANGEMENT

Shanghai–Hong Kong Stock Connect is the shortened name for "the pilot project of the Shanghai and Hong Kong stock exchange connection mechanism," referring to the technical connection established between Shanghai Stock Exchange (SSE) and Hong Kong Exchanges and Clearing Limited (HKEx) which enables investors on the mainland and in Hong Kong to buy and sell stocks listed on each other's exchange through local securities companies or a prescribed range of brokers. The main arrangements of Shanghai–Hong Kong Stock Connect are as follow:

Jianjun Li has a PhD in Economics, and is a postdoctoral researcher in finance and a special researcher at the CASS Financial Law and Financial Regulation Research Base.

J. Li
Bank of Kunlun, Beijing, China

© The Editor(s) (if applicable) and The Author(s) 2016
B. Hu et al. (eds.), *Development of China's Financial Supervision and Regulation*, DOI 10.1057/978-1-137-52225-2_7

1) transaction structure. There are two parts to Shanghai–Hong Kong Stock Connect : Shanghai Stock Connect and Hong Kong Stock Connect (Fig. 7.1). In Shanghai Stock Connect, Hong Kong investors entrust Hong Kong brokers with a request to SSE to buy and sell stocks listed on SSE within a prescribed range through the securities transaction service company set up by HKEx; this is known as a "northward transaction." In Hong Kong Stock Connect, mainland investors entrust Chinese securities companies with a request to HKEx to buy and sell stocks listed on HKEx within a prescribed range through the securities transaction service company set up by SSE,; this is called a "southward transaction."

2) types of stocks and investment quota. Stocks that investors from the mainland and Hong Kong can buy and sell from each other's market through Shanghai–Hong Kong Stock Connect are limited to a prescribed range.

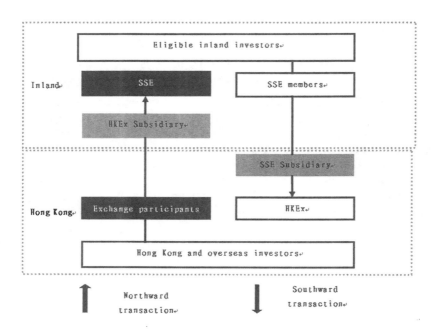

Fig. 7.1 Transaction structure of Shanghai-Hong Kong Stock Connect.
Source: HKEX (HKEX, Hong Kong Exchanges and Clearing Limited. http://www.hkex.com.hk/eng/index.htm)

Specifically, investment targets that mainland investors can consider include HSLI and HSMI constituent stocks and A+H stocks listed on both HKEx and SSE, which number approximately 266 individual stocks in total. Targets that Hong Kong investors can invest in include stocks of SSE 180 Index and SSE 380 Index and A+H stocks listed on SSE, which number approximately 570 individual stocks in total.

At the same time, the Shanghai–Hong Kong Stock Connect is subject to a total quota limit and daily quota limit. The total annual quota of Shanghai Stock Connect is 300 billion yuan, and the daily quota is 13 billion yuan; the total annual quota of Hong Kong Stock Connect is 250 billion yuan, and the daily quota is 10.5 billion yuan. The quota control is based on standards of "net buy-in;" once the quota is used up, the circuit-breaker mechanism will be activated.

3) investor eligibility and currency used in transactions. According to the relevant provision, investors in Hong Kong Connect should be mainland institutional investors, or individual investors whose total balance of securities accounts and capital accounts exceed 500,000 RMB. All overseas institutional investors and individual investors from Hong Kong can be investors in Shanghai Stock Connect.

The Shanghai–Hong Kong Stock Connect adopts RMB settlement for transactions in both directions, i.e. stock transactions made by mainland investors in Hong Kong Stock Connect offering in Hong Kong Dollars are settled in RMB, while stock transactions made by Hong Kong investors in Shanghai Stock Connect are both offered and settled in RMB (Table 7.1).

7.2 Main Features of Shanghai–Hong Kong Stock Connect

1. Shanghai-Hong Kong Stock Connect embodies China's growing economic strength and the principle of mutual benefit.

    There have been several historical attempts to open up China's domestic capital market. However, neither the "Hong Kong Stock Thorough Train" pilot scheme in Tianjin in 2007 nor the subsequent international board made any substantive progress. This time, the successful implementation of Shanghai–Hong Kong Stock Connect is closely related to China's overall economic strength. China has become the second-largest economy in the world, and its standing in the global economy is significant as confidence in its

Table 7.1 Relevant provisions and main arrangements of Shanghai-Hong Kong Stock Connect

	Shanghai Stock Connect	Hong Kong Stock Connect
Investment object	SSE 180 Index constituent stocks	HSLI
	SSE 380 Index constituent stocks	HSMI constituent stocks
	A + H stocks	A + H stocks
Numbers of stocks involved	Approximately 570 individual stocks	Approximately 266 individual stocks
Total quota	300 billion yuan RMB	250 billion yuan RMB
Daily quota	13 billion yuan RMB	10.5 billion yuan RMB
Investor eligibility	Hong Kong and overseas institutional and individual investors	Mainland institutional investors and eligible individual investors (whose securities accounts and capital accounts with total balance of no less than 500 thousand yuan RMB)
Transaction currency	RMB quotation and settlement	Hong Kong Dollar quotation and RMB settlement

Source: Data collected by the author

market grows. As China pushes ahead with financial reform, RMB exchange rate marketization is making significant progress with more fluctuation on both the mainland and Hong Kong. The RMB is gaining recognition in the global market, and interest rate liberalization has also hit milestones. China's foreign exchange reserve is approaching 4 trillion USD, further strengthening its ability to resist the impact of financial shocks. All these factors combined to allow a smooth implementation and a solid foundation for the Shanghai–Hong Kong Stock Connect.

Shanghai–Hong Kong Stock Connect drew on lessons from "Hong Kong Stock Thorough Train" and the international board. The program started with cooperating and sharing, to avoid resource competition. The mutual investment by mainland and Hong Kong investors in each other's stock market will not only help to eliminate the doldrums seen in the mainland stock market, but also benefits the revitalization of the Hong Kong stock market, creating a win–win situation for both sides.

2. Shanghai–Hong Kong Stock Connect is an innovative breakthrough in institutional cross-border capital flow arrangements

As an institutional arrangement for cross-border capital flow, Shanghai–Hong Kong Stock Connect shares certain similarities with previously launched QFII, QDII, and RQFII systems, all being special arrangements intended to enhance forms of cross-border investment and increase capital market openness in a Chinese landscape where capital accounts were previously less open. However, the Shanghai–Hong Kong Stock Connect has achieved breakthrough and innovation in three respects (Table 7.2), in comparison with QFII.

First, when it comes to the cross-border capital management method, Shanghai–Hong Kong Stock Connect uses a "closed-loop operation" requiring that capital gained from the sale of securities cannot remain in the local market but should return to its originating account. Such "channelization" management of cross-border capital allows the Shanghai–Hong Kong Stock Connect to maintain a balance in its capital account opening and control over cross-border capital liquidity risk.

Second, the Shanghai–Hong Kong Stock Connect lays more emphasis on the flow of communication and capital in the market. On the one hand, mainland investors can invest in the Hong Kong stock market via "Hong Kong Stock Connect"; on the other hand, Hong Kong investors can invest in the mainland stock market via "Shanghai Stock Connect." This facilitates the opening of China's

Table 7.2 Comparison of Shanghai-Hong Kong Stock Connect and QFII/QDII/RQFII

	Shanghai-Hong Kong Stock Connect	*QFII/QDII/RQFII*
Business carrier	Exchanges in Shanghai and Hong Kong	Assets management company
Investor	Free, direct investment	Indirect investment relying on assets management company
Investment direction	Bilateral investment	Unilateral investment
Mode of management	Closed-loop operation allowing no capital to remain at the local destination of investment	Capital can remain at the local destination of investment

Source: Data collected by the author

capital market from both directions and is an unprecedented institutional design for the opening up of the securities market.

Third, clearing and settlements are handled in domestic currency. This applies to both mainland investors and Hong Kong investors buying and selling stocks via Shanghai–Hong Kong Stock Connect. Only RMB is used for clearing and settlement in the cross-border capital flow. With RMB as the sole currency in the cross-border capital transactions, the market is effectively enacting capital market internationalization and currency internationalization.

3. The market impact of a relatively seismic reform

Shanghai–Hong Kong Stock Connect is not a small-scale pilot reform project. From the perspective of either breadth of participation or market depth, its reform efforts are fairly substantial. Compared with the institutional arrangements for QFII which set limits on investor eligibility and market access, the Shanghai–Hong Kong Stock Connect expands the range of participants by eliminating conditions for institutional investors and allowing individual investors to participate.

As to quota limits, at present the Shanghai Stock Connect allows a total investment quota of 300 billion yuan RMB to enter the mainland stock market, amounting to one-fifth of the current limit for QFII which is 216 billion USD, but equivalent to the actual volume for QFII and RQFII (Fig. 7.2). The investment quota in the Hong Kong stock market via Hong Kong Stock Connect is 250 billion yuan RMB, close to about 50% of the current volume for QDII (Fig. 7.2). As for transaction volume, Shanghai Stock Connect allows 13 billion yuan RMB to enter the mainland stock market on a daily basis, equivalent to 14% of the average daily transaction volume in the Shanghai stock market. Hong Kong Stock Connect allows 10.5 billion yuan RMB to enter the Hong Kong stock market on a daily basis, equivalent to 20% of the average daily transaction volume in the Hong Kong stock market. When it comes to stock investing levels, market values of stocks available in Shanghai–Hong Kong Stock Connect are 90% and 82% of the total values of the Shanghai and Hong Kong stock markets respectively. The Shanghai–Hong Kong Stock Connect wields a certain influence on the capital markets of both the mainland and Hong Kong.

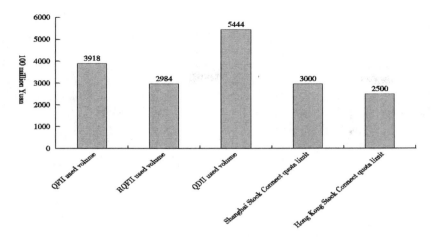

Fig. 7.2 The quota limits of Shanghai-Hong Kong Stock Connect are close to QFII volumes, etc.
Source: WIND

7.3 THE STRATEGIC SIGNIFICANCE OF SHANGHAI–HONG KONG STOCK CONNECT

Since the Shanghai–Hong Kong Stock Connect began, apart from the opening day of Shanghai Stock Connect when the daily investment quota limit was exceeded, both Shanghai Stock Connect and Hong Kong Stock Connect have had large surpluses way below the daily transaction quota. By the end of 2014, the Hong Kong Stock Connect had only utilized less than 5% of the total quota limit; while Shanghai Stock Connect has a relatively higher utilization ratio, it transacted no more than 25% of the total quota limit. Market activity was much lower than expected. Reasons attributed are the following short-term market factors: differences between the Shanghai and Hong Kong stock markets in terms of investment transaction conventions, laws and regulations, etc.; and need for investors to be familiar with a new open market narrowing its differences in valuation and short-term arbitrage.

Even so, we must realize that Shanghai–Hong Kong Stock Connect is not a short-term measure to stimulate the market, but a major political initiative. It is intended to comprehensively deepen reform in China's capital markets from a macro-economic perspective. It would be misleading to think about major reform initiatives in terms of their short-term effects. To understand the importance of this reform a long-term overall perspective is required.

To sum up, Shanghai–Hong Kong Stock Connect is an important and unprecedented institutional change in the capital market; it has achieved the facilitation of a convenient working operation and controllable risk in an investment securities landscape that previously had no convertibility. This is of significant and far-reaching impact.

7.3.1 An Important Link in China's Deepening Financial Reform

The opening of capital markets and securities markets has always been a major step in a country's financial internationalization progress towards economic globalization. Objectively speaking, the degree of internationalization of a country or a region's securities market reflects the actual level of development of its financial industry, an important manifestation of the integration of its economy and financial institutions into the global system. The internationalization of the securities market facilitates the internationalization of financial institutions and businesses and the standardization of the financial market of a country or a region, and contributes to the improvement of market regulation and legal systems that not only promote global competitiveness and development of the country's securities market, but also enable the country's enterprises to raise capital at a lower cost. Enterprises are helped to raise their global competitiveness and this favors the economic development of the nation.

There were two important stages of internationalization in the market during the latter part of the last century. The first occurred in the early 1970s when the Bretton Woods system came to an end. To counter the global dollar crisis, developed countries abolished restrictive measures on interest rates, loan limits, and securities investment limits to allow the private sector to better withstand the financial crisis. For this reason, many developed countries completed the process of opening their securities market before the mid-1980s. In the late 1980s, along with the rise of global financial liberalization, emerging economies also opened their securities markets one after another, welcoming the challenge of globalization.

However, unlike the mechanisms of developed countries such as the USA and the UK, the opening of Shanghai–Hong Kong Stock Connect means that China chose to gradually open as befitted its stage of development: though overseas investors are allowed to hold, buy and sell stocks in China's listed companies, there are limits on investor eligibility, size of investment, investment objective and so on which can be gradually lifted should the timing be appropriate to achieve the opening of the securities market. Learning from international experience, emerging markets including South Korea, India, Brazil and Taiwan have adopted similar strategies towards financial openness with relatively positive results.

Shanghai–Hong Kong Stock Connect can be described as a special arrangement which aims to further enrich overseas forms of investment and enhance the degree of the opening of the capital market under China's current capital account model, which is not as yet completely open. Its successful opening not only enables investors from the mainland and Hong Kong to buy stocks from the other side, but also plays a significant exploratory role, testing the waters in the current stages of China's financial reform.

7.3.2 Favoring the Deepening of Reform and Opening of the Domestic Capital Market

In recent years, China has carried out a series of reforms in the capital market with certain outcomes, but it still lags behind those of mature capital markets. Since the launch of Shanghai–Hong Kong Stock Connect, the connection has facilitated the integration of domestic and overseas markets. This opening up accelerates capital market reform and provides new stimulus for the financial sector to develop institutionalization, standardization, and marketization.

First, it stimulates activity in the mainland stock market and promotes the steady development of the whole market. Hong Kong's unique position as a global financial center lies behind the influence of Shanghai–Hong Kong Stock Connect. The range of overseas investors is very broad, including both local investors in Hong Kong and investors from all over the world, both individuals and various institutional investors. Therefore, the capital inflow brought by Shanghai–Hong Kong Stock Connect comes not only from the Hong Kong market but also from overseas. It will certainly introduce a large quantity of long-term, low-priced investment funds and will stimulate a surge in trading volumes in the mainland stock market.

Meanwhile, Shanghai–Hong Kong Stock Connect also favors the creation and development of new financial products in the mainland capital market. At present, the mainland stock market functions mainly as a spot market. Only one derivative was rolled out from the CSI 300 stock index futures. On the other hand, the Hong Kong securities market has a more complete and richer product system which includes not only stocks but also structured products, derivative warrants, callable bull/bear contracts, equity-linked notes, futures and share options, etc. When the two markets are connected, the differences between them will help accelerate the reform and innovation of the mainland capital market and the promotion of products including ETF futures, revitalizing the inland capital market and making it more competitive.

Second, it speeds up the process of internationalization in the domestic capital market. The Hong Kong capital market is a completely open and international mature market with a complete legal system and rules of market conduct. It has also established the foundations of market credit and a market culture. From capital, talent, information and rules, Hong Kong is able to connect to markets across the world. The Hong Kong market is a window for mainland investors, and global investors can be introduced to the mainland via the Hong Kong market. This promotes exchange and information sharing between the domestic and overseas markets. It also helps the domestic market establish laws and regulations that conform to international standards, and accelerates the internationalization of the domestic capital market, raising the impact of its global influence.

Third, it helps improve investment philosophy in the mainland capital market towards maturity and reason. In recent years, the investment philosophy of the mainland stock market was one of short-term speculation. This runs counter to the philosophy in the capital markets which stresses value creation and long-term investment.

In contrast, the Hong Kong stock market is a relatively mature investment market which stresses value investment. Different stock market philosophies are closely related to investor structures. The mainland stock market is still dominated by retail investors, with institutional investors comprising less than 20% of the market. Hence the strong culture of short-term speculation. Meanwhile 80% of the Hong Kong stock market consists of institutional investors, who hold a more mature investment philosophy and value longer-term investments. The launch of Shanghai–Hong Kong Stock Connect will undoubtedly boost foreign investment in the mainland capital market, expand the scale of institutional investors in the mainland capital market, optimize investor structure, drive transformation toward a market investment philosophy, and tame excessive speculation on the market. In the long term, it will facilitate the formation of a value investment philosophy and improve the transaction skills of investors.

Fourth, it is favorable to the development of corporate governance and a more standardized market. More overseas investors entering the market is likely to also mean that many of them will make suggestions as to cash flow management, corporate governance, and related-party transactions in listed companies. Though these overseas investors may not necessarily be large stock holders, their proposals can drive corporate governance, market regulation transparency, further restrictions on related parties and large shareholders, protection of small shareholders, etc., which to some degree can promote the standardization of development and governance of China's stock market and listed companies.

Fifth, it favors the recovery in the value of A shares. In the past, the Shanghai and Hong Kong markets could realize domestic and overseas investment through QFII of QDII, but due to various restrictions, the two markets are in fact divided from each other, so the pricing of A shares and H share in an A + H share are not the same. The opening of Shanghai–Hong Kong Stock Connect integrates the two markets which will encourage consistent stock valuations within the same company or comparable companies in Shanghai and Hong Kong. It especially favors blue chips on the A share market "revising discounts upwards and revising premiums downwards" to support the stock valuations of A shares.

Sixth, investors can make diversified investments. It was always the case that domestic mainland investors could only invest in limited financial products, so the Shanghai–Hong Kong Stock Connect opens up more investment options and greatly expands their investment channels. Domestic investors can allocate both their domestic and overseas stocks and financial assets. This provides a diversified tool for wealth management and new channels for asset safety protection and value preservation.

7.3.3 Further Exploration of Capital Account Opening

China's capital account opening is a major part of the country's financial reform. According to the experience of other countries, the opening of the capital account carries a high risk. Mismanagement of the capital account opening will inject serious financial risk or even cause a financial crisis.

Though China has opened its current account for a long time, the opening of the capital account has been occurring only slowly over the past decade. Currently, QFII and QDII are the only channels allowed between domestic and overseas financial markets. With the Shanghai–Hong Kong Stock Connect, individuals can invest in overseas securities, opening a new door for the RMB to flow freely at home and abroad.

The daily upper limit of 20,000 yuan for RMB exchange per Hong Kong resident was abolished to support the opening of Shanghai–Hong Kong Stock Connect, breaking down the RMB exchange barriers. That is to say, the operation of converting RMB and HK dollars in the Hong Kong market has become the same as international currencies such as the USD and the euro, and is free of special limitations. The RMB is now completely exchangeable in Hong Kong. Besides, since a large amount of offshore RMB in markets other than Hong Kong is also seeking proper investment channels, the special channel of the Shanghai–Hong Kong Stock Connect enables a large quantity of offshore RMB held by overseas investors to enter the domestic capital market, which is of marked significance in promoting the opening of the capital account.

7.3.4 Significant Support for RMB Internationalization

There has been important progress in international settlements made in RMB in the last few years. In the first ten months of 2014, the figure for RMB settlements in cross-border trades hit 5.4 trillion yuan, the number of overseas banks providing RMB payment and settlements exceeded 2,000, and offshore RMB centers were successively established in, among other places, Hong Kong, Singapore, London and Luxembourg. A report by the Bank of International Settlements (BIS) reveals that the RMB become one of the Top Ten active currencies in global foreign exchange market transactions, jumping from seventeenth place in 2010 to seventh currently. As RMB gains recognition in international markets gradually and its scale expands overseas, broadening the scope of RMB investment transactions in the financial market becomes a key step towards RMB internationalization.

To a certain degree, expectations of steady RMB appreciation favored the early stages of RMB internationalization. However if RMB internationalization depends simply on dividends made from RMB appreciation, more arbitrary and speculative measures will occur in the market, and this is unsustainable. In 2012, for example, as the European debt crisis deepened and China registered dismal foreign trade figures, speculators expected the RMB to depreciate. That led to a slowdown in the scale of overseas RMB growth. That same year, RMB deposits in Hong Kong stood at 602.9 billion yuan, an increase of 14.4 billion yuan on the previous year. That compared to an increase in 2011 of 273.6 billion yuan, an amount roughly nineteen times that of 14.4 billion. RMB deposit growth in Hong Kong in recent years has shown a downward trend in both the scale and speed of growth, reflecting the challenges faced by overseas investors holding and using RMB.

Presently, as exchange rate marketization reform deepens, with the RMB at an equilibrium exchange rate, the trends in fluctuations on both sides are gradually being established. The main driver for overseas investors holding RMB currency is no longer an anticipation of its appreciation. Currently, the QFII mechanism also has certain shortcomings, with such an inconvenient transaction system (limitations on eligible institutional investors, 3-month or 1-year capital lock-up periods, designated domestic bank trusteeship, free exchange) that it is difficult for capital from overseas to be allocated to the Chinese market, resulting in a relatively small proportion of Chinese assets in their global portfolio allocation. According to PBC's (2014) research, in mid-2013, financial assets valued in RMB available to overseas investors were worth 250 billion USD, accounting for only 0.1% of the global capital market, and falling far behind the 55 trillions' worth of USD financial assets for global investment.

The continuing advance of RMB internationalization also requires new avenues for overseas investors to invest or use their RMB. The Shanghai–Hong Kong Stock Connect creates an innovative breakthrough in return mechanisms for RMB, opens up circulation channels for domestic and offshore RMB markets, and encourages global investors to utilize RMB and invest in RMB products. More importantly, we have also found that the Shanghai–Hong Kong Stock Connect establishes an RMB circulation cycle based on financial investment, i.e., capital circulation whereby RMB goes out via Shanghai Stock Connect lands in an offshore market, and returns via Hong Kong Stock Connect. The establishment of this circulation channel will definitely encourage more market entities to use and hold RMB as part of the goal of promoting RMB internationalization (Fig. 7.3).

7.3.5 Promotes the Profile of Shanghai and Hong Kong as International Financial Centers

As the two most influential financial centers in China, Shanghai and Hong Kong play important roles in the economic development of the country.

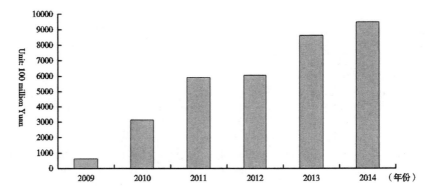

Fig. 7.3 RMB deposit scale in Hong Kong.
Source: WIND

For a long time, Shanghai and Hong Kong cooperated well in the area of finance. The opening of the Shanghai–Hong Kong Stock Connect business marks a new stage in cooperation between the two financial markets. The Hong Kong market is relatively more mature and open, with more international investors, as well as more legal and regulatory frameworks. The mainland market economy is on a larger scale, with the potential to tap large demands for capital market financing, richer resources for IPO, and large demands for investment and money management, owing to and supported by the high savings ratio of mainland residents. Therefore, the launch of Shanghai–Hong Kong Stock Connect plays an important role in strengthening the cooperation of the Shanghai and Hong Kong financial markets and elevating their positions as international financial centers in the long run.

It will contribute to accelerating the construction of Shanghai's international financial center. Under the 12th Five-year Plan, Shanghai needs to begin the building of an international financial center in 2015. The city has to strive to establish its position as a global center for RMB product innovation, transaction, pricing, and settlement. However, with limitations in terms of an incomplete market mechanism, underdeveloped innovation capacity, and insufficient degree of openness, the Shanghai international financial center will be unable to meet the development objective. In addition, many institutional investors are still lagging behind, with a great deal of room for improvement in resource allocation, competitiveness, influence, and degree of financial internationalization. The launch of Shanghai–Hong Kong Stock Connect will greatly improve the internationalization level and overall quality of the Shanghai capital market when it comes to accelerating RMB internationalization, promoting international development of the capital market, facilitating cross-border capital flow, and improving investor structure, thus contributing to the construction of the Shanghai financial center.

It also helps reinforce and elevate Hong Kong's position as an international financial center. As a major constituent of the economy, the stock market contributes 16% of Hong Kong's GDP. As the economy develops and wealth increases on the mainland, the demand for financial investment also gradually increases among residents, with Hong Kong as an important overseas investment market for mainland investors. The launch of Shanghai–Hong Kong Stock Connect enables mainland investors to enter the Hong Kong market more easily and efficiently, injecting new capital into the entire Hong Kong market. This will significantly improve market transaction volume and activity, offer more opportunities for business expansion to securities traders, funds, and other financial institutions in Hong Kong, and thus magnify the overall economic and financial strength of Hong Kong. The launch of Shanghai–Hong Kong Stock Connect will also reinforce Hong Kong's position as an RMB offshore market. Since RMB is used in transactions, the Shanghai–Hong Kong Stock Connect will further expand the usage of offshore RMB in Hong Kong, enlarge the RMB capital pool, promote the development of RMB business in Hong Kong, and reinforce and enhance Hong Kong's position as the largest RMB offshore business center in the world.

7.4 Suggestions for the Regulatory Framework and Response for Shanghai–Hong Kong Stock Connect

The ultimate goal of the Shanghai–Hong Kong Stock Connect is to have a long-term institutional arrangement that will connect both capital markets and lead to mutual prosperity. The bilateral connection mechanism, however, means that the mainland stock market has to tackle challenges arising from international rules. At the same time, cross-border capital flow also implies potential risk. Therefore, the steady development of Shanghai–Hong Kong Stock Connect requires close cooperation by governments and regulatory departments of the two markets to continuously improve institutional arrangement, laws and regulation, as well as bridging gaps in regulation and controlling risks.

7.4.1 Regulatory Framework of Shanghai–Hong Kong Stock Connect

To counter possible risks from the opening of Shanghai–Hong Kong Stock Connect, regulatory departments in the mainland and Hong Kong have already made suitable arrangements in the design of their institutional framework in three principal respects:

First, the transaction mechanism benefits a steady market operation. In the design of the Shanghai–Hong Kong Stock Connect mechanism, the regulatory departments have already considered possible risks and made arrangements accordingly. Objects selected for transaction are all of above-average market quality in terms of value creation, corporate governance, and liquidity, which reduces the risk of stock selection. Meanwhile, the Securities and Futures Commission of Hong Kong has limited domestic investors participating in Hong Kong Stock Connect to institutional investors and individual investors whose securities accounts and capital accounts total at least 500,000 yuan, as the Hong Kong market has always been dominated by institutional investors. These requirements limit Shanghai–Hong Kong Stock Connect participants to institutional investors with professional experience and non-retail individual investors, avoiding speculation by retail investors and reducing the risk of fluctuations in the capital market.

Second, transaction methods are convenient for real-time surveillance. Shanghai–Hong Kong Stock Connect relies on Shanghai Stock Exchange and Hong Kong Exchanges and Clearing Limited as business carriers to establish mutual market connections. All order requests for Hong Kong Stock Connect in the Shanghai stock market are gathered at SSE and then sent to HKEx. Equally, all order requests for Shanghai Stock Connect in the Hong Kong market are gathered at HKEx and then sent to SSE. Because all transactions must be gathered at the two exchanges, both exchanges and regulatory authorities can conduct real-time surveillance of investors' participation in Shanghai–Hong Kong Stock Connect and the cross-border flow of RMB. Should any abnormality occur in Shanghai–Hong Kong Stock Connect transactions, both the Shanghai and Hong Kong exchanges can act quickly for effective regulation.

Third, the regulation method facilitates risk control. To manage cross-border capital flow, the regulatory departments adopt an enclosed management mode, that is, capital earned from selling securities must be returned to its source and cannot be retained in the local market. This means cross-border capital can only be used to buy financial assets; the "enclosed circulation" of this investment path minimizes the threat of short-term international speculative capital. It alleviates threats to China's financial system and economic stability and guarantees order in cross-border RMB flow and controllability of risks.

In addition, regulatory departments from the mainland and Hong Kong have signed a "Cooperation Memo of the CSRC and the SFC on Strengthening Regulation and Law Enforcement under the Shanghai–Hong Kong Stock Connect Program," which stipulates arrangements for cross-border law enforcement regarding regulatory objects, investor rights and interests protection, emergency mechanisms for abnormal condition, etc. (Table 7.3).

The establishment of the above regulatory measures, mechanisms and systems marks the establishment of the regulatory framework of Shanghai–Hong Kong Stock Connect. To some extent, restrictions are imposed to circumvent various risks introduced into the domestic financial market and investors; they provide certain guarantees for the steady and efficient operation of Shanghai–Hong Kong Stock Connect.

7.4.2 Potential Risks Facing Shanghai–Hong Kong Stock Connect and Suggestions for Its Regulation

As a new initiative, Shanghai–Hong Kong Stock Connect will inevitably face certain unpredictable risks during its operation, which requires the regulatory authority to pay close attention and activate appropriate counter-measures.

First, the regulatory authority should continue to pay attention to risks incurred by cross-border capital flow. The Shanghai–Hong Kong Stock Connect has enclosed cross-border capital management; it is not a perfect capital flow control system and faces some operational difficulties. This is because, in China's experience of capital control, there has been

Table 7.3 Cooperative regulation in Shanghai-Hong Kong Stock Connect

	Content
Regulatory object	The regulatory object includes listed companies, securities companies, and SPV. Listed companies: they are regulated according to principles at the place where they are listed. Securities companies: by principle, they are regulated by the regulator at the place where they held licenses. Overseas regulators can also supervise their cross-border transactions. SPV: they are regulated by local regulator.
Investor protection	Investor protection follows the principles of transaction locality. Investors should be protected by the market which they have invested in. Civil procedure law concerning foreign affairs can be abided by, and legal proceedings of civil compensation can be initiated in the court with jurisdiction.
Response to abnormality	Dual regulation of the transaction amount and the price reduces the possibilities of abnormal occurrence such as "fat finger".

Source: CSRC

large-scale capital inflow and outflow whenever there were opportunities for arbitrage. More significantly, the QFII, QDII, and RQFII quotas of some institutions have yet to be used up. The "bilateral investment" mechanism for domestic and overseas capital in the Shanghai Free Trade Zone might also bear similarities to the Shanghai–Hong Kong Stock Connect, which might be popularized to more free trade zones in the future, ultimately presenting multiple outgoing investment channels and capital flow channels and creating cross-border capital flow risk. For this reason, there should be a general arrangement for the bilateral investment of domestic and overseas capital to prevent new financial risks arising from "channel scrambling" around the country. The "enclosed circulation" design does not mean that monitoring and regulation of capital should be relaxed.

For this reason, cross-border regulation cooperation should continue to be deepened. On the international level, cooperation needs to be strengthened not only between regulatory departments on the mainland and in Hong Kong but also with other countries so as to expand the scope of inter-regional and international financial regulation cooperation and the joint monitoring of international capital flow. On the domestic front, close cooperation between the central bank or People's

Bank of China, the CSRC, and relevant financial institutions is required for data monitoring, analyzing RMB outflow and inflow, and to make timely policy adjustments in response to abnormal changes, so as to avoid the negative consequences of international speculative activity.

Second, reform of the transaction system should be accelerated to conform to international practice. There are considerable differences in terms of current transaction rules, laws and regulations, regulatory systems, etc. between the Shanghai and Hong Kong markets. For example, at present the Shanghai Stock Exchange and Shenzhen stock exchange adopt the T+1 transaction system for stocks and funds and set the limit at 10% up or down, while capital markets internationally do not impose such limits. The H stock transaction system on the Hong Kong market is also T+0. The differences between systems in the various capital markets may lead to contradiction and risks. To achieve a better connection with the international capital market, precautionary measures must be taken, including research and institutional innovation to improve the regulatory system.

Third, regulatory cooperation needs to be strengthened. Currently, the Shanghai–Hong Kong Stock Connect stresses the principle of "localized" regulation: when investors are in the opposite market, they must comply with the transaction rules and practices and be protected under the regulations of that market. However, for day-to-day transactions, it is hard to determine whether it is the mainland or Hong Kong that takes responsibility for regulation. In cross-border investment transactions, once illegal activity such as false statements, insider trading, or market manipulation surfaces, cross-border law enforcement cooperation intended to ensure the compliance of entities subject to regulation can introduce complexities for the parties.

To improve the efficiency of joint regulation, some key issues should be clarified: whether the regulatory department of the other side should totally recognize such measures and decisions; whether authentication is required before recognition;and how to deal with legal risks when the regulatory department of one side makes disciplinary decisions concerning a market entity from the other side. Meanwhile, specific cross-border regulation and law enforcement measures should be issued. The regulatory department should also consider the differences between the two markets in terms of laws and regulations, listing rules, transaction rules, and so on, in order to educate investors and protect their rights and interests.

Fourth, due attention needs to be paid to the risk of large fluctuations in the capital market. The opening of the global financial capital market, especially the stock market, usually involves large market fluctuations in the early stages, with a certain impact on and risks to the stability of the financial market. The regulatory department should step up the monitoring of the stock market and guard against such large fluctuations that can impact negatively on its economy and the financial sector generally.

References

People's Bank of China (PBC), 2014. The report of RMB Internationalization. July 2014.

CHAPTER 8

Stock-Issue Registration System Reform: International Experience and China's Choice

Limei Wan

The general purpose of the construction of capital market systems put forward in Premier Li Keqiang's report of March 5, 2014 is to "speed up multi-level capital markets and promote the reform of the stock-issue registration system." Most noteworthy in the report is the reform of the stock-issue registration system. Following the Third Plenary Session of the 18th Central Committee, another "top-design" policy to promote the IPO registration system was set out, following which numerous financial reform proposals have appeared on the agenda.

In an interview at the Review Conference of the Anhui Delegation of National People's Congress on March 5 2014, Xiao Gang, Chairman of the China Securities Regulatory Commission (CSRC), stated that the implementation plan for the registration system reform would be completed in 2014. The State Council has apparently set up a special team for this task, with the CSRC leading relevant ministries. A detailed pre-

---

Wan Limei, Ph.D. of Management, Institute of Finance and Banking, Chinese Academy of Social Sciences.

L. Wan
China Securities Regulatory Commission, Beijing, China

© The Editor(s) (if applicable) and The Author(s) 2016
B. Hu et al. (eds.), *Development of China's Financial Supervision and Regulation*, DOI 10.1057/978-1-137-52225-2_8

liminary plan for a Chinese-style registration system may be submitted for discussion in the middle of 2014, which implies that reform of the system is drawing closer. However, due to the legal conflict with the Securities Law and the huge fluctuation happened in June-July 2015, the registration system was delayed twice. Till March 2016, the plan is still suspended.

China has much to learn from the registration system practices of other countries. According to traditional theories of verification and registration systems, countries such as the USA, Japan, and Taiwan mostly follow the stock and IPO registration system, and enterprises can be listed on the stock market so long as they meet the requirements for listed companies and fully disclose the information required by law, while regulatory institutions only play a supervisory role. The UK, France, Switzerland and some emerging economies like China, Hong Kong, the Philippines, and other Southeast Asian countries adopt a verification system or a similar system where verification by regulatory institutions plays a decisive role.

However, a deeper analysis of the UK's and Hong Kong's issue systems shows that under the verification system, their stock-issues still rely on disclosure of information enabling market participants to make value judgments and undertake risk assessment—in effect a registration system. This chapter will examine the new stock-issue systems of various countries and regions around the world, with the aim of learning lessons that will benefit the reform of China's registration system.

8.1 The History of Chinese Stock-issue System Reforms

Since 1994, China has conducted several experimental rounds of reform of its stock-issue system. The review system has evolved from local approval through quota management, target management, and channel systems to the current sponsor system. The two phases of "quota management" and "target management" were included in the review. And the "channel system" and "sponsor system" were part of the approval system.

8.1.1 The Approval System Period

China's securities market was established during a unique period which historically marked the transition from a planned economy to a market economy. It was a time of immature issuers, intermediaries, and investors, and the market was unable to price in all its functions. Therefore in the early stages, regulation of stock-issue clearly showed some characteristics of a heavily planned economy.

8.1.1.1 The "Quota Management" Phase (1993–1995)

For issue of stock under the approval system, the Securities Commission of the State Council would decide annually on the total volume of stock issue (quota or target) according to the country's macro-economic circumstances and market forces. A planning commission would issue an overall quota, approved by the State Council, to each administrative region, municipality, and municipality with independent planning status, as well as to relevant ministries and commissions. Provincial governments, ministries and commissions recommended selected enterprises for examination and approval by the CSRC. During this process, the enterprise was vetted and due diligence carried out to evaluate and arrange the scale, price, method and timing of the stock issue.

8.1.1.2 The "Target Management" Phase (1996–2000)

The stock-issue framework was established in 1996 by the State Planning Commission and Securities Commission. Stock was issued to each provincial government and industrial administrative department based on market conditions and in accordance with CSRC guidelines. Following recommendation by the provincial government or industrial administrative department, companies that meet the requirements of the CSRC were then eligible for the issue of shares and to have their records audited. In 1997, a procedure whereby pre-selection materials were examined was added, during which the CSRC vetted companies recommended by local government or competent administrative departments in charge of central enterprises. Thus the previous practice of local recommendation and approval at two administrative levels was changed and the process of pre-examination of enterprises began.

8.1.2 The "Verification System" Period

The approval system had played an active role in the development of the capital market, but it did not help to improve its efficiency because of lack of clarity on the role of market participants. The verification system that took effect from 2001 represented a breakthrough on, for example, price, methods of issue, and types of companies and industries that would go public.

8.1.2.1 The "Channel System" Phase (2001–2004)

Under the channel system, the regulatory department directly determined the number of channels for each securities company based on their strength and performance. The "channel system" changed the practice of selecting and recommending issuers by administrative methods, diluted the strength of stock-issues, and increased the transparency of stock-issue regulation. It required lead underwriters to assume some of the risk of stock issues and gave them the power to select and recommend stock issuers. In addition, to some extent, with the abolition of targets and quotas the channel system resolved the conflict and incompatibility between the large number of issuing companies and the limited market capacity.

8.1.2.2 The "Sponsor System" Phase (2004–Present)

The key point of the sponsor system is to clarify the responsibilities of sponsoring institutions, the responsibilities of its representatives and the establishment of accountability mechanisms. Compared with the channel system, the sponsor system has broadened the scope of the liabilities that the sponsor had to undertake during the IPO process.

Global stock markets contain three main kinds of issue systems: approval systems, verification systems, and registration systems, each of which is appropriate to a particular level of market development. The approval system is suitable for a completely planned issue, the verification system operates during the transition from the approval system to the registration system, and the registration system is widely adopted in mature stock markets. The goal of whichever system is in place is to protect the rights and interests of investors and give due consideration to the financing rights of issuers. This in turn works towards realizing a freely operated, stable capital market. It also facilitates the development of the economy. The stock-issue system should therefore change and evolve to accommodate the requirements of the market as it develops and matures (Table 8.1).

With the formal release of the "Opinion on Further Promoting the Reform of New Share Issue Systems" on November 30, 2013, the stock-issue system in China has taken on characteristics of both verification and registration systems. The registration system will be the future direction for the reform of China's stock-issue system. Its suits the requirements of market mechanisms; it can also keep pace with the acceleration of securities marketization in China and with the basic principles of stock-issue system reform decided by the Third Plenary Session of the 18th Central Committee. The registration system is already widely employed and plays

Table 8.1 Examples of three kinds of issue systems

Examination system for stock-issue	Representative countries
Approval system	China (before 1999)
Verification system	The UK, Germany, Hong Kong, Taiwan (before 2006), China (from 2001)
Registration system	The USA, Japan, Taiwan (from 2006)

Source: Public data

an important role in mature securities markets such as the USA, Japan, and Taiwan. The lessons that China can learn from mature markets in this respect will benefit the development of a stable, risk-assessed capital market, as well as the country's economic progress.

8.2 International Experience and Lessons of the Registration System

The stock-issue and IPO mechanisms within a particular country or jurisdiction often suit the context in terms of the historical background or phase of development. Therefore not all markets will have the same characteristics when it comes to audit and operational procedures. The USA operates the most typical type of registration system.

8.2.1 American Stock-issue Registration System

The American registration system is based on a management system defined by law. The Securities Act of 1933 clearly states that information disclosure underlies the registration system for stock issues. Supervision and regulation of stock issues and public listing are under the purview of the federal government, state government, and industrial self-regulation associations. These three levels manage the efficient operation of the registration system, providing institutional guarantees and a legal basis for the system (Table 8.2).

It took more than a century for the American centralized legislation system to come to fruition, and in its early stages, the securities market came under a generally loose administration. The American registration system, which should be viewed as part of the entire securities regulatory

Table 8.2 The three-level legal system in the USA

Three levels	Four kinds of laws and regulations
Centralized administration of the federal government	*Basic laws on securities* Securities Act of 1933 Securities Exchange Act of 1934 Securities Act Amendment of 1965 Securities Act Amendment of 1975 Securities Act Amendment of 2005 *Supporting laws* Public Utility Holding Company Act of 1935 Trust Indenture Act of 1939 Investment Company Act of 1940
Local state administration	*Stock-issue and exchange activity-related laws and regulations*
Industrial self-regulation	Rules and regulations of New York Stock Exchange Regulatory systems of National Association of Securities Dealers

Source: Shenyin and Wanguo Securities Research Institution

framework, consists of two levels: (1) registration at federal level based on disclosure; and (2) registration at state level based on substantive audits. The former was set up by the Securities Act of 1933 and is regulated and implemented by the US Securities and Exchange Commission (SEC) which was established in 1934. The latter actually came into being before federal regulation, with a history dating back over a hundred years: it was first established in Kansas in 1911 with all other states then following suit. In its early days, the federal registration system was only supplementary to regulation at state level.

8.2.1.1 *The Core of the American Registration System: Formal Examination*

A formal examination means only checking [of] the completeness of the disclosure and required format regardless of the accuracy or truthfulness of the disclosure or the state of business of the company. The principle of trade freedom in the market economy is upheld in the belief that the government has no right to curtail the issue of a stock regardless of its quality.

A widely accepted definition of substantive examination is a regulatory system of authorization, under which the regulatory institution can reject the application for new share issue unless the specific condition of stock issue and related transaction guarantees a fair relation between the originator and public investors and provides earnings to public investors in reasonable proportion to risk assumption. From the standpoint of regulating the public listings of American local companies, the federal registration system and substantive examination at the state level work in tandem.

8.2.1.2 *Federal Level: SEC Mechanism for IPOs*

The SEC assigns the task of reviewing registration statements to a team usually consisting of lawyers, accountants, analysts, and industry experts. The SEC has experts in various industries, for example, oil, gas, or mining, who examine application reports filed by companies in their respective specialisms. In contrast, the CSRC's examination team for IPO preliminary review consists entirely of staff with legal and financial backgrounds, with no industry professionals. As of 2009, its IPO preliminary review team still had no industry professionals on board. Only five industry experts from the Chinese Academy of Sciences, the Ministry of Science and Technology, and universities were added to the Issue Examination Committee that same year.

Under the terms of the Securities Act of 1933, the SEC has the right to reject any application for registration. The SEC favors opinion letters to delay corrections and other amendments that need to be made. When it comes to the review process, the registration system at federal level is not ideal, in that IPO registration with the SEC takes effect automatically within 20 days of the submission date. Once the SEC issues its opinion, the issuer submits amendments or supplementary materials, which generates a further 20-day limit. It is quite common for the SEC to raise questions.

8.2.1.3 *State Level: Substantive Examination of IPOs in Each State*

In reality, stock issues must be registered within the securities regulatory agencies of the state, because they neither fall under the preferred federal administration as provided for by the National Securities Markets Improvement Act of 1996, nor do they qualify for exemption of registration within the state. If the stock issue involves more than one state, it will also involve the administration of the federal securities regulatory institution.

Generally speaking, the principle of auditing stock issue in states across the USA is meant to ensure fairness, justice, and equality for investors. In some states with stricter audit practices, when the proportion of insider or originator investment in the issue is significantly less than that of public investors, or when insiders are able to buy into the stock at a substantively low price, the state securities regulatory agency will decline the registration or specify extra conditions (e.g., earnings from internal transactions should be entrusted to a third party for a period of time until certain requirements are met). Even when the offer price proposed by the issuer is deemed to be excessive (e.g. because the issuer's profit history does not support its offer price), or the stock issue gives unequal voting rights to the public, or the underwriting fee is unreasonably high, these circumstances could lead the state securities regulatory authority to veto the stock issue.

8.2.1.4 Coordination Between Federal Regulation and State Securities Regulation in the USA

The National Securities Market Improvement Act solves some problems where federal and state jurisdictions overlap. For example, according to the Federal Securities Act, though some transactions exempted from federal registration can also be exempted from state registration, federal exemption does not automatically mean exemption at state level, so the issuer still needs to register in the relevant state. The logic is that transactions with federal exemption are subject to the administration of state registration only when the stock issue is geared towards unsophisticated buyers. In addition, the Securities Act of 1956 has been adopted by 36 states, and recognizes the New York Stock Exchange, American Stock Exchange, Midwest Stock Exchange, or other stock exchanges to be exempt from state registration obligations. Later, some states had the NASDAQ Global Select Market and Chicago Board Options Exchange included in the range of registration exemptions.

8.2.2 The Examination System of New Share Issues in Japan

The Japanese review system is very similar to that of the USA. From the Securities Exchange Law to the Financial Product Exchange Law, the review of stock issues in Japan complies with the registration system.

8.2.2.1 A Similar Issue Procedure to the USA, but more Effective

An application by an issuing company to the Financial Services Agency (FSA) takes effect and the issuing company can sell new shares 15 days after submission, if the FSA finds no objections. If the review process finds that the application materials are comprehensible to the public or if related information pertaining to the applicant has already been widely disclosed to the public, the application can take effect on the same day or the next day with notice, or the 15-day period can be shortened. In such circumstances, the audit notice will dictate the effective date.

When application files are incomplete, the applicant can be ordered to submit an amendment. Amendments pertaining to important items are required if any record is incorrect or where such items are missing. Under these circumstances, the provision regarding effective date does not apply, and the application will take effect after the day designated by the agency conducting the audit. If the application is already effective, the examining agency orders that the stock issue is halted until the issuing company submits an amendment deemed appropriate by the auditing authority.

8.2.2.2 Simpler Requirements on Information Disclosure than Those in the USA

Information disclosure for new share issues in Japan includes: application statement, registration statement, supplementary materials, and prospectus. Application statements for new share issues should include the following: items offered; the company's operating purpose; trading name; parent company; corporate capital; state of the business; and other important matters concerning the business specified by the FSA in the public interest and for the protection of investors. The registration system can be used instead of the securities application in circumstances where the issuer continuously discloses the state of its finances and operations, and relevant information for the purpose of raising funds. The Japanese registration system resembles shelf registration in the USA.

8.2.2.3 Dual Regulation for New Share Issues

Japan's securities registration system has a divided regulation structure involving the FSA and self-regulatory organizations in the securities market. Public offering registration and audit, which are part of the FSA's responsibilities, and listing verification, which stock exchanges and Japan Securities Dealers Association are authorized to conduct, represent the initial regulation of offering and listing activities and the advanced control system.

The FSA is responsible for registering and examining the public offering of joint-stock companies, while each stock exchange and the Japan Securities Dealers Association are, respectively, responsible for the examination of applications filed by companies listed in relevant stock exchanges and those in the over-the-counter (OTC) market. Stock exchanges in Japan have all formulated detailed regulations with generally similar frameworks for listed companies. The second level is routine regulation of market dealings, information disclosure and so on by the Securities and Exchange Surveillance Commission under the FSA, the key point of which is to investigate possible criminal behavior such as insider trading, market manipulation, and fraudulent information disclosure practices. This forms part of the regulatory and law enforcement process. The two-level regulatory system has ensured the quality of listed companies and that their operations meet legal and compliance standards.

8.2.2.4 Specific Responsibility for Illegal Conduct by Issuers
The Securities Exchange Law contains comprehensive stipulations on illegal conduct during the issue of negotiable securities, covering not only offering companies but also various intermediaries involved in the offering such as securities companies, accounting firms, law firms, etc. The stipulations cover: (1) illegal fund raising or securities selling; (2) making false statements or omitting significant issues of importance in the prospectus; and (3) making false statements or omitting significant issues of importance in the application statement.

8.2.3 Taiwan's Successful Transition from Verification to Registration System

8.2.3.1 1960s–1980s: Implementation of the Examination and Approval System in Taiwan
Taiwan established a securities management committee in 1960 and issued the Measures for Administration of Securities Dealers in 1961—the same year that the Taiwan Stock Exchange (TWSE) was founded. In its first six years, the Taiwanese stock market was controlled by big corporate shareholders and speculators and experienced fluctuations that could be attributed to speculation. From 1963 to 1968, the Taiwanese government imposed a "mandatory listing system" requiring listing of over-the-counter-traded securities in the stock exchange so as to support centralized trading of securities. In 1968, the Taiwanese authorities published the Securities Exchange Law, which provided important legal protection and support in the development of Taiwan's securities industry. The Securities

Exchange Law officially changed the "mandatory listing" practice to "free listing", that is, publicly offered shares could be traded over the counter without being listed on the stock exchange. However, as they still adopted a verification system for the audit of new stock issues, which limited the number of approved companies, the over-the-counter market failed to prosper, and the number of listed companies in the stock exchange did not increase dramatically. The Taiwan securities market could not grow at this stage, because the slow growth it had undergone in its infancy resulted in an underdeveloped market.

8.2.3.2   1980s–2006: Concurrence of Verification and Registration Systems

In the 1980s, however, the securities market in Taiwan experienced significant changes. Over 30 years various underlying problems had developed in the securities industry and its legal system. At the same time, developed countries and regions around the world were also advancing their securities industries and legal systems which acted as a catalyst for reform and improvements in the legal system for the securities industry in Taiwan.

In 1983, the Taiwanese authorities made major amendments to the Securities Exchange Law. One of the most important improvements was the introduction of a registration system for the examination of new share issues, which simplified the examination procedure for negotiable securities offerings. The 1983 amendments changed the stock-issue examination system from sole verification to a concurrent verification and registration system. Stock issues in Taiwan could be subject to either the registration or the verification system at the discretion of the authorities. The authorities wanted to simplify issue procedures, improve efficiency, and foster prudent investment with the registration system, and at the same time were conscious of the emerging securities industry and market in Taiwan which still demanded a verification system to control the quality of listed companies. The concurrent implementation of two systems combined the strengths of both and acted as a gradual transition to overall implementation of the registration system.

8.2.3.3   2006–Present: Sole Registration System in Taiwan

On January 11, 2006, the Taiwanese authorities again amended the Securities Exchange Law. Article 22 on the examination of stock issue stipulates that "the offering of negotiable securities, government bonds and other negotiable securities approved by competent authorities excluded, cannot be done unless the application to competent authorities takes effect." This means that the stock-issue examination system in Taiwan has completed its transition from the concurrent system of 1983 to today's registration system, and a major step forward has been taken in the construction of Taiwan's securities market system. The reason that the Taiwanese authorities effected this transition was that although the laws and regulations of Taiwan's securities market had been completed after a number of amendments, securities issuers, intermediaries, investors and regulatory institutions were continuing to gain experience in the securities market.

8.2.4 Lessons from Stock-issue Registration Systems in Other Countries

The registration system has become the mainstay of new stock-issue systems in capital markets outside China, and is not only widely adopted by mature markets but is also gradually being introduced by many emerging markets as part of the process of development. The stock-issue system of each country or region is closely related to its economic, social, and historical backgrounds and the stage of capital market development, so no two stock-issue systems are exactly alike. Even if they all conduct registration systems, each market may involve different registration procedures, examining institutions, and specific processes. The essence of the registration system can at first be better understood by examining the shared characteristics of stock-issue registration systems in overseas markets:

1. *The regulatory institution still needs to examine stock issues, but the core of the audit is information disclosure and the regulatory institution does not make a value judgment on the issuer.* The regulatory institution should protect the interests of investors, examining the relevance, completeness, and readability of disclosed information but taking no responsibility for its accuracy. In the case of possible contradictions, omissions or misleading messages in the information disclosure, the regulatory institution has the right to ask the issuer to clarify or further disclose, or even ask it to withdraw the registration file, decline the application or reject the registration file.
2. *Value judgment is exercised mainly by the investor.* The investor needs to make the investment decision according to the information disclosed by the issuer. The investor is the key factor determining the

success of an offering. In the American market, there are tens of thousands of institutional investors, so if investors have no interest in investing in the issuer, or if there are wide expectation gaps between investor and issuer, registration with the regulatory institution will make no difference to the success of the offering.
3. *The issuer and the intermediary are responsible for the truthfulness of the disclosed information.* The issuer takes main responsibility, while the intermediary should share the liability if it fails to exercise due diligence and can even be liable to prosecution.
4. *Stock offerings and listings are separate, distinct activities.* Offerings are mainly checked by the regulatory institution under a review standard. When it comes to listings, especially where there is a multi-tiered capital market, stock exchanges can set different thresholds for listings according to their framework. Businesses can also choose to be listed at whichever stock exchange best accommodates their requirements.
5. *The registration system makes the stock-issue process more institutionalized, transparent, and predictable, enabling the regulatory institution to manage the market along more advanced and modern lines.* Registration system reform is meant to alter the relationship between the government and the market. As regulatory institutions decentralize administration and control, the market can then regulate itself to balance the forces of supply and demand.

    Responsibilities that are not meant to be borne by regulatory institutions will gradually be delegated to various bodies such as stock exchanges, intermediaries, issuers, investors, etc. This will demarcate more clearly the boundary between government and market. Emerging markets from India and Taiwan have gone through similar reforms and experienced the deregulation process.
6. *The implementation of the registration system is related to the legal system of the market, its disciplinary mechanisms, and the level of investor protection. Supervision needs to be strengthened in the immediate aftermath if the system is to be relaxed.* The experience of other countries has shown that the implementation of the registration system and the relaxation of market access restrictions necessitates the continuous refinement of supporting laws and regulations, as well as the strengthening of supervision and law enforcement, and the protection of investor rights and interests in the later stages. These can better guarantee the successful implementation of the registration system.

There are six reasons why the American registration system is so effective. First, the government does not need to authorize the rights of issuers: the issuers themselves already hold their rights. Second, the registration and issue process is simple, and relevant agencies work efficiently. Third, the examining institution only conducts a formal examination but does not issue a substantive judgment. Fourth, the supervisory function of the securities regulatory institution is highlighted, whereas its administrative function takes a back seat. Fifth, the federal government, state government, and industrial self-regulatory associations are involved in regulation. Finally, there is an emphasis on the control of stock registration and offering after the registration.

The information disclosure system, cumulative tender book-building system, independent share placing system, and overallotment option under the American registration system are all market-oriented mechanisms to which China can refer for the implementation of the country's registration system. The detailed US information disclosure rules lay the foundation for the implementation of a registration system. On the premise of protecting the interests of investors, the American cumulative tender book-building system actually gives the market a freer hand. The independent share placing mechanism improves the pricing ability and standard of underwriters; the overallotment option helps to offset the fluctuations created by new share offerings. Relevant systems have already been implemented in the Chinese market but improvements are still required, since they are not completely effective.

8.3 The Reality and Practicalities of Exploring the Stock-issue Registration System in China

Presently, China uses a verification system and review processes similar to those of other countries that have also adopted the verification system, conducting a substantive review of securities offerings. However, in several respects China differs from other countries: the CSRC carries out the review, while in other countries it is done by the stock exchanges. The review timeframe is much longer than in other countries. The stock-issue system in China also encompasses many characteristics of a "registration system." When it comes to pricing and placing mechanisms, China has borrowed the cumulative order book-building mechanism from registration systems, but with its investor structure and information disclosure measures, China is very different from other countries that adopt the registration system: in China, individual investors make up a relatively high proportion of the market and information disclosure is mainly mandatory. In countries with a registration system, the market is largely composed of institutional investors, and there is mandatory information and resource disclosure. To sum up, stock issue in China still faces problems with its long cycle, low efficiency, high barriers to entry, incomplete information disclosure, and so on. According to international stock-issue registration systems, capital markets have relatively high operational efficiency under the registration system. These learning points are beneficial to the contemporary Chinese capital market and will contribute to improvement of the status quo, where there is a relatively low proportion of direct financing, and and to optimizing the existing social financing structure.

8.3.1 The Reality for Registration System Reform—to Improve the Scale of Direct Financing and Optimize Social Financing Structure

Reform of the registration system will help improve the scale of direct financing of enterprises and optimize social financing structures. The excessively large proportion of indirect financing, mainly from bank loans, and the relatively low proportion of direct financing, constitute the long-term problem of structural imbalance facing China. Though direct financing has been on the increase in recent years, it constitutes only 11.4% of the total financing market, far below the average level of mature markets. Previously, on the pretext of listing threshold and efficiency issues, direct financing channels for Chinese enterprises were blocked. In order to meet financing demands, enterprises have sought indirect financing channels, including bank loans. The high cost of capital has thus raised the overall indebtedness of society. The introduction of the registration system will lower the financing cost of enterprises, diversify financing methods, improve the financing structure in China, and promote the effective allocation of social resources.

8.3.2 Practical Exploration of Stock-issue Registration System Reform

To further improve the quality of stock issues in China, it is important to deepen the reform of the stock-issue system. Reforms should be carried out before, during and after stock issue, and this should include lowering market barriers so as to let the market decide the offer price and pace of the stock issue.

8.3.2.1 Lowering the Listing Threshold and Constructing a Diversified Market with Multiple Levels

The listing thresholds of both the main board and GEM (growth enterprise market) in China are higher than those of overseas markets. Financing requirements in China dictate that companies seeking listing should directly meet the requirements of net profit, cash flow, and revenue, while the NYSE only requires a minimum of one of the three aspects to be met.

Generally speaking, in comparison with overseas markets, the main board in China imposes relatively strict financial requirements on companies seeking listing but has relatively loose requirements for the protection of investors. More importantly, different boards' listing requirements do not differ significantly, which does not help in the construction of diversified market levels. In future, the securities market in China intends to optimize the listing threshold in two ways: by lowering the listing threshold and relaxing access standards to allow more enterprises to enter the capital market for fund raising and reduce the high costs of financing; and by reconciling the listing requirements of different boards to break the existing mould, build diversified listing requirements, streamline connections between different boards and levels, and connect different boards with board transfer mechanisms.

8.3.2.2 Improving the Quality of Information Disclosure and Laying the Foundations of the Registration System

The registration system centers on information disclosure and due diligence. High-quality information disclosure supports the efficiency of stock issues in the registration system. In recent years, we have gradually strengthened the quality of information disclosure but standards still lag below those of mature markets. Research indicates that problems still exist with listed companies when it comes to information disclosure, such as insufficient disclosure, generally poor disclosure of background or industry information, insufficient corporate social responsibility by the listed companies, etc. At the same time, in the 20 years since the securities market was established, the continuous improvement of its regulatory system has promoted continuous improvements in the information disclosure requirements of listed companies. However many listed companies have developed "innovative" ways of avoiding disclosure, operating many steps ahead of the policies set by securities regulation. Future registration system reform in China should have as its main focus the improvement of the quality of information disclosure, in order to transform the current system of examining financial and accounting data into a business framework that supports profit making, facilitating risk assessment and review audits from the perspective of investors.

8.3.2.3 Improving Market-Oriented Pricing Mechanisms and Relaxing Administrative Control over Offer Prices

At present, China controls the offer price through soft pricing constraints or via a "window operation." Soft constraints include setting the price-to-earnings ratio of the offer price below the industry average, where the issuer and the lead underwriter exclude the highest quote in the total subscription amount, which should not be less than 10% of the total subscription amount. In addition, constraints of the particular issue volume, net amount of fundraising and so on effectively determine the offer price, allowing little scope for the influence of market pricing mechanisms. Therefore, one of the top priorities in the reform of the registration system is to also reform the offer pricing into a market-oriented one. In future, direct limitations and indirect soft constraints on the general price-to-earnings ratio of the offer price, the amount of fundraising, the issue volume, etc. should all be discounted to allow intermediaries to play a professional role in pricing and reduce the price variation between primary and second markets.

8.3.2.4 Promoting the Implementation of Board Transfer and Delisting Mechanisms, Improving Market Mechanisms

A delisting mechanism acts as the "outflow" channel; few companies have delisted since stocks were first listed. However, the reform of the stock-issue system should ease both "outflow" and "inflow" channels to ensure the vitality and quality of the market. Overseas markets have free entry and exit. The USA, which is a mature market, has relatively advanced methods of stock exchange transfer and delisting mechanisms. Between 2000 and 2011, the average annual number of companies transferring from OTCBB to NASDAQ stood at 110; transfers from the NASDAQ to OTCBB were 205. When it came to delisting, as of 2001, the average number of delisted companies annually hit 2,109, much higher than the average number of IPOs. Hence the inflow and outflow of listed companies can effectively ensure the quality of listed companies and improve the efficiency of resource allocation.

8.3.2.5 Improving the Function of Intermediaries, Optimizing the Placing Structure

The principal way of promoting market-oriented reforms of the offer price and improving issue efficiency would be to improve the function of intermediaries. The existing offline price inquiry procedure drives price discovery and improvements in trading efficiency. Offline placing compensates institutional investors who are researching the new stock's investment value and price . The fairness and effectiveness of the process will influence the effectiveness of the new stock pricing. Meanwhile, independent placing of underwriters decides the degree of marketization of the placing. The higher the degree of marketization, generally the more effective the placing. Both underwriters and institutional investors can calculate their own pricing in offline placing. The accuracy of the price derived largely depends on the function optimization of intermediaries.

8.3.2.6 Promoting the Transition of Regulation Mode, Improving the Construction of Supporting Mechanisms

The reform of the securities issue registration system should be based on the improvement of supporting mechanisms, which includes changes in the rationale behind the regulation concept and the establishment of disciplinary mechanisms. The registration system emphasizes that the previous system of reviewing stock issues should rest on the due diligence of intermediaries and the disclosure of information by issuers; this weakens regulation under the verification system, demonstrates the shift toward regulation in the intermediate and later stages, and makes investor protection one of the major objectives of financial regulation. There is a shift from the previous concept of regulation by function towards managing by function. Disciplinary measures are strengthened and the disciplinary mechanisms of sponsors and intermediaries made comprehensive so as to ensure the healthy and orderly development of the market. Effective civil compensation, class action, law enforcement, amicable settlement, and criminal accountability systems, etc. deal with illegal conduct related to securities rapidly and effectively, and better protect the lawful rights and interests of investors.

Reference

Shenyin and Wanguo Securities Research Institution 2014. http://www.swsresearch.com/EN/Default.aspx

INDEX

A
accounting system, 18, 25, 160, 167, 191, 195, 198–199, 206
administrative licensing system, 69
Agricultural Bank of China, 61, 96
Alipay, 31, 35–36, 41
all-in-one window, 190
approval system, 102, 106, 150, 230–233, 238
A share, 112–114, 116–117, 120–121, 147, 149, 219
asset management, 6, 9–11, 35, 81, 89, 108, 141
asset securitization, 1, 6, 8, 10–11, 26, 38, 106
ATM, 35

B
bad-debt write-offs, 86
Bank of China, 20, 36, 54–55, 57–58, 61, 90, 161, 191, 195–196, 198, 200, 202–203, 227
Bank of Communication, 61, 80, 84
Bank of International Settlements, 220
bank-dominated financial system, 24, 46
bank-trust cooperation, 15–18
bank-trust wealth management, 16
Basel Committee, 60, 68, 77–79, 91
Basel Committee on Banking Supervision, 78
Basel III, 60, 76–80, 84–85, 90
big data, 34, 48–49, 136, 139–140
bilateral opening up, 109, 144, 150, 160
Bitcoin, 38, 55, 58
Board Transfer Mechanisms, 148, 150, 244
Bohai Bank, 91
bond market, 102, 111, 136, 144, 160
BRICS countries, 154
butterfly effect, 53

C
capital account, 114–116, 120, 154, 156–162, 168, 174–175, 178–180, 183–188, 200, 204–205, 207, 211–213, 217, 219–220, 224

capital account convertibility, 115, 159, 161–162, 175, 186–188, 200
capital adequacy ratio, 64, 78–79, 180
capital arbitrage, 206
capital control, 160, 162, 180, 182, 186–187, 225
Capital Flow Monitoring Report, 80
capital inflow, 154, 172, 176, 178, 181–182, 184, 186, 217, 226
capital regulation, 60, 78, 84
capital requirements, 14, 19, 127
Capital Rules, 60, 79, 91
capital structure, 80, 93
Capital Supplement, 60, 85, 93, 96
capital surcharge requirement, 90
The Central Economic Work Conference, 143
centralized management, 83
certificate of deposit, 26
channel system, 230–232
Chicago Board Options Exchange, 236
China (Shanghai) Free Trade Pilot Zone, 147
China Banking Regulatory Commission, v, 1, 3, 20, 98–99, 191
China Construction Bank, 61
China Development Bank, 63, 170
China Insurance Regulatory Commission, 20, 82, 191
China Merchants Bank, 61
China Securities Comprehensive Bond Index, 111
China Securities Depository and Clearing Co, 109, 112
China Securities Regulatory Commission, v, 20, 82, 102, 151–152, 191, 229
China's Financial Futures Exchange, 103
circuit-breaker mechanism, 211
clearing and settlements, 214
Clearing Limited, 20–22, 112, 228
CNH, 166
CNY, 166
commercial banking system, 6, 11
commodity derivative, 160
concentration-ratio management, 19
consumer protection mechanisms, 26, 49, 53
convertible bonds, 111, 126, 128
Corporate Bond Index, 111
corporate governance, 24, 66, 71, 73–74, 96–97, 127, 219
counter-cyclical, 182
credit intermediaries, 3–7, 9, 20, 27–28
credit-risk transfer, 2, 10
cross-border capital flow, 115, 154–155, 166, 177–185, 206, 213–214, 223, 225–226
cross-border guarantees, 157, 161, 171, 173
cross-border RMB business, 156, 171–172, 183
cross-market business, 20
cross-over effects, 44
crowd funding, 32–34, 37–39, 44–46, 50, 52
Crude Oil Futures, 107, 147–148
current account, 154–155, 179–180, 183, 196, 199, 204, 220

D

delisting indicator, 103, 108, 129, 132
Delisting Opinions, 128, 131–134
deposit-to-loan ratio, 77
derivatives trading, 93, 167
Didi Taxi, 43, 55
digital finance, 3, 31–39, 41–44, 46–58, 93

direct financing, 4, 12, 31, 46, 51, 106, 111, 144, 148, 150, 243
diversified financing system, 23–24, 51
domestic non-resident account, 199
double surpluse, 172, 179
Dow Jones Industrial Average, 114
duration management, 81

E
eBay, 38–39
economic structural adjustment, 97, 170
electronic finance, 31
enclosed circulation, 225–226
Energy Trading Center, 147–148
ETF, 103, 107, 218
European Central Bank, 2
Eurozone, 2, 104, 142, 165
Everbright Securities, 104
Evergrowing Bank, 91
Exchange Surveillance Commission, 238

F
Facebook, 38
Federal Securities Act, 236
finance companies, 8–9, 11, 61, 96
financial innovation, 1, 3, 5, 13–14, 22, 31, 40, 46, 48, 82, 98, 198, 207
financial regulation, v, ix, 1, 5, 32, 54–58, 71, 78, 80, 98, 153, 182, 205–206, 209, 226, 246
Financial Services Agency, 236
Financial Stability Board, 2, 90, 140
Financial Times Ordinary Shares Index, 114
financing guarantee, 8–9, 11, 28, 61, 176, 198
firewall systems, 72

the first line, 190, 198
foreign banks, 63, 69–70, 75, 77–78
foreign debt, xiii, 157, 161, 171–172, 174–179, 181, 185–187, 201–203
foreign debt management, 174–179, 186–187, 201, xii
foreign exchange, v, vii, xiii, 82, 153–187, 191, 195–196, 202, 205, 212, 220
foreign exchange derivative, 162, 167–168, 182
foreign exchange reserves, 154, 170
Fourth Plenary Session, 95
free convertibility, 161
free trade account, 160, 180, 198–200, 206–207
FSA, 236–238

G
G-SIBs, 90–91
G20, 90
GEM (growth enterprise market), 102, 121, 244
Germany, 36, 104, 233
global financial crisis, 71, 78, 178
Global Systemic Importance of Commercial Banks, 91
going out, 150, 168, 170, 172–173, 184
Google, 38
governance structure, 71, 77, 97
Green Credit Guidelines, 61
Guangfa Bank, 91

H
H share, 147, 219
Hong Kong, 104, 109, 112–121, 143–144, 147, 149, 159, 163, 165, 177–178, 192, 203, 209–211, 213–228, 230, 233

Hong Kong Exchanges, 112, 209–210, 224–225, 228
Hong Kong Stock Connect, 104, 109, 112–121, 143–144, 147, 149, 159, 209–227
Hong Kong Stock Thorough Train, 112, 211–212
hot money, 177–178, 206

I
IC cards, 35
inclusive finance, 95, 97
independent accounting, 82–83
indirect financing, 4, 12, 31, 243
individual investor, 113, 116, 120, 150, 211–212, 214, 224, 243
Industrial and Commercial Bank of China, 61
information asymmetry, 13, 37, 48–49, 72
information disclosure, 14–15, 21, 26, 51–53, 73–76, 103, 108, 124, 131–132, 134, 146, 151, 233, 237–238, 240, 242–245
information technologies (IT), 33
institutional arrangement, 127, 133, 171, 197, 213–214, 223–224
institutional investors, 104, 113, 116, 121, 159, 211–212, 214, 217–219, 221–222, 224, 241, 243, 246
interbank business, 5–7, 10–14, 18–20, 23–25, 66, 81–82, 87, 93
interest-rate liberalization, 159
Internal Control Guidelines, 63
internal controls, 67–68
international balance of payments, 153–155, 166, 173, 179–180, 183–184
international financial center, 114, 207, 221–223
International Monetary Fund, 140

internet credit financing, 9
investor protection, 116, 150, 226, 241, 246

J
Japan, 36, 39, 104, 142, 181, 206, 230, 232–233, 236–238
Japan Securities Dealers Association, 237

K
Kuaidadi, 43, 55

L
legal risk, 52, 56, 58, 227
Lending Club, 38
leverage, 2, 5–6, 12–13, 78–79, 81, 106, 202
leverage ratio, 5, 78–79, 202
liquidity crisis, 13, 77
Liquidity Risk Regulation, 77
liquidity risks, 13, 21, 65, 77, 81
liquidity transformation, 2, 6, 10

M
macro-prudent management, 198
macroprudential financial framework, 22
macroprudential management framework, 23, 25–26, 175
macroprudential regulation, 66, 77, 98, 138, 205
marketization reform, 22, 41–42, 163–166, 183, 191, 206, 221
maturity mismatch, 5, 12–13, 23, 25, 53, 81
maturity transformation, 2, 6, 10
microprudential regulation, 78–79, 205

Ministry of Commerce, 172, 174
Ministry of Finance, 68, 83, 117,
    174–175
mobile payment, 34
money drought, 13
money-market funds, 3, 8–11
moral hazard, 13, 21, 53
MSCI1, 14, 149
multi-tier capital market, 51, 105–106,
    144–145, 150

N
NASDAQ, 129, 236, 245
National Development and Reform
    Commission (NDRC), 74, 172
the National Equity Exchange and
    Quotations, 133
National Securities Markets
    Improvement act of 1996, 235
The National Share Transfer System,
    107, 148
negative list management, 19,
    184, 202
network finance, 31
network investment banking, 38,
    45–46
new normal, 59, 106, 122, 125, 143,
    145, 162, 183, 185–187
new third board, 107, 110, 148
New York Stock Exchange, 234, 236
non-performing loans, 62, 64, 85–86
non-traditional credit, 6–13,
    17–27, 29
non-traditional credit financing, 1–7,
    9–13, 17–18, 20–23, 25–27
NYSE, 129, 244

O
off-balance-sheet, 1, 5, 7, 12, 16–19,
    26, 86–89, 91, 98
off-site regulation, 52, 67, 94–95, 98

offshore account, 192, 199
offshore, xiii, 163–165, 168, 177,
    185, 187, 192, 199, 220–221,
    223
on-balance-sheet, 5, 7, 12, 18,
    26, 88
on-site investigation, 67, 139
one bank and three commissions, 20,
    191, 205
One Belt, One Road, 105, 143,
    168–169, 173, 184
online finance, 31
operational risk, 48–49, 52, 87
over-the-counter, 238
overseas investment, 157–158,
    169, 172–173, 183, 190,
    219, 223

P
parallel banking system, 2
Paul McCulley, 2
payment and settlement, 33–36, 40,
    44–45, 49, 220
PE, 37, 114, 125
peer-to-peer, 32
People's Bank of China, 20, 36,
    54–55, 57–58, 161, 191,
    195–196, 198, 200, 202–203
performance assessment, 93
pre-warning mechanisms, 65
pressure testing, 65
Price Law, 74–75
private equity funds, 2, 9, 11
Prosper, 38, 46, 239
provision, 12, 14, 16, 19, 24–25, 42,
    46, 60, 64, 74–77, 79, 84,
    88–89, 117, 123, 127, 132,
    157–158, 160, 162, 171, 174,
    176, 211–212, 237
provision coverage, 64
prudential regulation, 66, 77–79, 95,
    98, 135

Q

The Qualified Foreign Institutional Investors, 104
quantitative management, 154
quasi-credit, 11, 13, 16, 19, 24
quota limit, xi, 116, 119, 157, 203, 211, 214–215
quota management, 161, 205, 230–231

R

real-time monitoring, 116, 207
registration system, 103, 106, 108, 122, 125, 128–130, 134, 144, 146, 150, 157, 190, 192, 220, 229–246
regulation failure, 52–53
regulatory arbitrage, 5, 12, 17–18, 22, 42, 98
regulatory framework, 15, 42, 49–52, 54, 58, 60, 77, 98, 190, 205–206, 222–225, 233
regulatory vacuums, 5
risk isolation, 82–83, 98
RMB Cross-Border Payment Management Information System (RCPMIS), 171
RMB exchange rate, 155–156, 163, 166, 212, xi
RMB internationalization, 115, 154, 156, 161–164, 169, 173, 177, 184–185, 187, 203, 207, 220–221, 223
RMB Qualified Foreign Institutional Investor, 104
run-away, 49

S

the second line, 190, 198–199
Securities Act of 1933, 23, 234–235
Securities and Exchange Commission, 234
the Securities Exchange Law, 236, 238–239
the Securities and Futures Commission of Hong Kong, 109, 224
securitization, 1–3, 5–6, 8, 10–11, 26, 38, 106
shadow banking, 1–4, 6–14, 17, 19–23, 25–29, 31, 61, 63, 81, 88
Shanghai Composite Index, 110
Shanghai Futures Exchange, 147
Shanghai Stock Connect, 109, 112, 115–121, 210–215, 221, 224
Shanghai Stock Exchange, 103, 110, 112, 209, 224, 227
Shanghai–Hong Kong Stock Connect, 104, 109, 112–121, 143–144, 147, 149, 159, 209–227
Shenzhen Composite Index, 110
Silk Road Fund, 170
SMEs, 103, 107, 122–123, 125, 141, 148
sovereign debt, 174–175
special purpose vehicles, 157–158, 171
spillover effects, 53
sponsor system, 230, 232
SSE T-Bond Index, 111
State Administration of Foreign Exchange, 82, 176, 178, 185–186
The State Council, v, 2–3, 25, 62, 69–70, 79, 81, 83, 102, 105–106, 109, 133, 144, 146, 160, 170, 174, 193, 201, 207, 229, 231
State Taxation Administration, 117
stock market, 109–112, 114–116, 118–121, 129–130, 134, 140–141, 144, 149, 159–160, 212–215, 217–219, 223–224, 228, 230, 232, 238
sub-prime crisis, 77

systemic importance, 90–91, 94
systemic risk, 5–6, 12–13, 19, 21,
    23–24, 26, 50, 65, 81, 84, 95,
    98, 140, 168, 205, 207

T
target management, 230–231
technical risk, 51–52
third financing mode, 31
Third Plenary Session, 22, 105, 113,
    125, 144, 146, 168, 175, 193,
    229, 232
third-party guarantees, 19
third-party payments, 33, 36, 43–46, 50
third-party wealth management, 3,
    8–9, 11, 83
tobin tax, 181, 186–187
trade facilitation, 19, 169, 184,
    189–190, 194
transparency, 19, 24, 61, 81, 94, 96,
    139, 172, 178, 184, 219, 232
trust, 3, 8–11, 14–18, 20, 28–29, 49,
    61, 63, 81, 83–84, 87–88, 95,
    98, 160, 234
Tsinghua University, 36
The 12th Five-Year Plan, 113, 222
two-dimensional code payments, 50

U
UK, 32, 36, 39, 114, 149, 165, 216,
    230, 233

Unified ID account, 141
USA, 6, 11, 31–33, 36, 38–40, 42,
    45, 77, 104, 129–130, 142, 155,
    165, 181, 205, 216, 230,
    232–234, 236–237, 245

V
value-added tax, 192
VC, 37
virtual credit card, 50
virtual currency, 34, 38, 44, 46,
    49–50

W
wholesale market, 13, 23
window operation, 245

X
Xiao Gang, 105, 135–136, 138,
    145–146, 149, 229

Y
Yu'ebao, 31, 33–35, 39–44, 46,
    49–50, 53, 55, 58

Z
Zheshang Bank, 91
Zopa, 36